This engaging and well-researched book explor[es] make complex social and environmental issue[s] With a focus on critical thinking, intercultural l[earning] projects, it offers an inspiring approach that pro[vides a] contribution to current practice.'

Dr Stephen Scoffham, Faculty of Education, Canterbury Christ Church University

'This book argues powerfully for the role of picturebooks in teaching critical literacy, and also for incorporating global and justice perspectives in the classroom. It makes fascinating reading and is a rich resource for teachers of all ages of children.'

Margaret M. Clark, Emeritus Professor, University of Birmingham

You, Me and Diversity

IOEPress

Trentham Books

DICE
Development & InterCultural Education

Irish Aid
An Roinn Gnóthaí Eachtracha agus Trádála
Department of Foreign Affairs and Trade

This book is dedicated to my two daughters Emily and Laura, my husband, Dr Padraic Kenna, and my mother Margaret Dolan.

It is written in memory of my father, Ignatius Dolan 1929–2005 RIP.

You, Me and Diversity

Picturebooks for teaching development and intercultural education

Anne M. Dolan

A Trentham Book
Institute of Education Press

First published in 2014 by the Institute of Education, University of London,
20 Bedford Way, London WC1H 0AL
www.ioe.ac.uk/ioepress

© Trentham Books in association with the DICE Project (Development and Intercultural Education within Initial Teacher Education) 2014

British Library Cataloguing in Publication Data:
A catalogue record for this publication is available from the British Library

ISBNs
978-1-85856-522-4 (paperback)
978-1-85856-610-8 (PDF eBook)
978-1-85856-611-5 (ePub eBook)
978-1-85856-612-2 (Kindle eBook)

All rights reserved. No part of this publication may be reproduced, stored in a retrieval system, or transmitted in any form or by any means, electronic, mechanical, photocopying, recording, or otherwise, without the prior permission of the copyright owner.

Every effort has been made to trace copyright holders and to obtain their permission for the use of copyright material. The publisher apologizes for any errors or omissions and would be grateful if notified of any corrections that should be incorporated in future reprints or editions of this book.

The opinions expressed in this publication are those of the author and do not necessarily reflect the views of the Institute of Education, University of London.

Typeset by Quadrant Infotech (India) Pvt Ltd
Printed by CPI Group (UK) Ltd, Croydon, CR0 4YY
Cover image and photographs: © Anne M. Dolan

Contents

Acknowledgements

This book would not have been possible without the help and support of many people. Both the research and publication costs were funded by Irish Aid through the Development and Intercultural Education (DICE) project. I am grateful to Mary Immaculate College, Limerick, Ireland for providing study leave, and to the Research Office for additional funding through its Seed Funding Scheme. These valuable supports would not have been possible without the assistance of Professor Michael Hayes, President of Mary Immaculate College, Professor Teresa O'Doherty, Dean of Education, and Professor Michael Healy, Assistant Vice President for Research.

Special thanks are due to Deirdre O'Connor, Irish National Teachers' Organisation (INTO) and Carol Grewal, Principal of St Brendan's School, San Francisco, for providing encouragement and a listening ear when it was needed. I am grateful to my friends and colleagues in Mary Immaculate College who have shared their ideas with me and to many of our students who have tried out some of the ideas from this publication. Thanks to all the enthusiastic teachers and children who have listened to these stories and shared their responses with me.

A special acknowledgement is due to many people who helped me both directly and indirectly, in recent times and over the past few years, who provided inspiration, a word of advice, a cup of tea or a glass of wine when it was most needed. These include Niamh Armstrong, Dr Sandra Ryan, Dr Carol O'Sullivan, Professor Claire Lyons, Dr Paddy Fullam, Dr David O'Grady, Fr Michael Wall, Professor Peadar Cremin, colleagues from the Department of Learning, Society and Religious Education, members of the Management Committee from DICE, Deirdre O'Rourke, Aoife Titley, Dr Maeve Martin, Valerie Coughlin, the primary geographers from the Charney Manor conferences, members of the Irish Association of Social, Scientific and Environmental Educators (IASSEE) and all the mums from Roscam. Thanks to Dr Gillian Klein and all at Trentham Books and IOE Press, for their expertise and willingness to travel this journey with me. I am grateful to the staff in Ballybane Library, Galway, for sharing their expertise with me and providing my family with a weekly supply of picturebooks.

Finally, thanks to my wonderful family, to my mother for always being a source of encouragement, to my husband Padraic for his generous support, his love and patience, and to my two wonderful daughters Emily and Laura, who listen to these stories every day.

Anne M. Dolan

I have had the privilege of working in many parts of Africa, including Lesotho, The Gambia and Zambia, both on long-term and short-term placements. During these times I have met many inspirational people who are trying to improve their local communities, their societies and ultimately their world. I have written this book to honour much of the outstanding work that is taking place around the world today through aid programmes, community initiatives and local heroes.

About the author

Anne Dolan is a lecturer with the Department of Learning, Society and Religious Education at Mary Immaculate College, University of Limerick, Ireland. Currently she teaches methodology courses in primary geography and modules in adult and community education, lifelong learning and development and intercultural education. After working as a primary teacher for a number of years, Anne worked in the area of development studies in Ireland and abroad. She spent two years in Lesotho with the Agency for Personal Service Overseas (APSO) working in the Lesotho College of Education (LCE) as a lecturer in development studies. Anne's doctoral research focused on the experience of mature student teachers undertaking the BEd degree in the context of lifelong learning. Anne has also conducted research and consultancy for several non-governmental organizations in Ireland. Current research interests include development education, primary geography, participatory approaches to education and children's concepts of place. Her research for this publication supports her lifelong commitment to development and intercultural education.

Change it happens slowly.

One

small

step

at

a

time.

Extract from the picturebook *Climbing Lincoln's Steps: The African American journey* (Slade, 2010)

Irish Aid and DICE

Irish Aid is the Irish government's official aid programme administered by the Department of Foreign Affairs and Trade, working on behalf of the Irish people to address poverty and hunger in some of the poorest countries in the world. The programme is managed by the Development Co-operation Division of the Department of Foreign Affairs and Trade. Irish Aid's work in fighting global poverty and hunger is integral to Ireland's foreign policy. Its policy for international development – *One World, One Future: Ireland's policy for international development* – was launched in May 2013 following a Review of the White Paper on Irish Aid. This new policy sets out Ireland's vision, goals and priority areas for engagement in international development over the coming years. It also outlines the steps that will be taken to maximize the effectiveness and impact of Ireland's efforts in this area.

The DICE (Development and Intercultural Education) project is a collaborative initiative between five colleges of education in Ireland that is supported and funded by Irish Aid. The five colleges of education are: Mary Immaculate College, St Patrick's College, Froebel College of Education, Marino Institute of Education and Church of Ireland College of Education. The overall aim of the DICE project is to provide support to five primary colleges of education in Ireland, to utilize, develop and further extend staff capacity and expertise in integrating development education and intercultural education into existing initial teacher education programmes. The DICE project aims to equip student teachers with the necessary values, ideas, skills and capacities to integrate development education and intercultural education across all relevant areas of the primary school curriculum. By targeting the skills, knowledge and values of people involved in education, the project seeks to promote global solidarity, human rights and environmental awareness and tries to develop the ability to recognize and challenge discrimination and inequality, globally and locally. The project also tries to challenge perceptions and assumptions of those engaged in education in relation to the world and the society we live in. In addition, the DICE project undertakes research into the theory and practice of development education and intercultural education. This research is framed in the global contexts of rapid change and unequal development.

More information about Irish Aid and DICE is available on the following websites: www.irishaid.ie and www.diceproject.ie/

Introduction

This book has been written as a resource for student teachers and primary teachers. It facilitates the promotion of development and intercultural perspectives in primary education through picturebooks. A powerful resource for children, a picturebook can allow them to interrogate a range of global issues, in an age-appropriate manner. Never before has the quality, scope and relevance of picturebooks been as good as it is today, increasing the opportunities not only for literacy but also for teaching development and intercultural education. While picturebooks tend to be associated with early childhood education, the range of issues they address ensures their relevance for all primary classes. This book presents the range of picturebooks with development education and intercultural themes available for children in primary schools. Other books that are regularly used for literacy time can also be used to illustrate complex issues such as power, oppression and perspective. Teaching contemporary development issues such as the 9/11 tragedy, the Japanese tsunami, Hurricane Katrina or the Haitian earthquake can be challenging for teachers. Some excellent picturebooks deal with these topics. This book demonstrates how such picturebooks can be used as resources that promote critical thinking, intercultural learning and action-based projects in line with contemporary thinking in development and intercultural education.

Multicultural literature can be used to promote teaching and learning that values all children, rather than children of one particular race or creed. I use the term *multicultural* to describe the resources this book discusses, because there is no other term that sufficiently encompasses them. The word, however, is problematic and so is unpicked at the beginning of Chapter 2. Making multicultural literature available to children can develop mutual understanding, as well as self-esteem and confidence. Through the themes, characters and dilemmas of such books, and in conjunction with perceptive teaching, children can learn to respect their own cultural group, empathize with other groups, add their own personal voices to the collective dialogue and value multiple perspectives and experiences, as part of their lifelong learning process.

During a recent visit to the Holocaust Memorial Museum in Washington DC, I looked at illustrations and stories from *Der Giftpilz* (The Poisonous Mushroom) (Hiemer, 1938), published by Julius Streicher, who was executed as a war criminal in 1946. The publication is an example of Nazi anti-Semitic propaganda directed towards children. The book was intended to 'educate' children about the Jews – the poisonous mushroom of the title referring to a Jew. Historically, education in general and children's literature in particular have been used to promote a range of political messages and agendas. Reflecting on *The Poisonous Mushroom* has led me to consider my reasons for writing and for choosing the books in this publication. So to avoid duplicity or accusations of propaganda, I wish to articulate my personal motivation for writing this book. We live in a complex, diverse world with many different people and perspectives. This book is written to promote respect for, and understanding of, multicultural and diverse societies. It is written to help children and teachers understand and read the world critically, empathically and independently. Through this book, I hope to inspire teachers and children to accept that we all have a role to play as citizens and that we can make a difference.

You, Me and Diversity aims to provide student and primary teachers with a comprehensive choice of picture story books to use for teaching development/intercultural education and education for sustainability. Ultimately, the book aims to promote the use of a wide range of multicultural literature, both with children and with student teachers. References to children are made in terms of age rather than stage, class level or standard, as each jurisdiction has its own categorization system within formal education. The following grid (Table i) is provided as a means of assisting readers in a variety of educational settings. However, the age guide for each book is only a suggestion. Many picturebooks can be used with all class levels if teachers differentiate their methodological and conceptual approaches. According to Anthony Browne (2011: 235), 'picturebooks are for everybody at any age, not books to be left behind as we grow older'. Picturebooks that have been designed for younger children can promote rich insights and debate among older children.

Table i: Guide to comparative age of children in different geographical jurisdictions

Age	Ireland	Northern Ireland	California State, USA	Great Britain	
4–5	Junior Infants	Primary 1	Pre-Kindergarten (PK)	Foundation Stage	Reception
5–6	Senior Infants	Primary 2	Kindergarten	Foundation Stage	Year 1
6–7	1st class	Primary 3	Grade 1	Key Stage 1	Year 2
7–8	2nd class	Primary 4	Grade 2	Key Stage 1	Year 3

Age	Ireland	Northern Ireland	California State, USA	Great Britain	
8–9	3rd class	Primary 5	Grade 3	Key Stage 2	Year 4
9–10	4th class	Primary 6	Grade 4	Key Stage 2	Year 5
10–11	5th class	Primary 7	Grade 5	Key Stage 2	Year 6
11–13	6th class	Year 8	Grade 6	Key Stage 3	Year 7

Many excellent picturebooks enhance the teaching of development and intercultural conceptual development in an integrated, effective manner, while also addressing a range of literacies – oral, verbal, visual and critical. Picturebooks can bridge the gap between geographically distant places and the lives of children in the classroom. They can give children an understanding about how and where people have lived in the past, in the present, and how they might live in future (Zeitler Hannibal *et al.*, 2002). By bringing some of the methods, values and approaches advocated by development educators and intercultural education to the exploration of these books, classroom teaching can be enriched for the benefit of all children.

However, simply increasing the use of multicultural literature in general, and these books in particular, will not automatically improve multicultural and intercultural awareness and understanding in schools. Nor will it automatically improve schools' participation in development education actions, projects and approaches. These books need to be introduced in classrooms and schools as part of whole-school programmes designed to address development and intercultural education. Incorporating and critically interrogating these books with children, as part of a broader approach to culturally responsive teaching, will extend and enrich the global and justice perspectives of teachers and children.

In our increasingly diverse world, classrooms and schools reflect diversity. Including multicultural literature is no longer an option: it is a necessity. For the first time, racial and ethnic minorities make up more than half the children born in the US. In Ireland, where this book was written, more than 10 per cent of the population come from different ethnic backgrounds. Classrooms inevitably mirror broader society. In Fecho and Allen's words:

> The world outside the classroom transacts daily with the world inside the classroom and each reflects, shapes and is shaped by the other. In other words racism, classism and a whole range of *isms* feature in classrooms today, but they don't get discussed in complicated ways in many classrooms.

> (2003: 233)

Children are shaped by their experiences of cultural identity, socio-economic status, family background, geographical location, language, culture, religion and politics. Their experiences intersect with their abilities and opportunities to learn. Gopalakrishnan argues strongly that there is consequently an urgent need for multicultural literature right across the curriculum and especially:

> for genuine accounts that address many of these issues from an insider's point of view, to give children a way to validate their feelings and experiences; to create understanding, empathy and tolerance; to break debilitating stereotypes; to give equal voice and representation.
>
> (2011: 34)

There is a range of multicultural books that can assist teachers to devise and develop their own intercultural and development education strategies in the classroom. Development education is about living a life of social responsibility or, in Berman's terms, 'personal investment in the well-being of people and the planet' (1997: 15). In this context, the phrase 'personal investment' means that we *care* about the world, from the local to the global, and that we take actions to make it a better place. I would also add Maxine Greene's (1995: 5) notion of teaching 'social imagination', which she defines as 'the capacity to invent visions of what should be and what might be in our deficient society, on the streets where we live, and in our schools'. Since books in general, and picturebooks in particular, nurture the imagination, they offer an unlimited resource for inspiring and creating visions of a better world for all its citizens.

Multicultural picturebooks can help teachers raise complex issues in an age-appropriate manner for all levels in the primary school. The books I mention in this publication have, with some exceptions, been published or reprinted since 2000. In some cases I make reference to classic picturebooks that have stood the test of time or have been recently reinvigorated. For instance, Dr Seuss's book *The Lorax* (2009) was originally published in 1971 and is now the inspiration behind the internationally acclaimed film of the same name. All the books can be ordered through school libraries, local bookshops and online. Once these books are available to teachers, the challenge remains to maximize opportunities for development and intercultural learning. Teachers can design activities that move beyond the realm of description to deeper skills of analysis, comparison and evaluation. This book is written to support teachers in this important task.

Chapter 1 offers a detailed rationale for the book. I provide an overview of picturebooks, including definitions and an outline of the elements that make them up. I highlight the ingenuity of the genre, while also acknowledging some criticisms, and indicate how picturebooks can potentially contribute to teaching intercultural and development education in primary classrooms. In Chapter 2, I explore a number of definitions, values and concepts of multicultural, intercultural and development education in the context of culture and culturally responsive teaching. Child labour and access to education are highlighted as two important development education topics that can be explored in picturebooks through a critical lens.

In Chapter 3, I consider diversity, multiculturalism, multicultural literature and gender. As well as examining some of the debates around authenticity, I also include criteria for assessing multicultural literature. In Chapter 4, I address the concepts of critical literacy and critically reading the world. I advocate the use of critical thinking, philosophical thinking and creative thinking in the classroom as an appropriate development education response to complex development issues. I also explore critical issues of power, agency and action through the representation of different groups in children's literature, and briefly introduce my curriculum framework.

In Chapters 5, 6 and 7, I present a detailed application of my curriculum framework for using picturebooks to teach intercultural and development education. Each chapter deals with one of three core concepts: *respect*, *understanding* and *action*. In Chapter 5, I present a number of picturebooks that illustrate self-esteem, self-respect and identity. I discuss the issue of bullying in relation to a number of picturebooks that illustrate this controversial topic. Teaching about respect and human rights is discussed with particular reference to some powerful stories about respect and hope. Finally, I consider picturebooks about environmental respect and Education for Sustainable Development (ESD).

In Chapter 6, I examine a number of development and intercultural themes and topics including: contemporary events, gender, climate change, apartheid and the Holocaust. In Chapter 7, I present the final part of the curriculum framework – action – and explore different elements of authentic action. I discuss a number of picturebooks offering examples of the actions children can take and which present a range of people who took important actions in their own lives. This section requires teachers to encourage children to reflect on the implications of their actions.

In Chapter 8, I look at a number of picturebooks that highlight the experiences of refugee children. Many are based on real-life accounts of events that took place. A framework for curriculum building is set out in Appendix 1. Appendix 2 contains a list of resources.

Picturebooks engage the minds of children as well as their hearts. The most challenging make children think in new ways (Salisbury and Styles, 2012).

Anne M. Dolan

A quiet revolution has been occurring in the world of picturebooks. This book aims to share the diversity of picturebooks suitable for development and intercultural education, with the hope of increasing their use in primary classrooms.

Chapter 1

Picturebooks

> Throughout history, stories have transported people across time
> and space through the power of imagination. They take us into
> other lives, lands and centuries, connecting us with the experiences
> of individuals and communities affected by circumstances quite
> different from our own. As we are moved by the joys and ordeals
> of stories' protagonists, we grow to see the Other in ourselves and
> ourselves in the Other. Once we make that leap, we are changed
> forever, sometimes with extraordinary social consequence.
>
> (Glasgow and Rice, 2007: xiii)

Introduction

Picturebooks have traditionally been used for supporting literacy. Many
offer multiple opportunities for supporting development and intercultural
education. Recently published picturebooks are engaging, thought provoking
and provide an excellent means of bringing the world into the classroom.
Consequently, picturebooks have the potential to make abstract ideas and
intercultural concepts more accessible for children. However, many teachers
don't know such books exist. Recent research indicates that many primary
teachers do not feel confident in their ability to select contemporary literature
for children and tend to rely on the books they enjoyed as children (Cremin
et al., 2008). In a survey of 1,200 teachers, the United Kingdom Literacy
Association (UKLA) found evidence that teachers relied on a narrow repertoire
of children's authors, and in particular knew of only a small selection of
poetry and fiction picturebooks. Furthermore, children's literature tends to
identify strongly with European and Euro-American cultures, thus rendering
other cultures invisible. In this chapter, I set out my rationale for writing
this book, look at the nature of picturebooks and highlight the potential
contribution of picturebooks to intercultural and development education.

Rationale for this book

Air travel, migration and economic realities have combined to ensure greater
mobility around the world today. Whether we travel or not, the world and its
varied cultures come to us in our home environments through contemporary

events, trade and economics, popular culture (such as movies and television), technology (such as the internet), politics and foreign policy and migration. We are a global community, and the inability of borders to protect us has become increasingly evident in light of issues such as climate change, the so-called 'war on terror' and the international banking collapse. In this new world order we need better understanding and cultural awareness if we are going to coexist peacefully. Children's books *can* bridge cultural divides. In her book *Against Borders*, Hazel Rochman writes:

> Books can make a difference in dispelling prejudice and building community: not with role models and literal recipes, not with noble messages about the human family, but with enthralling stories that make us imagine the lives of others. A good story lets you know people as individuals in all their particularity and conflict; and once you see someone as a person – flawed, complex, striving – then you've reached beyond stereotype. Stories, writing them, telling them, sharing them, transforming them, enrich us and connect us and help us know each other.
>
> (1993: 19)

Children's literature does make a difference in children's lives, for not only does it entertain, it also stretches children's imaginations, reminds them of their humanity and exposes them to other cultures (Martinez *et al.*, 2001). As Reynolds (2007: 3) comments, 'children's literature provides a curious and paradoxical cultural space: a space that is simultaneously highly regulated and overlooked, orthodox and radical, didactic and subversive', Within this curious cultural space, picturebooks can bridge the gap between complex development issues and the daily experiences of children. According to Morris and Coughlan:

> Whether you and your children, or the children you work with, live in the multicultural inner city or in the heart of the countryside, the talk, investigation and activity that can be engendered by fine picturebooks will lay good foundations for the development of informed and positive attitudes to racial identity – the child's own and that of other groups in our society.
>
> (2005: 10)

Children learn so much about the world they live in through the books they read but are sometimes presented with only a narrow selection chosen on the basis of the teacher's world view. A fundamental step, therefore, is having a selection of high-quality, engaging, multicultural picturebooks that must be appealing to children and should share stories about universal experiences to which they can relate. Dowd (1992: 220) affirms that 'from reading, hearing, and using culturally diverse materials, young people learn that beneath surface differences of colour, culture or ethnicity, all people experience universal feelings of love, sadness, self-worth, justice and kindness'. According to McGinley *et al.* (1997: 43), 'stories can be a means of personal and social exploration and reflection – an imaginative vehicle for questioning, shaping, responding, and participating in the world'. The challenge of teaching children to read the world needs to be addressed in a holistic, comprehensive manner that prepares them for the global world they inhabit.

Some commentators have highlighted the link between children's books and adult writing since adult authors have been influenced both consciously and unconsciously by the books they read as children. As Reynolds (2007: 9) notes, 'like childhood itself, these stories do not disappear, but continue to unfold and inform how we interpret the world'. Ultimately it is important for development and intercultural educators to recognize the importance of children's literature. On one end of the continuum of development and intercultural education, it can contribute to intercultural understanding, while towards the more progressive end of the continuum, it has the potential to encourage children to think about alternative constructions of society. Such potential may only be realized in conjunction with the astute adult who selects the book and facilitates a critically engaged discussion with the text, illustrations and messages from the book.

Picturebooks feature in all pre-school and early childhood classrooms. Although generally associated exclusively with younger children, several have been written for older children, adolescents and, in some cases, adults (Cianciolo, 1997). However, Haynes and Murris (2012: 102) note that picturebooks are still 'pigeon-holed' as resources for young people, rather than appreciated as visual resources that can provoke deep philosophical responses from people of all ages. It could be argued that picturebooks are even more effective in promoting creativity and critical thinking with older children. Johnson and Freedman (2005: 25) argue that picturebooks are particularly effective for developing critical awareness with 11–14-year-olds. These authors maintain that picturebooks can 'create an accessible way for middle-level students to begin understanding the issues of social justice in relation to themselves as students, as citizens of a society, and as human beings sharing a planet with others who may not be like them'. Mourão (2013) illustrates how 16–18-year-olds can learn to appreciate visual messages by working with *The Lost Thing* (Tan, 2000). Picturebooks can help older children to develop their comprehension skills and can assist them to read critically (Courtney and Gleeson, 2010). Older readers can also use the pictures to predict what's going to happen next. The images can teach children to watch, look and listen for clues, warning signs and exciting things they might otherwise miss. Older readers – including those with a reading age lower than their cognitive age – can learn how to cross-reference the text and pictures to read between the lines. Accordingly, this book demonstrates the potential use of picturebooks with all ages within primary schools.

The complex relationship between words and images

A picturebook is typically 32 pages long with a balance between text and illustrations (Lewis, 2001). In high-quality picturebooks the relationship between text and illustrations is tightly interconnected, complementary and seamless. Bader describes picturebooks as follows:

> A picturebook is a text, illustrations, total design: an item of manufacture and a commercial product; a social, cultural, historical document; and foremost an experience for the child. As an art form, it hinges on the interdependence of pictures and words, on the simultaneous display of two facing pages and on the drama of the turning page.
>
> (1976: 1)

Today, an extraordinary diversity of picturebooks features in genres including fiction, poetry, informational and traditional literature (Lewis, 2001). Three types of picturebooks have been identified: (1) wordless books, which rely solely on illustrations to tell a story; (2) picture story books, in which illustrations and text work together to tell the story; and (3) illustrated books, in which the text supplies most of the information but the illustrations augment and support what is said by the text (Temple *et al.*, 2010).

According to illustrator Uri Shulevitz (1985: 15), a picturebook 'could not, for example, be read over the radio and be understood fully. In a picturebook the pictures extend, clarify, complement, or take the place of words.' Shulevitz highlights the importance of the visual as follows:

> By telling a story visually, instead of through verbal description, a picturebook becomes a dramatic experience: immediate, vivid, moving. A picturebook is closer to theatre and film, silent films in particular, than to other types of books. It is a unique type of book.
>
> (*ibid*: 16)

Both the words and the pictures are read, so it is this relationship between pictures and words, this inter-animation (Lewis, 2001), that makes picture story books so special. Indeed, the compound word 'picturebook' is used to denote the integrated relationship between written text and visual images (Serafini, 2009). High-quality picturebooks contain illustrations that are accomplished works of visual and graphic art, and texts that are written in expressive, carefully crafted language.

Many authors have commented on the interdependence between text and illustrations in the picturebook. Lewis (2001: 4) likens it to 'a single fabric woven from two different materials'. Bader (1976) defines picture story books in terms of the interdependent relationship between words and pictures, which creates an experience that is greater than the sum of the parts. The term *parallel storytelling* is used to describe picturebooks where the text and the drawings tell the same story simultaneously. In picturebooks with interdependent storytelling, there are clear differences between the way in which information in the text and the illustrations is conveyed (Agosto, 1999), and this dissonance provides a gap between the message of the picturebook and the reader's interpretation.

Nikolajeva and Scott (2001) suggest that there are at least five ways in which words and pictures interact in picturebooks: *symmetry*, where the words and pictures are on equal footing; *complementarity*, where words and pictures each provide information; *enhancement*, whereby each extends the meaning of the other; *counterpoint*, where the words and pictures tell different stories; and *contradiction*, when the words and pictures appear to directly oppose each other. These terms – symmetry, complementarity, enhancement, counterpoint and contradiction – can provide a language through which teachers and children can engage with a picturebook's complexity and sophistication. As Lewis (2001: 36) states, 'a picturebook's story is never to be found in the words alone, nor in the pictures but out of their mutual interanimation'.

Postmodern picturebooks

In postmodern picturebooks or picturebooks influenced by postmodernism (Allan, 2012), authors and illustrators 'deliberately work against a linear story-telling pattern' (Wolfenbarger and Sipe, 2007: 275). Postmodernism is generally characterized by the sardonic interpretation of traditional art forms. Postmodern picturebooks tend to have a non-linear structure with multiple storylines or narrators and components of self-reference. They extend the traditional borders of a picturebook. Each book can include a variety of designs, typography and surrealistic illustrations or images, and may also juxtapose unconnected images. The reader is recognized as an active agent in the reading process rather than a passive recipient of predetermined messages, as a producer rather than a consumer of text. Some postmodern texts contain intertextual references, which require the reader to make connections to the texts or require knowledge to understand the picturebook. Gaps are left so the reader can fill in or create the missing part of the story. These texts are often sarcastic or cynical in tone and poke fun at traditional formats.

Postmodern picturebooks appeal to a wide mix of ages and a range of reading levels. They also appeal to the cyber child and the internet generation, as they call on the reader to interact with the book. Postmodern books do not have a linear format – readers can choose how to read them by choosing their own paths through the stories, thus replicating hypertexts in webpages. So, as if clicking a mouse, the reader is enticed to move in any direction and thereby construct their own narrative. This genre of books challenges the reader to go beyond the obvious in finding meaning, thereby engaging higher cognitive skills. Classic postmodern picturebooks include *Black and White* (Macaulay, 1990); *The Three Pigs* (Wiesner, 2001) and *Voices in the Park* (Browne, 2008). Sipe and Pantaleo (2008) suggest that some picturebooks – for example, *The Stinky Cheese Man and other Fairly Stupid Tales* (Scieszka, 2007) – feature many of the characteristics or qualities of postmodernism. Others, like *The Paper Bag Princess* (Munsch, 2009), only exhibit one or two. Sipe and Pantaleo (2008: 4) therefore suggest that it makes sense to consider picturebooks along 'a continuum of postmodernism'.

Postmodern picturebooks are ideal for introducing development education and intercultural perspectives, and for promoting creative thinking and critical analysis and a personal sense of agency. The anti-authoritarian nature of these books is liberating for children and teachers. Children have an opportunity to consider a range of alternative perspectives. These books facilitate a space to consider alternative settings and endings for storylines, to address important 'what if?' questions. They allow opportunities for children to create new scenarios that address a range of social challenges and issues.

Criticism of picturebooks

Criticism of environmental picturebooks is provided by Marriott (2002). He questions whether the mediated experience provided by picturebooks contributes towards or hinders a realistic and appropriate appreciation of the natural world. Based on an examination of 1,074 books, he argues that picturebook makers typically transform and domesticate animals and their habitats in ways that give readers misleading images and impressions. While noting a few exceptional books that give an accurate and sensitive account of the animal kingdom and the natural environment, Marriott argues that many more are needed. However, he acknowledges a number of books that contribute effectively to the theme of environmental conservation, including Simon James's *The Wild Woods* (2008), which is about a child learning to respect animals in their natural habitat. This idea of mediated experience is supported by Benson, who observes that:

> The picture, especially the picture as a work of art, is a mediation of an idea. That idea is embodied in the perceptible qualities of that picture, qualities which are so presented by the artist to the spectator as to guide the experience along particular paths. Talk of the picture is further mediation.
>
> (1986: 135)

While these concerns are valid, I contend that teachers need to be aware of the limitations imposed by mediated experiences. From a symbolic interactionist perspective (Blumer, 1969) one can extend this argument if one recognizes that all the material covered in school is mediated by teachers, schools and society at large. The teacher's influence is paramount in determining the means through which the child interacts with the picturebook.

Elements of picturebooks

The picturebook as we know it in the twenty-first century has been made possible due to advances in printing technology, which allow an illustrator's drawings to be faithfully reproduced and to sit alongside words on the same page. This did not happen until the 1960s, and since then the world of the picturebook has evolved beyond all expectations.

To read a picture story book, the reader must attend to both the written and visual texts. In addition there are other elements of the picturebook that contribute to the overall narrative experience. Title page, covers, endpapers, dedication, author notes, book jacket, advertisements, promotional materials, associated websites and such make up what is known as the paratextual features of the book (Genette, 1997). The paratext is composed of those features contained within the covers of a book (peritext) and those outside the book itself (epitext).

Peritext refers to the physical features of a picturebook apart from the verbal and visual texts (Sipe and McGuire, 2009: 62). These include front and back covers, dust jackets (if the book is a hardback), the endpapers and the title and dedication pages. Endpapers are the pages immediately inside the front and back covers. In some cases, they represent the introduction to, and conclusion of, the story. In other cases, endpapers are used decoratively or symbolically. Some paperback editions are published without endpapers.

Epitext refers to discussions about the picturebook that take place outside the book, such as authorial correspondence and book reviews. In many contemporary picturebooks, the endpapers and other paratextual features are used by the authors, artists and book designers to extend the narrative beyond the written text itself (Sipe and McGuire, 2009).

Many children's books tell their stories through double-page spreads, which may not be obviously organized on the principle of left and right. Other codes and conventions are used to communicate the central message and to support the text and illustrations (Goodwin, 2008). These include: the format of the book – its presentation in portrait or landscape style; the presence of a frame, a border around the illustration; whether pictures break through the frame or take up the whole page or whether, to use the technical term, the picture *bleeds* or *is bled* to the very edge of the paper with no frame and no margin. Colour tone and the level of brightness, lightness or darkness in the images are used to support the central message. Viewpoint – the position from which the reader views the illustrations – is crucial for the illustrator and author, since turning the page requires the reader to pause and peruse the picture. Sometimes a sentence is continued over two pages, so urging the reader to turn the page to find out what happens next. While there are several wonderful books that explore themes relevant to development and intercultural education, knowledge of these codes and conventions will enable teachers to gain maximum potential from their work with picturebooks.

We live in an increasingly multimodal world, where word and image work together to give meaning. This is seen in everything we are expected to read, from newspapers to computer screens. Multimodal texts convey meaning through a combination of elements that draw upon several semiotic systems – linguistic, visual, gestural, audio and spatial. Picturebooks are good examples of multimodal texts in that they include multiple modes of representation including text, visual images and design. As well as recognizing that picturebooks need to be read multimodally, teachers should understand how these different modalities separately and interactively construct different dimensions of meaning. Picturebooks cross the boundaries between the arts, literacy and subject disciplines, so providing wonderful resources for cross-curricular work in primary schools.

Picturebooks are produced in all shapes and sizes. Some are available in Big Book format, designed to be used as teaching aids for a whole class. Others come with a collection of merchandise, puppets and stickers. However, the potential for educational engagement with picturebooks has dramatically increased through the enhanced potential of ICT. Picturebooks can now be shared with children via the interactive whiteboard in the classroom, and several companies are creating apps to accompany their picturebooks. YouTube has provided a forum for bringing more picturebooks and storytellers into the classroom. But, while the digital age brings many opportunities, no digital resource can ever replace the experience of sitting holding a book together with a child, and sharing the suspense initiated by the page turn and enjoying the physical nature of the picturebook.

Despite the excellence of the genre, picturebooks are facing a number of challenges. Anthony Browne (2011: 230) notes the threats of 'cutbacks in library spending, cutbacks in the number of picturebooks stocked by the major book chains, the threat of the ebook, computer games, TV and DVDs, as well as the apparent decline in the popularity of picturebooks among parents'. While the digital age is bringing opportunities to the picturebook arena, it also brings thinly veiled threats of which teachers and parents should be aware. Lane Smith's *It's a Book* (2010) is a charming manifesto on behalf of the printed page in the midst of challenges and opportunities presented by the digital era. This book will help teachers and children re-value the picturebook. It should not be left behind just because the computer has arrived.

In *It's a Book* a jackass with a laptop is baffled by a monkey's unrecognizable possession. 'What do you have there?' 'It's a book.' 'How do you scroll down?' 'I don't. I turn the page. It's a book.' When the monkey is asked 'Where's your mouse?', a live mouse appears cheekily from under the monkey's hat. The back page shows a picture of the jackass with the book, alongside the text:

Can it text?

Blog?

Scroll?

WI-FI?

Tweet?

No…it's a book.

(Smith, 2010)

Visual literacy and the power of picturebooks

Visual images are becoming the predominant form of communication in schools and on the internet – through social media – and television. Pictures exist all around us. They surround us. In an increasingly visual world it is important for children to become visually literate, to learn the skills of looking, appreciating and interpreting visual design. Visual literacy levels determine our level of visual comprehension and ability to read images in a meaningful way. From a young age, children unselfconsciously draw, their pictures combining the seen and the imagined (Salisbury and Styles, 2012). Sadly, once children have mastered print, then drawing and work with visual resources are less valued in primary classrooms. But children need to continue reading and 'writing' visual images so they can continue to understand and analyse visual material from media, computers and advertisements. Picturebooks provide invaluable resources for looking at and evaluating visual texts. Illustrators combine many visual elements and techniques. Aspects of artwork children can learn about include colour, shape, line, layout, borders, patterns, frames, perspective and typography (Pantaleo, 2008).

A picturebook is a work of art whose strength lies in the interrelationship between pictures and text. However, many teachers tend to focus on 'reading the text' to the point of excluding the illustrations. The influence of the teacher is paramount in guiding the child's interactions with the picturebook. Arizpe and Styles (2003: 249) underline the importance of teaching children to deconstruct pictures. Their research confirms that 'children can become more visually literate and operate at a much higher level if they are taught how to look'. The challenge for the primary teacher is to interrogate images from picture story books in a manner that promotes enquiry-based learning and creative thinking and develops skills of critical visual literacy. When picturebooks are used in primary classrooms, they tend to be restricted to the literacy hour and are often interrogated in very superficial terms. Kiefer (1993) also highlights the important role of the teacher in encouraging children to extend their initial reactions to books by allowing them the opportunity and time to respond beyond formal reading and read-aloud sessions. While the potential of picturebooks for supporting literacy is irrefutable, the additional potential for discussing a range of social issues is too often disregarded.

Picturebooks are immensely complex. It is important not to underestimate their power. Words and illustrations do not simply tell stories. Together, they create potentially powerful images of human beings and places. The child sees representations of people, male and female, adult and child, in illustrations that foster a range of interpretations. These interpretations might be internalized to a different degree by each child and propagate often unrecognizable stereotypes (O'Neil, 2010). Thus any picturebook that features people and places might have a didactic outcome different from that its editors intend (Mendoza and Reese, 2001). The challenge for the primary teacher is to interrogate these images in a manner that promotes enquiry-based learning and develops skills of critical visual literacy. Effective engagement with picturebooks, facilitated through effective teaching, will counter concerns such as those raised by Marriott (2002).

The potential of picturebooks for teaching intercultural and development education

While the value of picturebooks in developing language and literacy is widely accepted, I argue that picturebooks also provide a powerful medium for teaching development and intercultural education. Picturebooks demonstrate meaningful concepts and represent the world a child is coming to know. According to Galda *et al.* (2013), concept development, language development and the child's storehouse of experiences are strengthened through books. Thus picturebooks have the potential to supplement the work of primary teachers in the development of a variety of development education concepts and skills.

Picturebooks appeal to children. By connecting development and intercultural ideas to their personal experience, they can accommodate children with different styles and promote critical thinking. Lewis (2001: 137) claims that 'the picturebook is thus ideally suited to the task of absorbing, reinterpreting and re-presenting the world for whom negotiating newness is a daily task'. One central concern of development and intercultural education for primary children is to present a world that is constantly changing. While the quality and diversity of picturebooks has improved in recent years, so too has their ability to deal with contemporary global issues. The events of 11 September 2001 had a devastating impact all over the world and the date represents a significant milestone in international relations. The issue was very difficult for teachers to discuss in class, but a number of picturebooks – such as *Fireboat: The heroic adventures of the John J. Harvey* (Kalman, 2002), *The Man who Walked between the Towers* (Gerstein, 2003), *September Roses* (Winter, 2004) and *The Little Chapel that Stood* (Curtiss, 2003) – highlighted the events in a child-friendly manner. However, it is important to remember the power of the single image (Griffith and Allbut, 2011) or, in Marriott's (2002) terms, 'the mediated experience'. Therefore, to avoid presenting one side of the story, picturebooks such as Jeanette Winter's *Nasreen's Secret School: A true story from Afghanistan* (2009) are important for presenting different cultural perspectives.

There are also a number of picturebooks about Iraq that offer a Muslim perspective. In *Silent Music: A story of Baghdad* (Rumford, 2008), Ali finds comfort in practising his calligraphy during the turmoil that has reigned in Baghdad since 2003. Ali describes how he loves soccer – 'loud, parent-rattling music' – and calligraphy, forming the elegant Arabic letters, pen 'gliding and sweeping, leaping, dancing to the silent music in my head'. Two picturebooks deal with the efforts of Alia Muhammad Baker, the 'Librarian of Basra' who helped save the Basra Central Library during the invasion of Iraq: *The Librarian of Basra: A true story from Iraq* (Winter, 2005) and *Alia's Mission: Saving the books of Iraq* (Stamaty, 2004).

The events of 9/11 had serious implications for cultures all over the world, so discussions about such events need to address the multidimensional context in which they have taken place. By presenting a number of perspectives, teachers can represent how multidimensional 9/11 was, rather than a narrow, one-dimensional view of the event.

Such an alternative perspective is given in *14 Cows for America* (Deedy, 2009), a picturebook based on the true story of a gift of 14 cows to the American people by the Maasai in Kenya. In 2002 an American diplomat in Kenya accepted 14 cows during a special ceremony in western Kenya just nine months after 9/11. The picturebook features the story of Kimeli, who returns to his small Maasai village for a visit. He had been studying medicine in the United States and was there during the attack on the Twin Towers. He tells the story to his people and they try to imagine the tall buildings, the deadly fires and the air dark with smoke and ashes. They want to do something for the American people who suffered the attacks, and when an elder voices that sentiment, Kimeli points out the importance cows have to the Maasai. Kimeli asks the elders for their blessing on offering his only cow but the elders do more than give a blessing. An American diplomat is invited to visit, and in a splendid ceremony the Maasai offer 14 cows to America. An afterword by Wilson Kimeli Naiyomah, the Maasai warrior at the centre of the story, provides additional information about his tribe and their generous actions. This book subverts the narrative of charitable deeds by richer countries for poorer countries and demonstrates that everyone has the power to show solidarity with people in difficult situations.

By selecting picturebooks for children, teachers and parents are consciously or unconsciously selecting particular world views for them to experience. Children can be introduced to the diversity of world religions through picturebooks. *One Green Apple* (Bunting, 2006), *The Colour of Home* (Hoffman, 2002), *My Name Is Bilal* (Mobin-Uddin, 2005) and *Nadia's Hands* (English, 2009) all feature Muslim children. These books are useful for introducing children to Muslim characters and the culture of Islam. Rukhsana Khan (2009) points out that the characters in these books tend, however, to be self-conscious in one way or another. She would like to see a move away from 'Muslim as victim' and advocates the use of children's literature in which Islamic identity is part of the setting or the 'wallpaper' rather than the problem. Khan is an author and storyteller, a Muslim born in Lahore, Pakistan, who immigrated to Canada at the age of 3. In her own books *Silly Chicken (2005)* and *Ruler of the Courtyard* (2003) she has adopted humour as a strategy for promoting multicultural understanding. Racial and religious prejudice can be explored through such books as *My Name Was Hussein* (Kyuchukov, 2004). Based on the life story of a Muslim Roma boy growing up in Bulgaria during the Communist regime, this book provides a glimpse of what life is like for many ethnic minorities. Children need to experience a variety of books from a range of perspectives. Through interrogation and discussion, these books can lead to fruitful discussions in the classroom and deepen children's understanding of the complexities of particular issues and development topics.

Some picturebooks present interesting perspectives on war and peace. One of the classic anti-war picturebooks is *The Butter Battle Book* (Seuss, 1984), which tells the story of a land where two hostile cultures, the Yooks and the Zooks, live on opposite sides of a long curving wall. The Yooks wear blue clothes, the Zooks wear orange. The main dispute between them is that the Yooks eat their bread with the butter side up, while the Zooks eat their bread with the butter side down. The conflict between the two sides leads to an escalating arms race, each competing to make bigger and better weapons to outdo the other.

A young Yook listens to his grandfather's disgust at a culture that chooses to spread butter on the bottom of the bread rather than the top:

> It's high time that you knew
> of the terribly horrible thing that Zooks do.
> In every Zook house and in every Zook town
> every Zook eats his bread
> with the butter side down!
> But we Yooks, as you know,
> when we breakfast or sup,
> spread our bread', Grandpa said,
> 'with the butter side up.
> That's the right, honest way!'
> Grandpa gritted his teeth.
> 'So you can't trust a Zook
> who spreads bread underneath!

Waterloo and Trafalgar (Tallec, 2012) is a wordless picturebook. The two main characters take their names from two of the most famous French defeats in the Napoleonic wars. They appear as enemy soldiers, one dressed in blue, the other in orange. They spy on each other through rain, snow and storms. They learn to tolerate battles, colds and boredom. Soldiering is, after all, quite tedious nonsense most of the time. Tallec sets up the two enemies across terrain that invokes the futile trench warfare of the Great War, sketching winter, Christmas and spring, their feeble attempts at progress and the appearances of characters caught in a trap. Then one day, a blue bird lands on Trafalgar's wall and deposits a blue and orange spotted egg. Out hatches a mixed-breed blue and orange bird! The hatchling tweaks Trafalgar's nose and then flies away to avoid his wrath. A furious Trafalgar follows the bird straight into Waterloo's turf! Only at the end of this wordless graphic story does Tallec's pencil pan back and we see that the two warriors snagged in endless conflict are actually inside an enclosure within peaceful, blossoming parklands. If only we could see beyond ourselves.

The War (Vaugelade, 2007) is a picturebook allegory about the futility of war. The Blues and the Reds have been at war for so long, neither side can remember why they started fighting. Prince Fabien of the Blues is faced with his father's disapproval, as he tries to end the war. Armed only with a pen, paper and his wits, Prince Fabien bravely accomplishes what years of war have failed to achieve and becomes an unlikely hero. The theme of futility is continued in *The Enemy: A book about peace* (Cali, 2009), a powerful anti-war book. Set in two war trenches loosely based on a First World War scenario, two lonely soldiers face each other across a barren battlefield. What each discovers, as the story unfolds, is that the enemy is not a faceless beast but a real person with family, friends and dreams. This picturebook uses images to make the connection between xenophobia and war.

In *The Conquerors* (McKee, 2005) the army of a large country invades those that are smaller. The mantra of their leader is, 'It's for their own good. So they can be like us.' Soon there is just one very small country left unconquered. The General marches in with his army. Instead of fighting, the inhabitants welcome the invaders and invite the soldiers into their homes. This unexpected, friendly reaction angers the General and he orders fresh troops. The same thing happens with unexpected results for the General and his big country. These books help children explore themes of conflict, oppression and xenophobia through the prism of war.

What Is Peace? (Damon, 2004) is a lift-the-flap book that examines peace from a child's perspective. Each page has a large picture with a definition of peace – 'Peace is playing together', for example – illustrated by a picture of children putting it into action. Lifting the flap reveals the opposite (not spoiling the game), also illustrated. The last double-page spread has a pop-up rainbow instead of flaps and the final page has instructions (for adults) on making an Origami peace crane. *Talk Peace* (Williams, 2005) introduces the vital notion of peace to very young children through a poetic text and bright, cheerful illustrations. It puts forward the idea that peace, racial harmony and understanding should permeate every word, action, place and time. Other books for younger children about peace include *Paulie Pastrami Achieves World Peace* (Proimos, 2009) and *The Peace Book* (Parr, 2005).

Radunsky's *What Does Peace Feel Like?* (2004) will inspire teachers and children to create their own images of peace. In *Peaceful Pieces: Poems and quilts about peace* (2011) Anna Grossnickle Hines illustrates a collection of peace poems with handmade quilts. The author/illustrator explores peace in many forms – from peace at home, to peace on a worldwide scale, to peace within oneself. The book invites the reader to consider the meaning of peace and its fleeting nature. In *Paths to Peace: People who changed the world*, Breskin Zalben (2006) sets the tone for each of the 16 peacemakers she profiles in the book with a stirring quote set within a stunning and incisive collage. Mahatma Gandhi, Eleanor Roosevelt, César Chávez, and Nobel-Prize winners Aung San Suu Kyi and Dr Wangari Maathai are some of the people she chose to represent different eras and parts of the globe. Many commenced their path to peace during their childhood, and all challenge us to think about improving the lives of others. Also included in this beautiful volume are art notes, a glossary, a bibliography, further reading and an index, making it an excellent resource for the classroom.

Archbishop Desmond Tutu was awarded the Nobel Peace Prize in 1984 for his lifelong struggle to bring equality, justice and peace to his native South Africa. He continues to play an important role as a spokesperson worldwide. The picturebook *Desmond and the Very Mean Word* (Tutu and Carton Abrams, 2013) is based on a real experience that occurred when Desmond Tutu was growing up in South Africa. The book begins with a letter from Archbishop Tutu to the reader:

Dear Child,

When I was growing up in South Africa, we were told something very strange. We were told that people with darker skin were not quite as wonderful as people with lighter skin. Can you imagine how silly? It's as if someone said that people with big noses were better than people with small noses. But that's the way it was for a long time, and many mean things were said and done during those bad old days. You are about to read a story of a young boy named Desmond who looks a lot like me although he doesn't have all this funny grey hair. In this story, Desmond learns the power of words and the secret of forgiveness.

Desmond Tutu

In this picturebook, Desmond rides through his neighbourhood on his new bicycle. His pride and joy turn to hurt and anger when a group of boys shout a very mean word at him. While the mean word itself is not revealed in the book, his conflicting emotions are highlighted: his wanting to fight back and his ultimate decision to forgive:

> Father Trevor sighed. "That is the problem, Desmond. You will get them back, and they will get you back, and soon our whole world will be filled with nothing but getting back."

The book shares timeless wisdom with readers about how to handle bullying and angry feelings while seeing the good in everyone.

A major concern of development education and education for sustainable development is the interrelationship between human and physical environments on a variety of levels from the local to the global. Lewis (2001) uses ecology as an analogy to explain the complex nature of picture story books. The words come to life in the context of the environment, the pictures and vice versa. Thus this complex relationship between words and illustrations serves as a useful frame through which children can come to grips with the global concept of interdependence.

Values underpinning *You, Me and Diversity* are those that are promoted by development and intercultural education, outlined in Figure 1.1.

Conclusion

Picturebooks are extraordinarily diverse. Some have been created principally for humour, while others present sensitive issues in a way that promotes empathy and understanding. Some picturebooks leave the reader reflecting about a particular perspective, while others have no message at all. In certain cases the pictures tell the story with a little assistance from the text, and in others the text does most of the work with some help from the illustrations. Some picturebooks include illustrations that are magnificent works of art in their own right, while others use photographs and digital media. According to Goodwin (2008: 104), 'the picturebook has developed into a versatile medium capable of conveying narrative at a variety of levels and to different effect'.

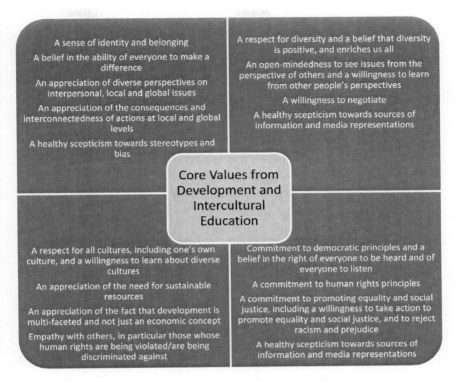

Figure 1.1: Development education and intercultural education: core values

Source: Adapted from Fitzgerald (2007)

From a literacy perspective, regular encounters with picturebooks expand the children's vocabulary, extend their command of sentence structures and give them a sense of the shape of stories and poems, while enlarging their sense of the world and how people live in it (Purcell-Gates, 1988). Good literacy education – including reading, writing, talking and listening – is arguably fundamental for development and intercultural education. Literacy education should involve artistic and enthralling endeavours for all involved. For children, engagement with picturebooks should ultimately be an enjoyable experience. As Bishop observes:

> Reading literature, especially fiction, no matter what culture it reflects, ought to be an aesthetic experience. In our search for social significance and our desire for social change, we dare not forget that a well written piece of literature is a work of art. It may be serious and cause readers to reflect or to become angry or to see something familiar in a new way; it may be informative and

diminish ignorance; but it does so through readers' engagement with the literary work. In classrooms where multicultural literature is to have an effect, that experience is primary. Other goals can be achieved when readers are given time and the opportunity, with a knowledgeable teacher as facilitator, to make thoughtful responses to their reading and to enrich their own readings by interacting with others whose responses may or may not be similar.

(1997: 6)

While excellent picturebooks are available for teaching a broad range of development and intercultural themes, these books are rarely found in primary classrooms because many teachers are unaware of their existence and potential links with the primary curriculum. Culturally diverse picturebooks can extend children's perspectives in preparation for active citizenship in a diverse and globalized society. Choosing high-quality authentic picturebooks is the first step. It is important that we, as educators, approach this task with a critical eye to ensure that the picturebooks used in class are accurate, dispel or challenge stereotypes, avoid generalizations and provide authentic settings and language.

You, Me and Diversity is designed to help student teachers and primary teachers select picturebooks effortlessly, efficiently and expertly. Once teachers have made their selection from the high-quality picturebooks that are available, they will find here a range of avenues through which these books can introduce, support and underpin a range of development education and intercultural topics, themes and perspectives for primary classrooms.

Chapter 2

Culture, intercultural education and development education

In this chapter, I explore a number of definitions, values and concepts of multicultural, intercultural and development education in the context of culture and culturally responsive teaching. I focus on the development education topics of child labour and access to education, and highlight selected picturebooks that deal with these topics.

Culture

The concept of culture is common to both interculturalism and multiculturalism and a constant backdrop for all discussions within development education. Culture essentially refers to the way of life of a group of people. Arnove and Torres define culture as:

> A reference to all aspects of life including the mental, social, linguistic and physical forms of culture. It refers to ideas people have, the relationships they have with others in their families and with larger social institutions, the languages they speak and the symbolic forms they share, such as written language or art/music forms.
>
> (2003: 116)

Culture is often compared to an iceberg, which has both visible (on the surface) and invisible (below the surface) parts. Elements of culture we can plainly see, such as food or clothes, are represented by the upper portion of the iceberg. Those elements that are not as obvious – such as why someone eats or dresses the way they do – are represented by the much larger portion of the iceberg underwater. Referred to as *surface* and *deep*, *visible* and *invisible*, *overt* and *covert*, these observable and non-observable parts of culture need to be identified and understood as part of one's identity. Failure to understand and recognize these parts of culture – the layers that compose them and how they influence each other – is the main reason for cultural misunderstandings and, in some cases, cultural conflict.

Multicultural education

Multicultural education is a school reform movement that arose out of the Civil Rights Movement of the 1960s and 1970s in the USA. Its transformative potential has been noted in the literature. If implemented in thoughtful, creative and effective ways, multiculturalism has the potential to transform schools and other educational institutions in ways that will enable them to prepare children and young people to live and function well in the future (Banks, 2008).

The initial motives of multiculturalism were cultural pluralism – i.e. incorporating the perspectives of traditionally unrepresented groups. However, the term *multiculturalism* as discussed by James Banks (and initially in Europe) was always centred on issues of equality. Banks and McGee Banks (2009) have traced four historical stages of multiculturalism in America:

- phase 1: ethnic studies, whereby students learn about histories and cultures of ethnic minorities
- phase 2: equality and equity, which involves an attempt to promote a change of attitude towards diverse histories and cultures of ethnic minorities. Promoting equality and equity in education is also considered a priority in this stage
- phase 3: equity for all previously under-represented groups including disabled, gay and lesbian and feminist groups. At this point all under-represented groups are included under multiculturalism
- phase 4: theory, research and practice of multicultural education. This stage involves a critical investigation of the intersections of race, class and gender across cultures, histories and experiences.

I have stated earlier that the term *multicultural* is problematic. In Europe, in both policy and public discourses, there has been a shift away from multiculturalism to a demand for integration, cohesion and, in some cases, assimilationism. In numerous European countries there is currently a moral panic about immigration and ethnic and religious diversity. Throughout Europe the ideas about how we accommodate difference and diversity are being challenged (Vasta, 2007), and there has been much debate in the UK about immigrant diversity, multiculturalism, integration and segregation. Vasta argues that diversity, through multiculturalism, needs to be part of national policy and public symbolism. The City of Amsterdam, for example, has defined its 'diversity' policy as 'post multicultural', where 'everybody is entitled to participate, not as a member of a group, but as an individual with a multifaceted identity' (Uitermark *et al.*, 2005: 17–18). There is a stronger emphasis on diversity within intercultural education.

Intercultural education

Intercultural education is a synthesis of the learning from multicultural education and antiracist education approaches, commonly used internationally from the 1960s to the 1990s. Intercultural education has two key dimensions. It is:

- education that respects, celebrates and recognizes the normality of diversity in all areas of human life. It sensitizes the learner to the idea that humans have naturally developed a range of different ways of life, customs and world views and that this breadth of human life enriches all of us
- education that promotes equality and human rights, challenges unfair discrimination and promotes the values upon which equality is based (NCCA, 2005: 3).

On the basis of a review of key scholars in intercultural education and global education, Short (2009) defines intercultural education as an orientation in which learners:

- explore their cultural identities and develop a conceptual understanding of culture
- develop an awareness and respect for different cultural perspectives as well as the commonality of human experience
- learn about issues that have personal, local and global relevance and significance
- value the diversity of cultures and perspectives within the world
- demonstrate responsibility and commitment to making a difference in the world
- develop into inquiring, knowledgeable and caring human beings who take action to create a better and more just world.

Education itself is inherently a cultural process. While it cannot bear total responsibility for the development of intercultural competences, it nevertheless has an important role to play. An intercultural education is essential for all children in equipping them to live in a diverse, globalized society. Both the terms *multicultural* and *intercultural* describe a situation where there is more than one culture in a country. While the term *multiculturalism* is sometimes used to describe a society in which different cultures live side by side without much interaction, the term *interculturalism* expresses a belief that we all become personally enriched by coming into contact with and experiencing other cultures. Cultures can, and should be able to, engage with and learn from each other (Haran and Tormey, 2002). Some commentators have defined multicultural education in more radical terms. For example, Banks and McGee Banks (2009: 1) describe multicultural education as 'an idea, an educational reform movement and a process whose major goal is to change the structure of educational institutions so that male and female students, exceptional students and students who are members of diverse racial, ethnic, language and cultural groups will have an equal chance to achieve academically in school'.

Development education

There are a wide range of definitions and interpretations of development education. According to Irish Aid, development education:

- is an educational response to issues of development, human rights, justice and world citizenship
- presents an international development and human rights perspective within education here in Ireland and elsewhere
- promotes the voices and viewpoints of those who are excluded from an equal share in the benefits of human development internationally
- is an opportunity to link and compare development issues and challenges in Ireland with those elsewhere throughout the world
- provides a chance for Irish people to reflect on our international roles and responsibilities with regard to issues of equality and justice in human development
- is an opportunity to be active in writing a new story for human development.

(2006: 6)

Development education is also discussed through a range of other terms including *global education*, the *global dimension, citizenship education* and *global citizenship education*. Specific themes within development education include interdependency, global poverty, aid, trade and debt, social justice and human rights. Both development education and intercultural education have theoretical frameworks, issues, topics and values of common concern, as highlighted in Table 2.1.

Table 2.1: Development education and intercultural education:
core themes

Development education	Development and intercultural education	Intercultural education
Global knowledge	Equality, inequality and social justice	Identity and belonging
Global poverty	Human rights and responsibility	Culture, religions and value systems
Environment/ sustainable development	Peace, conflict and resolution	Racism, prejudice and discrimination
Aid and trade	Migration, asylum and refugees	
Globalization	Culture, diversity and similarities	
Interdependence		

Source: Adapted from Fitzgerald (2007)

From my perspective, development education is about fairness, equality and justice, with a particular reference to the so-called *developing world*. I choose this political term to maintain the important link between developing countries and the discipline of development education. Terms such as the *global south* and *the majority world* are also used by other writers. To understand global equality and justice, children need to examine these issues in their own schools, homes and local areas. It is impossible to interrogate development issues without examining key factors such as gender and the environment. This leads on to the vital theme of resources, control of resources and political power, where this power is located and how it is exercised and distributed. Culture is a key element underpinning development education, and culturally responsive teaching is important if we wish to eliminate racism and discrimination and promote more positive approaches to living in diverse communities.

Culturally responsive teaching

Studies from America illustrate that teacher education has been slow to respond to the shifting demographic landscape. According to Villegas and Lucas (2002: xiii) the lack of action 'helps to perpetuate the persistent achievement gap between white, middle class, English-speaking children and their poor and minority peers'. Villegas and Lucas have written extensively about the 'culturally responsive teacher', maintaining that all those entering the teaching profession must be prepared to teach a racially, ethnically, economically and linguistically diverse population. Equally, the number of students from minority groupings should be encouraged and enabled to gain access to initial teacher education. Britain has a long tradition as a multicultural society. In Ireland, where this book was written, approximately 10 per cent of the student population in primary education come from different ethnic backgrounds. This raises questions about 'the culturally responsive teacher', primary teachers who can take into account cultural, linguistic, economic and social factors in teaching and learning, classroom management and relationships with children and their parents. Culturally responsive teaching is a pedagogy that recognizes the importance of including children's cultural references in all aspects of learning (Ladson-Billings, 1994).

Villegas and Lucas define *culturally responsive teachers* as those who:

- have socio-cultural consciousness – that is, they recognize that the way we perceive the world is deeply influenced by race/ethnicity, social class and language
- have affirming views of students from diverse backgrounds
- have a sense that they are responsible for and capable of bringing about educational change
- embrace constructivist views of teaching and learning
- are familiar with their students' prior knowledge and beliefs
- design instruction that builds on what students already know.

(2002: xiv)

Culture plays a role not only in communicating and receiving information but also in shaping the thinking process of groups and individuals. All aspects of teaching and learning are mediated through culture. A pedagogy that acknowledges, responds to and celebrates fundamental cultures offers full, equitable access to education for students from all cultures. According to Nieto (2010: 215), teachers and prospective teachers, especially those who have not had extensive experience working with students of diverse backgrounds, 'need to learn to understand human differences in order to tap into the intelligence and capacity of all students'. Becoming competent and caring mentors for a broad range of students means developing specific skills and competences for teaching students who speak languages other than English and whose cultural and racial backgrounds differ from their own. Undoubtedly, the better prepared that pre-service teachers are to work with diverse populations, the more effective their teaching can be. But these competences are not acquired automatically: they need to be developed and nurtured.

Development education topics and picturebooks

Several picturebooks specifically address a range of development education topics: justice, equality, child labour, refugees and hunger. In the following section I consider the topic of child labour. I present three picturebooks that illuminate different aspects of the topic and suggest ways to promote the development of critical thinking with the assistance of these picturebooks.

Child labour

Child labour is an important development education topic. Through the Millennium Development Goals, the United Nations made a commitment that by 2015, children everywhere, boys and girls alike, should be able to complete a full course of primary schooling. But in some countries, such as Pakistan, where many families earn less than $1.25 per day, parents have to pay for their children to attend public school. Many schools also require children to wear special school uniforms. Extreme poverty means that several families cannot afford school fees or school uniforms.

Instead, many parents in Pakistan are forced to make difficult choices for their children, all in the hope of giving them a better life. Several send their children to work in factories making handmade rugs because the factory owners promise to take care of the children and give them the chance to earn money for their family. Although it is illegal for children under the age of 14 to work in carpet factories, many young children work for long hours weaving carpets. They can become sick from inhaling carpet fibres or hurt their hands and fingers by doing this intricate work. Most of these children don't have time to go to school, so have little hope of finding a better job when they grow up.

Child labour is not exclusive to Pakistan. In Ecuador thousands of children pick bananas, while in the US thousands work illegally in farming and certain industries. Child labour occurs in many parts of the world. The United Nations estimates that 250 million children between the ages of 5 and 14 work full time. In many cases, the wages that children earn help to feed their families. But some countries have no laws to protect children from working long hours in poor conditions.

Picturebooks and child labour

Three picturebooks tell the stories of children who work in carpet production: *Waiting for the Owl's Call* (Whelan, 2009), *The Roses in my Carpets* (Khan, 2004) and *The Carpet Boy's Gift* (Deitz Shea, 2006).

Waiting for the Owl's Call is about Zulviya, a young Turkoman child living in Afghanistan. She works all day long with her sister and cousin at the loom, weaving rugs by hand. They begin early in the morning, shortly after the call to prayer, and do not finish until dusk when they hear the call of the owl. The work of tying thousands of knots in a single day is tedious and difficult. It makes Zulviya's back ache and her fingers bleed. To keep her mind occupied, Zulviya imagines creating her own pattern full of the colours and symbols of her homeland. She longs for the chance to attend school some day.

The book communicates the real problem of child labour in Asia's rug-making industry. The information at the end of the book informs the reader of a non-governmental organization named RugMark that inspects rug production sites, issues certification labels for rugs made without child labour and helps rehabilitate child workers and send them to school. Readers will gain a deeper appreciation of Afghanistan's culture and the importance of education in meeting the needs of its children.

Roses in my Carpet (Khan, 2004) is about a young refugee boy from Afghanistan. At the mud house in the refugee camp, his days consist mainly of work, school, prayers and sharing what little there is to eat. He has nightmares about war and is learning the skill of carpet weaving, from which he hopes to derive a living for his family someday. His father is dead and the boy is embarrassed to admit that he accepts a little aid from an unseen sponsor. In his graceful narrative, he describes the colours he uses as he practises his skill as a carpet weaver:

> Each colour that I weave has a special meaning. The threads that line the frame, on which all the other threads are knotted, are white. White for the shroud we wrapped my father's body in. Black is for the night that cloaks us from enemy eyes. Green is the color of life. Blue is the sky. One day it will be free of jets.

> Everything in camp is a dirty brown, so I do not use brown anywhere in my carpets.

> Red is my favourite. Red is the colour of the blood of martyrs. But it is also the colour of roses. I have never grown flowers. Every bit of land must yield food. So I make sure there are plenty of roses in my carpet.

The colours chosen by the illustrator also reflect the tension in the book. Leaden skies and mud-coloured walls contrast with the bright colours of the carpet.

The Carpet Boy's Gift (Deitz Shea, 2006) is a sensitive introduction to the subject of human rights and the complicated issue of child labour. The central characters, Nadeem and Amina, are bonded child labourers who work in a rug factory in Pakistan. The following extract from the book highlights the financial exploitation that underpins child labour:

> Master says I have only two more months until my peshgi is paid back. With that thought, Nadeem quickened his knotting of the scarlet weft threads on the loom and then beat them tightly into place with his panja. I'm sure Master means it this time, Nadeem hoped. He must mean it.

> Nadeem pictured himself free, playing soccer with his little brother Hakim. In the daylight! Since his parents had to sell him three years ago for a loan of 1,000 rupees, Nadeem had worked in the carpet factory from dawn to sundown, seven days a week.

While their earlier efforts to win freedom have been thwarted, they are inspired after an encounter with Iqbal Masih to continue to try to change their lives for the better by insisting on their right to go to school. Although the story is fictional, it is inspired by the true story of Iqbal Masih, a 12-year-old boy and human rights activist who became a real-life hero to thousands in his short life. When Iqbal was 4, his family bonded him for a *peshgi* of about $12 to a rug maker near Lahore, Pakistan. Iqbal wove carpets 12 hours a day for six years, working in poor conditions and suffering from hunger and injuries like other children in the factory.

One day Iqbal escaped and attended a rally held by the Bonded Labour Liberation Front (BLLF), an organization working to help children like him. He learned that a law against child slavery had been passed in Pakistan in 1992, but the factory owners didn't obey the law and the police didn't enforce it. With help from the BLLF, Iqbal began to sneak into hundreds of rug factories so he could educate other child labourers about their rights. He was shot dead in 1995. The book includes detailed information about child labour issues and encourages children to support companies that work to make the world a better place for all. Readers can learn more about the facts of Iqbal Masih's life, examine their own consumer habits, explore what schools are like in different countries and develop new ideas about human rights. These resources can lead to valuable discussions about what is acceptable or unacceptable for children in a global economy.

Anne M. Dolan

Follow-on work based on the three books

COMPARATIVE ANALYSIS OF THE THREE PICTUREBOOKS
Ask children to identify common strands in the books. Discuss how the issue of child labour is explored by different authors and illustrators.

REFLECTING ON JOBS IN MY HOME
Children can reflect on the nature of the work they do at home and in school. Do they have jobs? If so, what kind and do they get paid? Discuss the issue of a minimum age for working and a minimum age for leaving school. List some reasons why children might be forced to work. List some jobs that children should never be permitted to do. Use a world map or globe to discuss the region of the world where the story takes place. Discuss the mountains and the difficulties of living in isolated areas.

LEARNING TO BE PART OF THE SOLUTION
Create a display that celebrates the lives of children who have made a difference like Iqbal Masih. As children investigate stories of others who have made discoveries and sacrifices, they might realize that they too can learn to make a difference in the world.

VISITING A LOCAL CHARITY SHOP
Take children to a local charity shop to investigate how clothing can be recycled and who benefits from the recycling.

UNDERSTANDING ISSUES IN THE WORLD OF WORK
Introduce children to what it means to work with wages and without. Explain that the *The Carpet Boy's Gift* depicts the realities of oppressive child labour. Ask readers to discuss what types of work are acceptable and unacceptable for children. Discuss the idea of a wage. Help children begin to understand that work can either give people a sense of dignity or make people feel demeaned.

CELEBRATING LABOUR DAY
Labour Day is an annual holiday to celebrate the achievements of workers. Some countries vary the actual date of their celebrations so that the holiday occurs on a Monday close to 1 May. Labour Day has its origins in the Labour Union Movement – specifically, the Eight-Hour Day Movement, which advocated eight hours for work, eight

hours for recreation and eight hours for rest. Children can plan a celebration to honour the different jobs they do in the home to help their parents and the type of paid and unpaid work carried out by their parents.

HISTORICAL ANALYSIS
Children can investigate child labour practices in the past and the campaigns that were organized to stop child labour.

MIDDLE EASTERN FOOD
Ask children to identify which foods come from the Middle East and Pakistan.

ART AND CRAFT
Children can design and sew one or more clothing items of their choice. Sewing will help children develop an appreciation for the hard work and skill involved in being a tailor.

WHERE DO YOUR CLOTHES COME FROM?
Map the sources of clothes the children wear. Survey the clothing labels to find where clothing is manufactured. Locate the major assembly places on a map. Compare the pros and cons of buying clothes made in places where the labour practices are unacceptable. This information may help children and their families become more thoughtful consumers.

MAKE A POSTER PROTESTING AGAINST THE USE OF CHILD LABOUR
Children are being exploited and forced to work in factories all over the world. Children can design a poster that makes people aware of the problem following a brainstorm about the impact of these practices on children and their families.

The Carpet Boy's Gift (Deitz Shea, 2006) is primarily about child labour in Pakistan, but of course this happens elsewhere too. A number of supplementary discussions can be inspired by the book:

- heroes, and learning to make a difference in the your community
- the world of work (for elementary-school-aged children)
- rug-making techniques and traditional designs for rugs
- the culture of Pakistan
- consumer awareness habits
- poverty and human rights

- the role of the UN and Universal Children's Rights
- ethics in the global economy
- trade issues and social justice
- history of child labour around the world (for middle-school-aged children)
- the important life opportunities that schools can afford children.

Education, schooling and picturebooks

These books about child labour also deal with education and the lack of it. For those who regularly go to school, this right can be taken for granted. It is important for teachers to encourage children to reflect on their experiences of schooling and how they would feel if they could not attend school, if they could not read or write or if they did not have access to electricity or the outside world through media and the internet. Conversations about basic human rights and the rights of children do not have to be in abstract terms. Children can produce a dialogue that predicts a future where the characters from these stories attend school. Teachers can encourage the children to write the dialogue and develop dramatic scenes. Teachers can challenge and assist children to prepare by researching the school experiences of children in other parts of the world.

The *right to education* is a universal entitlement to education, recognized as a human right. According to the International Covenant on Economic, Social and Cultural Rights (1966), the right to education includes the right to free, compulsory primary education for all. Education is power. It helps individuals be aware of their rights, make rational decisions and protect themselves against abuse and oppression. However, millions of people around the world are being denied access to education and the vast majority are women. Many girls have to help out with the housework and take care of their siblings instead of going to school or playing. Although the rates of girls' primary education have improved in most countries, only 43 per cent of girls in the developing world attend secondary school.

As a follow-on to these books, children could research the greatly differing provision of education in other countries. Children can bring in pictures and photographs of other schools. The children in the stories under discussion have never been to school. In *Waiting for the Owl's Call* (Whelan, 2009) the nearest school to Zulviya would take two days to reach. She has no idea what happens there. Children could be encouraged to think about the role of school and education in their lives and its advantages and disadvantages. They could write a letter to Zulviya telling her about their school. Children could discuss the issue of girls' access to education, and write a letter to

Zulviya's village outlining reasons why they should or shouldn't build a school for the girls in the village. Children will benefit from learning about the similarities and differences among schools, their resources and rules.

Several picturebooks deal with the issue of education as a development theme. *Running the Road to ABC* (Lauture, 2000) describes the arduous journey of six Haitian children on their way to school. These children have to wake up early and travel a great distance. Yet none of this bothers them because they are so eager to learn. In *Rain School* (Rumford, 2010), Thomas is excited about his first day of school in Chad, and has many questions for the other children about what to expect. When he gets to school on the first day, he discovers that there is no school and he and his classmates will have to build it. Once the school is built, the children learn and flourish throughout the school year. In the summer, the school is again torn down by wind and rain. The process of rebuilding starts once more. Rumford's book highlights the centrality of school to a community and that schools cannot exist without children, parents and teachers.

Bonyo Bonyo: The true story of a brave boy from Kenya (Oelschlager, 2010) is about a boy who overcomes incredible adversity. Growing up in western Kenya in a family of struggling farmers, Bonyo enjoyed the simple things in life and was a happy child. However, his sister died when he was 9 and her death changed the path of his life forever. Akinyi, Bonyo's sister, died because his village did not have access to clean water or medical care. From that day Bonyo swore that he would build a hospital in his village to help other children like Akinyi. But Bonyo's family could not afford the dollar it would cost to send him to school that year. A chance encounter with the principal of a school gave Bonyo an opportunity to get an education. He duly found himself at medical school in Texas, USA, with a blanket and some money in his pocket. Years later, he fulfilled his lifelong dream of becoming a doctor.

Nasreen's Secret School: A true story from Afghanistan (Winter, 2009) is about the importance of education, the healing powers of love and the ability of the human spirit to rise above oppression. Although set in Afghanistan with a distinct Middle Eastern backdrop, the themes and emotions it presents are universal. *Listen to the Wind: The story of Dr. Greg and three cups of tea* (Mortenson, 2009) is based on a real-life story. After failing to reach the summit of Pakistan's K2, the world's second-highest mountain, Greg Mortenson stumbled into the remote village of Korphe. Mortenson, a nurse by training, badly needed nursing himself, and the villagers obliged with kindness and grace. What started as a desire to reciprocate with an act of generosity has led, over time, to Mortenson raising money and building close to 80 schools in remote parts of Pakistan and Afghanistan. The first school was in Korphe, a village so poor that children were without a full-time teacher and had to write on the ground with sticks.

In *Running Shoes* (Lipp, 2009), Sophy is a young girl living in a remote low-income village in Cambodia, facing obstacles that prevent her from going to school. Only boys attend the nearest school, eight kilometres away, and the recent death of her father comes as a huge personal and economic blow. However, one day a government census worker who visits the village once a year notices Sophy staring at his running shoes and takes an interest in her situation. The running shoes that arrive at Sophy's home a month later help her overcome one obstacle, the long trip on foot along a narrow, rocky road to get to school. Her courage, intelligence and quick feet help her overcome an even bigger problem, namely the ridicule from the boys that a girl wants to join them at school. This unique book gives a compelling account of the multiple barriers that prevent children in developing countries, especially girls, from attending school. Getting past such hurdles can involve numerous steps, including a change in parents' willingness and ability to send a child to school, relaxing social norms about who can attend it and improving school access for children in remote villages.

Cline-Ransome's (2013) *Light in the Darkness: A story about how slaves learned in secret* is a story about a pit school. With no access to education, some African American slaves set up makeshift classrooms. These pit schools were disguised ditches, where slaves of all ages gathered to form letters out of sticks, scratch letters in the dirt and pronounce their sounds in whispers. Told from the perspective of Rosa, who makes the dangerous night-time journey to her tuition with her mother, the story effectively conveys the urgent dedication of the characters to their clandestine schooling and their belief in the power of literacy. It demonstrates the risks taken by the slaves for the sake of education and its associated value. Through this story, the author makes the point that learning was not just a dream of a few famous and accomplished men and women, but one that belonged to ordinary people willing to risk their lives.

Other books that deal with the right to education are as follows: *We Are All Born Free: The Universal Declaration of Human Rights in pictures* (Amnesty International, 2008), *For Every Child: The UN Convention on the Rights of the Child in words and pictures* (Castle *et al.*, 2001), *The Royal Bee* (Park, 2008), *Brothers in Hope: The story of the lost boys of Sudan* (Williams, 2005), *The School is Not White! A true story of the Civil Rights Movement* (Rappaport, 2005), *Beatrice's Goat* (McBrier, 2001), *Dancing to Freedom: The true story of Mao's last dancer* (Cunxin, 2008), *Josias, Hold* the *Book* (Elvgren, 2006) and *Armando and the Blue Tarp School* (Fine, 2007). Related books are *Biblioburro: A true story from Colombia* (Winter, 2011) and *Waiting for Biblioburro* (Brown, 2011).

Non-fiction picturebooks that feature education in different countries include: *My School in the Rain Forest: How children attend school around the world* (Ruurs, 2009), *A School Like Mine: A unique celebration of schools around the world* (Smith, 2007), *My Librarian is a Camel: How books are brought to children around the world* (Ruurs, 2005) and *Off to Class: Incredible and unusual schools around the world* (Hughes, 2011).

Conclusion

In this chapter, I have defined some of the important concepts that are central to this book. These include culture, multicultural education, intercultural education, development education and culturally responsive teaching. The process of becoming a culturally responsive teacher should begin during initial teacher education programmes. Student teachers and teacher educators need to be well versed in the concepts discussed in this chapter before they begin the process of selecting appropriate picturebooks for primary classes.

Chapter 3

A culturally diverse classroom

Introduction

As Fox and Short (2003) assert, 'stories matter'. Moreover, it is important to think about which stories we tell and why. In classrooms that promote intercultural and development education, picturebooks can provide an invaluable resource to promote global perspectives and values of justice. In recent years there has been a dramatic increase in high-quality multicultural literature that promotes perspectives on global issues and justice from a multitude of viewpoints. While some books dip into multiculturalism in a marginal way, others embrace key concepts and themes emphatically. More importantly, schools need to prepare children to live in a multicultural society and experience different cultural perspectives in all aspects of teaching and learning. Teachers need to critique picturebooks and assess which are best for their educational purposes. These stories need to be explored in the context of thoughtful curriculum planning. However, the inclusion of picturebooks that feature a range of culturally inclusive images will not in itself promote intercultural learning without some direction from the teacher. It is up to the professional primary teacher to maximize the opportunities for promoting intercultural understanding through enquiry-based learning. In this chapter, I explore diversity, multiculturalism and multicultural literature, and look at some of the debates around authenticity. I also include criteria for assessing multicultural literature.

Diversity

Authors such as Mem Fox are committed to promoting diversity in picturebooks such as *Whoever You Are* (2001). *Ten Little Fingers and Ten Little Toes* (Fox, 2008) eloquently epitomizes diversity alongside our common bond as human beings. Illustrated by Helen Oxenbury, each page has one baby from a different part of the world:

> There was one little baby who was born far away,
> and another who was born on the very next day.
> And both of these babies, as everyone knows,
> had ten little fingers and ten little toes.

There was one little baby who was born in a town,
and another who was wrapped in an eiderdown.
And both of these babies, as everyone knows,
had ten little fingers and ten little toes.

There was one little baby who was born in the hills,
and another who suffered from sneezes and chills.
And both of these babies, as everyone knows,
had ten little fingers and ten little toes.

There was one little baby who was born on the ice,
and another in a tent who was just as nice.
And both of these babies, as everyone knows,
had ten little fingers and ten little toes.

But the next baby born was truly divine,
a sweet little child who was mine, all mine.
And this little baby, as everyone knows,
has ten little fingers, ten little toes,

and three little kisses on the tip of its nose.

Picturebooks include a variety of stories and illustrations of a range of different ethnic groups and cultures around the world. The beauty of the illustrations and the quality of the stories provides a strong, visible statement that affirms the importance of valuing diversity. These books can be used to integrate multicultural content into the primary curriculum and in turn can help create an inclusive classroom atmosphere. The importance of the picturebook, as a conveyor of cultural values, is becoming increasingly significant in the lives of young and older children. Graham (1990: 27) points out that 'children *read* illustrations in much the same way as they interpret behaviour in real life' and, as such, these visual narratives can give children small insights into the way people from different cultures live and interact. The following account of one person's experience with diversity, related by a primary school teacher in Ireland during an intercultural education workshop, raises the importance of ensuring that all media – including picturebooks – used in the classroom feature several cultures:

> I got a call from the pre-school that my 4-year-old attends because there was some difficulty: there was a new child in the class and he didn't like her because she was black. I was embarrassed and perplexed. I was certain that our family was not racist and certainly no one would ever have said anything that might lead to

him not liking someone because of their skin colour. I knew that if I wanted to find out what was going on, I needed to be open and non-judgmental, so I didn't give out to him, I just asked him why he didn't like the new child. 'Because she doesn't wash herself, she is all dirty', he told me. I explained that was just the colour of her skin and that she did wash herself and was clean, but it made no difference to him. I thought about it for a while. Looking through the books we used at home when reading to him, I noticed that all the pictures were of white people. I checked the books they used in the pre-school, and all the pictures in those were of white people too. I realized that he had grown up with the idea that people were 'normally' white-skinned and, consequently, that people with a different skin colour were not normal. I needed to show him that people normally have different skin colour and there was nothing to dislike or be afraid of. So I got some new books to use when reading with him, books that had pictures of children with different skin colour in them. When reading, I pointed out that different children had different skin colour and that this was perfectly normal. In a short time, I could see that this was making a difference to his attitude.

(NCCA, 2005: 4)

Prior to the 1960s, people who were not white were virtually invisible in children's literature internationally. The multicultural movement involved a critique of literature, including that for children, to assess which stories were systematically included and excluded. The critique resulted in greater diversity in children's literature and the development of multicultural literature as a discipline in its own right. Sociocultural changes during the 1960s and 1970s, particularly in America, fostered renewed interest in multicultural literature for adults and children, which reflected 'the diverse life experiences, traditions, histories, values, world views and perspectives of the diverse cultural groups that make up society' (Grant and Ladson-Billings, 1997: 185).

The composition of families is increasingly diverse in contemporary society and includes same-sex and opposite-sex couples, single parents and mixed-race partnerships. International adoptions also further contribute to the diversity of families. Many who adopt children from other countries deal with ever-changing laws, policies and requirements that make the process extremely challenging. *Bringing Asha Home* (Krishnaswami, 2006) is a story about adoption told from a brother's point of view. Its backdrop is *Rakhi*, a special Hindu holiday celebrating the bonds between brothers and sisters.

Arun wishes that his soon-to-be-adopted sister could tie a shiny bracelet or *rakhi* on his wrists. But it takes nearly a year to receive governmental approval to bring Asha home and the wait is unbearable for Arun. Throughout the year Arun finds special ways to bond with his new sister.

Yafi's Family: An Ethiopian boy's journey of love, loss, and adoption (Pettitt, 2010) addresses many of the insecurities associated with adoption. Yafi was born in Ethiopia and remembers living with his Grandma Elsa before moving to the orphanage where his new family found him. In this straightforward tale of interracial adoption, Yafi is black, his adoptive family white. Yafi describes his early life and how he felt when first adopted, adding texture through the mention of Ethiopian food and culture. The story tells of his new sisters' delight in meeting him and the challenges that anybody who has adopted an older child can relate to, including the struggle of communicating in a new language. Yafi's birth family and country of birth are honoured in this picturebook.

Other perspectives on adoption can be found in *Sweet Moon Baby: An adoption tale* (Clark, 2010), *My Mei Mei* (Young, 2006), *Ryan and Jimmy: And the well in Africa that brought them together* (Shoveller, 2006), *Over the Moon: An adoption tale* (Katz, 2001) and *Jin Woo* (Bunting, 2001).

Gender

Gender is also considered in the context of multiculturalism and diversity. Childhood is central to the development of gender identity, and children's literature forms one piece in that socialization process. In terms of power, gender is a pervasive yet sometimes invisible aspect of every development education topic. Decision making, distribution of resources and environmental issues all have a gender dimension.

Education in general, and early years education in particular, continues to be remarkably gendered, with teachers reinforcing typical gendered behaviours. According to Banyard (2010: 54), girls receive harsh criticism from teachers when they don't conform to stereotypical gender behaviours. Teachers describe girls who misbehaved as 'bad influences', 'spiteful' and 'scheming little madams', yet when boys behave in similar ways, they are said to be 'just mucking about'. Gender is therefore a cross-cutting perspective that informs all aspects of education, including multiculturalism and children's literature.

Gender stereotyping can still be found in children's literature, even after several years of training, awareness raising and education initiatives. A study by Hamilton *et al.* (2006) recorded that gender bias is common in many children's books. In their study, they noted the following:

- there were nearly twice as many male as female title and main characters
- male characters appeared in illustrations 53 per cent more than female characters
- female main characters nurtured more than male main characters and were seen in more indoor than outdoor scenes
- occupations were gender stereotyped and more women than men appeared to have no paid occupation.

In a follow-up study Paynter (2011) found that most measures of stereotypes and under-representation had improved since the Hamilton *et al.* study. It noted that some indicators are still problematic, such as a greater number of male compared to female authors and illustrators, a larger proportion of male characteristics represented through the text, illustrations and animal characters, and the absence of female characters with assertive characteristics. Authors such as McCabe *et al.* (2011) highlight a widespread pattern of under-representation of females in children's literature.

In terms of fairy tales, Parsons (2004) considers the cultural messages embedded in this patriarchal canon of stories and their implications for the construction of gender-appropriate behaviour. While some people may dismiss the influence of fairy tales, she underlines their pervasive power. According to Parsons:

> In our high-tech, mass-media culture we are surrounded by the vestiges of fairy tales from the marketing of Disney products to the perpetuation of romance ideology, the binary positioning of women and men, and women's and girls' obsession to manifest socially defined beauty.
>
> (2004: 135)

From a feminist perspective, fairy tales in the patriarchal tradition portray women as weak, submissive and dependent, while men are powerful, active and dominant. McCabe *et al.* (2011: 198) argue that 'children's books reinforce, legitimate and reproduce a patriarchal gender system'. Adults have a role to play in that because they select books for children. Hence, it is important to choose books that include both female and male characters in a wide range of roles. From a global perspective, there are several quality picturebooks that feature the stories of prominent women such as Amelia Earhart, Harriet Tubman, Wangari Maathai and Rosa Parks.

Multicultural literature

Mendoza and Reese (2001: 1) define intercultural and multicultural books as 'picturebooks that depict the variety of ethnic, racial, and cultural groups within society'. According to Harris and Hodges (1995: 158) multicultural literature is 'writing that reflects the customs, beliefs and experiences of people of differing nationalities and races'. Other definitions are more inclusive, incorporating gender, disability and sexual orientation. For Cai (2006) multicultural literature should not just introduce students to a range of cultures, it should be used as a tool to focus on social equity, justice, prejudice, praxis and the development of an understanding of the experience of oppressed groups. Both Bishop (1997) and Nieto (2010) argue that multicultural education is for all children. Nevertheless, while multicultural literature is important for the dominant culture represented in any classroom, it is particularly beneficial for minority cultures. From reading stories about their own culture, children have opportunities to see how others go through experiences similar to theirs, develop strategies to cope with issues in their life and identify themselves with their inherited culture. It is important, therefore, that educators incorporate multicultural literature into the curriculum and make it part of children's everyday life. Through multicultural literature, teachers can develop understanding and empathy in the classroom.

Windows and mirrors

Several authors, including Bishop (1997), have referred to the imagery of windows and mirrors to reflect the dual role of multicultural children's literature. A child may see his or her own life reflected in a book or may have an opportunity to see into someone else's life. According to Gates and Mark:

> Through the window of literature, however, we are allowed to enter worlds not physically open to us to view, to empathize and to participate emotionally in ways that may emotionally change the way we see ourselves and the society in which we live. Only through repeated immersion into those other cultural experiences will we as a society begin to appreciate the struggles, the pain and the horror that our sisters and brothers of other backgrounds have suffered. Only then will we begin truly to develop the respect needed to appreciate and honor our unique diversity as a country.
>
> (2006: 2)

Books can be windows looking out to the world, showing how children grow up in different places, as well as highlighting difficult circumstances that children have to endure – perhaps because of war, poverty or extraordinary events (Gamble and Yates, 2008). Historically and internationally, children's literature has given white middle-class children the mirror but not the window. They can see themselves in the stories they read and hear, but other ethnicities are absent. Children from minority groups such as refugee children have had few literary mirrors that affirm their identities. According to Short (2009: 10), 'children's engagements with literature have the potential to transform their world views through understanding their current lives and imagining beyond themselves'. Children need to find their lives reflected in books, but without windows they cannot envision alternative ways of thinking and being. Access to a range of picturebooks is important for all children. Some excellent books that deal with different aspects of African culture are not available in parts of Africa as they are produced by British and American publishers (Yenika-Agbaw, 2008).

Levels of multiculturalism in children's literature
Multiculturalism exists within a broad spectrum of different levels. One way of categorizing these levels has been devised by Banks (2008).

LEVEL 1: *A CONTRIBUTIONS APPROACH*
This is the first and lowest level of multiculturalism in the classroom. Often referred to as *the tourist approach* or a *food and festival approach*, books in this category are produced during certain festivals and holidays. This literature is not necessarily evaluated for authenticity and representation.

LEVEL 2: *THE ADDITIVE APPROACH*
A limited amount of literature from different perspectives is on offer. Generally, this level involves reading folktales from around the world and bringing in guest speakers. However, there is no critical engagement with the literature.

LEVEL 3: *THE TRANSFORMATION APPROACH*
This level allows teachers and children to rebuild their curriculum. In transforming the curriculum, children and teachers learn to view themes, concepts and issues from a range of alternative perspectives including those of different ethnic and cultural groups.

LEVEL 4: *THE SOCIAL ACTION APPROACH*
This approach involves students in their curriculum and in social action by getting them to speak out against injustice or engage with power structures, albeit in an age-appropriate manner. This might be achieved by reading accurate accounts of historical events and following that up with an action initiative, such as writing a letter to the local newspaper or conducting more

detailed research or an awareness campaign within the school community (Banks, 2008).

Sims (1982) identifies three different categories of African American children's literature: *melting pot*, *social conscience* and *culturally conscious*. In general, the term *melting pot* refers to a fusion of cultures, ethnicities and experiences. Books in this category feature universal experiences such as the first day in school, birthday celebrations and experiences of sharing. These books do not cause controversy and are useful for introducing multicultural perspectives. *Socially conscious* books deal with social issues in a way that makes the reader empathize with the characters. These books loosely correspond with levels two and three of multiculturalism. *Culturally conscious* books are those which portray cultural traditions, languages and ethnicities of certain groups in an authentic manner, and generally from the insider's perspective. Several commentators, such as Banks (2008), argue that it is important to move beyond cultural awareness to social action that promotes decision making and advocacy.

Integrating quality multicultural literature into the curriculum

Jenkins and Austin (1987: 6) suggest that good quality multicultural literature reflects many aspects of a culture, its values, beliefs, ways of life and patterns of thinking. A piece of good literature can transcend time, space and language and help readers 'learn about an individual or a group of people whose stories take place in a specific historical and physical setting'. In addition, exposure to good multicultural literature also helps children appreciate other ethnic groups, eliminate cultural ethnocentrism and develop multiple perspectives. Through culturally diverse material, all children can learn that they have much in common with other people through a range of universal feelings such as sadness, love, fear, justice, kindness, anger and sympathy (Dowd, 1992).

Bishop (1997: 4–5) identifies five functions of multicultural literature in the curriculum. Multicultural literature:

- provides knowledge or information
- changes how students view the world by offering varying perspectives
- develops an appreciation for diversity
- promotes critical enquiry
- provides enjoyment and illuminates human experience.

Multicultural literature enhances children's language, literacy and literary development. It presents children with previously unexplored issues and new ways of exploring them. Such alternative scenarios help children to think more critically and creatively and, in turn, to be more open, sensitive and appreciative of new ideas.

As well as being a key to unlocking the past and the future, children's literature allows children to visit unfamiliar places virtually. Nevertheless, it is important for teachers to critically assess their choice of picturebooks, the images they convey and the potential impact of the story and images on children. By reading picturebooks about Tanzania, such as *My Rows and Piles of Coins*, (Mollel, 1999) or *Elizabeti's Doll* (Stuve-Bodeen, 2009), children might think that all Tanzanians live in small, rural villages. An idea of life in a big city, such as Dar es Salaam, may be difficult to imagine.

Identity and cultural identity

Identity refers to how individuals or groups see and define themselves. It is formed through a socialization process influenced by social institutions such as the family, the education system and the mass media. By validating the stories and experiences of children from different ethnicities, multicultural literature plays an important role in the development of identity. In *An Angel Just Like Me* (Hoffman, 2007), Tyler, an African American boy, wonders why all angels are girls (never boys), with golden hair and pink skin. On Christmas morning he receives a special gift, a beautifully carved black angel just like him. Authors such as Bishop (1997) maintain that children who do not see their culture reflected in the literature they read may not appreciate their own importance as human beings.

Multicultural literature has been described as a tool that 'helps children to identify with their own culture, exposes children to other cultures, and opens the dialogue on issues regarding diversity' (Colby and Lyon, 2004: 24). However, studies in multicultural education tend to exclude any discussion of what it means to be white. Indeed, there is a tendency to consider all groups except white people as 'ethnic' or multicultural. Multiculturalism should also include an examination of white Anglo-Saxon people.

Glazier (2003) refers to 'hot lava' topics, such as whiteness, social class, politics and religion, which are never discussed. Simply including culturally diverse literature in the classroom will not automatically generate respect for cultural differences. Aveling (2006) writes about the challenges and possibilities for critically constructing whiteness as part of an antiracist programme when working with predominantly white teacher education students. Shome (1999: 108) explores whiteness in terms of 'discursive practices of colonialism and neo-colonialism that privilege and sustain the global dominance of white imperial subjects and Eurocentric world views'.

Whiteness has been described as an ideology that consists of practices and beliefs that allow whites to maintain power. In terms of teacher education, Aveling (2006) maintains it is impossible for student teachers to address issues of race and culture without first of all deconstructing what it means to be white, a process which she admits many students find uncomfortable.

The issue of authenticity in multicultural picturebooks

In recent years, multicultural picturebooks have challenged the under-representation and marginalization of children from different ethnic backgrounds (Gamble and Yates, 2008). The issue of authenticity continues to be debated (Smolen and Oswald, 2011). Several multicultural books are written by authors from their own culture. Virginia Hamilton, an African American, writes about African Americans; Rukhsana Khan, a Pakistani woman (currently living in Canada), writes about Pakistan. Other books are written and illustrated by authors outside the culture portrayed in the book. Set in the USA, *One Green Apple* (2006) is written by Irish-born author Eve Bunting. The American writer Virgina Kroll, whose Catholic mother's father is from Poland and whose Presbyterian father is from Germany, is the author of *Masai and I* (2009) and *Faraway Drums* (1998). Doreen Rappaport, the award-winning author of *Martin's Big Words: The life of Dr. Martin King, Jr.* (2007), is a white American writer who was born in New York City. Books in the 'Grace' series about a girl of Gambian descent were written by Mary Hoffman, a white Londoner, and are set in a London setting, although the author did visit The Gambia for research purposes. This series includes *Grace at Christmas* (2011), *Princess Grace* (2008), *Grace and Family* (2007) and *Amazing Grace* (2007). A comprehensive review of African American literature has been written by Bishop (2007). It traces the development of African American children's literature – books written by African Americans – from its beginnings to the present. These books focus on African Americans and their life experiences and are intended for children up to the age of 14.

One question to consider is whether the outsider can legitimately tell the story of a group to which they do not belong. Authors such as Hancock (2008: 213) argue that in order to achieve authenticity 'the author must either be of the culture or take on the perspective of other people living in the culture'. Bishop (1997: 17) concurs with this and suggests that:

> The farther a writer's background, knowledge and experiences are from the culture of the person or people about whom he or she is writing, the greater the necessity for the author to fill in

the cultural gaps, the greater the effort needed to do so, and the greater the risk of mistakes.

Balanced against this, one has to consider by what other means these stories would be made available to children. Sometimes an outsider's point of view is important in terms of both objectivity and accessibility (Gamble and Yates, 2008). Ho believes that, irrespective of cultural lens, the issue of empathy is crucial:

> All things being equal, if the writer is of the same skin colour and speaks the same language as the people she writes about, then of course she is more likely to portray them with more sensitivity than someone who is completely different. Yet I feel that none of those factors – race, sex, class, even language – matters as much as experience and empathy. If someone has lived and worked so closely within another community that she has assimilated their experiences, then I think she can come to feel what they feel.
>
> (2002: 97)

I agree with Rochman (1993), who argues that accuracy and authenticity are essential in multicultural children's literature. Unfortunately, literature for children set in Africa continues to be dominated by stereotypes (Yenika-Agbaw, 2008). While several authors attempt to address the complexities of various cultures, their efforts are often thwarted by publishers whose primary concern is the sale of books rather than an authentic representation of cultures.

The special case of Africa

Africa is not a country. Africa is the second-largest continent in the world, three times the size of the United States of America. This vast continent includes 54 countries and at least 800 different cultures and dialects. Previously, the Republic of Sudan, north and south combined, was the largest country in Africa. Since South Sudan gained independence in 2011, the largest country is Algeria, with Nigeria the largest in terms of population. One-seventh of the world's population lives in Africa, yet its importance is not reflected in the classroom or the curriculum (Glasgow and Rice, 2007). It often surprises children to discover the size of Africa (as portrayed on the Peters Projection World Map) and to find out that Africa spans six time zones. It takes longer to travel from Dakar, Senegal, to Nairobi, Kenya, than to fly from New York to London. There are no tigers in Africa and most African children have never seen some of its wildlife except in a zoo. However, stereotypical images of Africa pervade in terms of wild animals and primitive cultures. Few people visualize places in Africa as panoramas of skyscrapers, busy city streets, business suits and success stories.

One book that might help in the classroom is *Africa is Not a Country* (Knight and Melnicove, 2002). Suitable for middle and senior classes, the book is an excellent resource for all teachers who would like to introduce aspects of Africa into their geography programme. *Africa is Not a Country* is perhaps the first picturebook about the African continent to respectfully present the diversity of people living in several countries. The authors have created a book that explicitly describes and illustrates the multidimensions of the continent. Referring to 25 countries in total, they begin with Eritrea and feature children from Cape Verde, Lesotho, Mauritania and Madagascar.

Dispelling the misconception that Africa is a country, the authors narrate the experiences of children at play, school and home from a range of African countries. Realistic illustrations are used to explore the cultural, environmental, ethnic and social diversity of countries that make up the African continent. Beginning with morning activities, the book depicts people having breakfast, going to school, doing housework, shopping and playing. Unique contemporary characteristics for each African country are highlighted. Rwandan children are shown making pictures of war, while two Kenyan children are illustrated as they run to school, dreaming of becoming professional runners some day.

Using maps and illustrations, the vast and varied African continent is shown with different people inhabiting a variety of environments. From vast deserts with camels in the North to lush agricultural lands in the central and southern regions, the authors introduce Africa to young children in this colourful and easy-to-read book that explains why Africa should not be conceptualized as a single nation, given its size, diversity and complexity. Each country is presented on a two-page spread, with some text and a large illustration. The text includes many facts about each country without being overly detailed. At the end of the book is an alphabetical text box for all the African countries – excluding the recently established South Sudan – listing capital city, population, Independence Day, currency, a pronunciation guide, national flags and unique facts about each country.

Several picturebook authors and illustrators have tried to create books that help readers identify with life in various parts of Africa. Cunnane's book *For You Are a Kenyan Child* (2006) puts it this way:

> Imagine you live in a small Kenyan village, where the sun rises over tall trees filled with doves. You wake to the sound of a rooster's crow, instead of an alarm clock and the school bus. Your afternoon

snack is a tasty bug plucked from the sky, instead of an apple. And rather than kicking a soccer ball across a field, you kick a homemade ball of rags down a dusty road. But despite this, things aren't that different for a Kenyan child than they would be for an American kid, are they? With so much going on around you, it's just as easy to forget what your mama asked you to do!

While this is a beautiful book and a winner of the Ezra Jack Keats New Writer Award, there are some spelling and contextual errors, as the following extract illustrates:

He lets you look at him cook.
"Una taka chepati?" he asks –
Do you want a pancake? –
And he gives you the first hot one of the day.

In this extract there is a spelling error. The correct spelling is *Unataka Chapati*. Alternative spellings for Chapati are Chapatti or Chapathi. Second, a chapati is not a pancake, it is a type of flat, round bread that originates in India. There are other linguistic errors in the book, errors that reflect a poor level of research and lack of consultation with a person who speaks Swahili.

Unfortunate issues have also been identified in other publications. *Mama Panya's Pancakes: A village tale from Kenya* (Chamberlin, 2005) depicts a young Kenyan boy's experience of visiting the market with his mother. Along the way, Adika, the boy, invites all their friends for pancakes, causing Mama to worry that she can't afford enough flour to feed the extra guests. Everyone brings gifts such as milk, butter and flour so there is plenty of food for everyone. This book is often used to promote development and intercultural education in classrooms. *Panya* is a Swahili word, which means a small mouse. (Some translators argue that the word can also mean a rat.) Mama Panya therefore translates into the mother of a small mouse. While this is an authentic Kenyan name, perhaps an alternative could have been chosen for the title of the book. However, the title may be more of an issue where English is the first language rather than Swahili, as I am evaluating this issue through my own cultural lens. I would like to note that this is a great book, but teachers should be aware of the issues associated with its title.

The story highlights the vulnerability of impoverished families in parts of Kenya. By using it to explore topics such as *food* and *journeys*, children can identify similarities with their own lives. The book presents the Kenyan landscape as well as sample Swahili words like *Jambo* (hello or greetings) and *Harambee* (all pull together). It also contains a map suitable for primary school children outlining some of Kenya's major geographical features – for example, rivers, mountains and major cities – and additional information about village life in Kenya such as typical animals, insects, reptiles and plants, instructions for pronouncing Kiswahili words and Mama Panya's pancake recipe.

There is a misspelling in *Masai and I* (Kroll, 2009). *Maasai* is the correct spelling of this noble tribe. It means people speaking *maa*. Masai was the incorrect spelling used by the British settlers and has remained in current use. The correct spelling can be found in *14 Cows for America* (Deedy, 2009) and *Papa Do you Love me?* (Joosse, 2005). An excellent non-fiction book about the Maasai (Reynolds, 2011) combines Maasai proverbs and beautiful photography to give us a detailed glimpse of modern-day Maasai life. In addition to the historical Maasai culture, Reynolds demonstrates how the Maasai way of life is changing due to outside pressures, and in showing how the tribe is adapting to this new world, he gives the story relevance in a broader context. Members of the Maasai tribe have a unique identity, beautifully described by Karen Blixen (Dinesen, 2001: np) in *Out of Africa:*

> A Masai warrior is a fine sight. Those young men have, to the utmost extent, that particular form of intelligence which we call *chic*; daring, and wildly fantastical as they seem, they are still unswervingly true to their own nature, and to an immanent ideal. Their style is not an assumed manner, nor an imitation of a foreign perfection; it has grown from the inside, and is an expression of the race and its history, and their weapons and finery are as much part of their being as are a stag's antlers.

Authors and illustrators

By researching authors and illustrators, teachers and student teachers can establish links between their personal life stories, the stories they write and the motivations for the stories presented in picturebooks. The following examples illustrate the links between authors and illustrators and their work in picturebooks.

Asma Mobin-Uddin, author of *My Name Is Bilal* (2005), wanted to read stories to her children based on Muslim characters. However, she found very few books, and those that she did locate often presented unflattering or incorrect information about Muslims. This motivated her to write books that presented a positive image of Muslim children and addressed some of the issues they face as minority children attending non-Muslim schools.

Belle Yang's book *Hannah Is My Name* (2004) is based on the author's personal experience. Yang and her family arrived in San Francisco in 1967, and she draws on her own experience to create the story of little Na-Li, whose parents give her the American name Hannah when she travels to America from Taiwan.

Jerry Pinkney is one of the most prominent African American children's book illustrators. Throughout his career Pinkney has dedicated himself to telling the stories of African Americans, portraying black people realistically as individual people with dignity (Bishop, 2007). Pinkney considers himself a multiculturalist, as he works with material from diverse cultural settings. He has also adapted some classical children's stories including *The Little Match Girl* (1999), *The Ugly Duckling* (1999), *Aesop's Fables* (2000) and *Noah's Ark* (2002).

Niki Daly is a South African author/illustrator whose picturebooks celebrate the imaginative powers of children and their everyday lives. Daly has the ability to view the world from a child's perspective and to see it in a rainbow of shades, reflective of multicultural modern South Africa. Many of Daly's solo efforts, as well as his illustrations for other authors, represent strong African themes. In books such as *Not so Fast, Songololo* (2001), *The Herd Boy* (2012) and *Jamela's Dress* (2004), he looks at the day-to-day interactions of the myths that shape the reality for many black South Africans.

Fly, Eagle, Fly! by Gregorowski (2008), which was republished several times, is one of the classics of South African children's literature. Illustrated by Daly, the book includes a foreword by Archbishop Desmond Tutu. A baby eagle is brought up with chickens on a farm and learns how to scrabble on the ground for grain. One day the farmer's friend points out that this eagle should be flying high in the sky. This book contains a powerful message of rising above one's imposed earthly restrictions. The illustrations are equally inspiring with their authentic portrayal of the South African landscape and people. Niki Daly is a middle-aged white South African man but is often thought to be a black woman. According to Daly (2011) himself:

> I wrote and illustrated a number of books which reflected the lives of the children on the other side of the racial divide. In retrospect, I see these books … as half-way bridges between white and black children who live[d] separate and unequal lives determined by the appalling apartheid system. In order to do these books I ignored the myth propagated through apartheid and some political activists who said that there are differences between people.

In *Jamela's Dress* (Daly, 2004) Jamela falls in love with the fabric her mother buys to make herself a dress for a friend's wedding. The child parades through town, wrapped in the flowing garment to cheers and chants of 'Kwela Jamela African Queen!'. Caught up in the moment, she doesn't realize that the beautiful fabric has been stained by bicycle grease and torn by chickens. Everyone is angry with her – 'Even Jamela was cross with Jamela' – but the day is saved by a young man who has captured the fun on film. A few days later, his photo wins a prize and the photographer offers Jamela some of the award money to replace the ruined fabric. Mama makes a magnificent dress for herself, as well as one for 'Kwela Jamela African Queen!'.

The orange, yellow and green patterns from Jamela's dress are repeated in the endpapers. Niki Daly adds an author's note at the end about the origin of the word *kwela*, which is a type of music played on the streets of Cape Town. The word originated from the Nguni word *kwhela*, meaning to start well or to get moving. So when the author calls Jamela 'Kwela Jamela African Queen', he could be referring to the beautiful music that is within Jamela or saying that her future is moving forward. Other books in the 'Jamela' series include *What's Cooking, Jamela?* (2001), *Where's Jamela?* (2004), *Happy Birthday Jamela* (2006) and *A Song for Jamela* (2009).

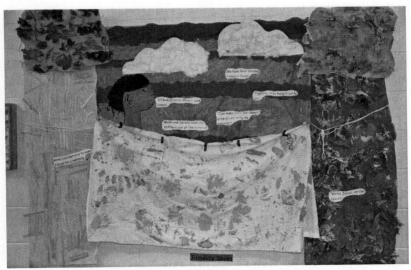

Children from Knocknacarra National School, Galway, Ireland, created this mural in response to the picturebook, *Jamela's Dress*.

Criteria for selecting picturebooks

Important criteria for selecting multicultural literature also apply to all children's literature. The following criteria have been informed by a range of established lists from Temple *et al.* (2010) and Derman-Sparks and the ABC Task Force (1989), among others.

Accuracy

Look for accuracy in stories about modern-day experiences, historical fiction and all non-fiction. Books should contain current, factually correct information that supports storylines. Try to source books about realistic, everyday events and activities that include characters from diverse groups. Modern stories should acknowledge recent events. For example, a book about South Africa should reflect changes in the apartheid system. While the age of children is a consideration, stories should not force artificially happy endings.

Authenticity

Ensure that a story features authentic perspectives by the author and illustrator. Consider your own views about the author's culture and experiences. Is the perspective in the picturebook patriarchal or feminist? Is it solely Eurocentric or do perspectives from developing countries also surface? Analyse the biographical material on the dust jacket or the cover. If a story deals with a minority theme, what qualifies the author or illustrator to deal with the subject? If the author and illustrator are not members of the minority being written about, is there anything in their background that would specifically recommend them as the creators of this book?

Stereotypes

A stereotype is an oversimplified and typically derogatory generalization about a particular group, race or sex. Avoid books featuring caricatures of a group's physical features or stereotypical roles and behaviours. Cultural groups should be presented in a multidimensional manner, to help readers realize the depth and breadth of experiences within cultures. Beware of reinforcing stereotypes. Books should reflect individual people's lives, rather than assigning general personality traits or behaviours to an entire group of people. Does the book reinforce or counteract positive associations with the colour white and negative associations with the colour black? Choose books that present a diversity of perspectives about race and ethnicity, including those about multiracial families, poor children, rich children, migrant children and refugee children.

Ideally, teachers should avoid picturebooks with stereotypical images and text, but as these are available they can be discussed alongside others in group work on picturebooks about Kenya or the African continent, for instance. After the children have examined a sample of picturebooks in their groups, they should draw or write what they have learned. The results from all groups should be compared in terms of similarities and differences, which books the ideas represented came from and whether the books' views and images were stereotypical.

Questions to discuss are:

- What stereotypes can we identify in our view of Kenya (or Africa) and its people?
- Why are these stereotypes so persistent?
- How accurate are they?
- How do we know?
- How might they affect the lives of Kenyan people living in the West?
- Why do we stereotype other cultures?
- How is stereotyping linked to prejudice about others?
- Can we identify stereotypical views held by others about our own country?
- Are they accurate?
- Are they positive or negative?
- Where do they come from?

Setting

Books should include accurate settings. A stereotypical image might present all Native American people in tepees, but throughout history Native Americans have lived in various types of homes and they are part of contemporary society. If these books are used, ensure that Native Americans are shown in a range of homes through alternative images and photographs. Similarly, there is a tendency to use picturebooks with images of mud huts from different parts of the continent of Africa. Ensure that such images are balanced with those of cities and skyscrapers from Nairobi, Johannesburg and other African cities. The issue of urbanization and living in cities can also be addressed through picturebooks. While the majority of the world's population live in urban settings, is this sufficiently represented in picturebooks?

Illustrations

Illustrations should convey that members of any ethnic group look different from one another. Choose books with photographs that accurately portray present-day events. Captions on all photographs should be correct and specific. For example, an appropriate caption for a photograph of a city might read, 'Maseru, Lesotho', not the more general 'Africa'.

Language

Is language used authentically? The language and dialect spoken by characters should authentically portray how they typically interact. Terminology that refers to aspects of culture should be acceptable by contemporary standards.

Controversial issues

In handling difficult topics, authors should present the complexity of issues and offer multiple perspectives. Also consider who holds powerful positions. Who has problems? Who solves problems? Men and people of European descent should not be the ones who provide all the solutions. What types of roles do girls, women and people of colour have? Look for sexist language and adjectives that exclude or in any way demean girls or women. Do the whites in the story possess the power, take the leadership and make the important decisions? Do minorities and females function in essentially supporting, subservient roles? Are the oppressions faced by minorities and women represented as causally related to an unjust society? Are the reasons for poverty and oppression explained, or are they simply accepted as normal and inevitable? Does the storyline encourage passive acceptance or active resistance? Is a particular problem that a minority person faces resolved through the benevolent intervention of a white person?

Cultural diversity

Look for stories that include a variety of cultures with different family compositions. Books that feature single parents, grandparents who play key roles in nurturing children, and extended families who share a home and each other's lives, are among the variety readily available. Are cultural details naturally integrated? These details are necessary to make the story come alive, but should not impede the flow of the story. Is the collection balanced? It is important to present children with a balanced collection of multicultural books.

Assess value judgements

If the minority group in question is depicted as different, are negative value judgements being implied? Are minorities depicted exclusively in ghettos, *barrios* or migrant camps? If the illustrations and text attempt to depict another culture, do they go beyond over-simplifications and offer genuine insights into another lifestyle? Look for inaccuracy and inappropriateness in the depiction of other cultures. Watch for instances of the quaint-natives syndrome – most noticeable in areas like clothing and custom but extending to behaviour and personality traits as well. Stereotyping is unacceptable and soon becomes easily recognized.

Conclusion

In this chapter, I have explored concepts of diversity, multicultural education and multicultural literature. I have presented various debates within multicultural literature, including about authenticity and cultural identity, as well as criteria for choosing high-quality, authentic books. Simply incorporating multicultural literature into the classroom will not necessarily promote intercultural thinking. First, one needs to be aware of the different levels of multiculturalism in children's literature. Second, one needs to choose a range of high-quality picturebooks that represents all such levels. Third, one needs to plan a curriculum that promotes culturally responsive teaching and critically interrogates the content and messages provided by these books. And fourth, the teacher has a central role in maximizing the learning potential from these books.

Chapter 4

Critical literacy and critically reading the world

Introduction

Development education and intercultural education can be seen as educational approaches that empower young people to think critically, independently and systematically. With a strong emphasis on values and perceptions, they also prepare learners to participate effectively in society, both locally and globally, so as to bring about positive change for a more just and equal world (Fiedler, 2008). The importance of critical thinking is thus a fundamental aspect of development education. In this chapter, I discuss different aspects of thinking – critical thinking, critical consciousness, critical literacy (Johnson and Freedman, 2005) and critical questions – with specific reference to picturebooks. I then present a framework for critically exploring development and intercultural concepts through picturebooks.

Critical thinking

Critical thinking has been defined as the ability to use logical thinking, analysis, comparison, questioning, evaluation and summarization. Lipman (1988: 40) sets out the difference between thinking and critical thinking (see Table 4.1). Critical thinking is not isolated from other important goals in education. If children are able to think critically, they will be more proficient in a range of curricular areas, including literacy, numeracy, history, geography, science and cross-curricular areas such as intercultural and development education.

Table 4.1: A comparison of general thinking and critical thinking

Thinking	Critical thinking
Guessing	Estimating
Preferring	Evaluating
Grouping	Classifying
Believing	Assuming
Inferring	Inferring logically
Associating concepts	Grasping principles

Noting relationships	Noting relationships within relationships
Supposing	Hypothesising
Offering opinions without reasons	Offering opinions with reasons
Making judgements without criteria	Making judgements with criteria

Source: Lipman (1988)

Critical thinking has been defined as an attitude or 'habit of mind' (Meier, 2003). Meier's 'habit of mind' approach allows students to develop problem-solving and thinking skills by addressing the following aspects of any situation, problem or issue: *significance* (why is it important?), *perspective* (what is the point of view?), *evidence* (how do you know?), *connection* (how does it apply to other situations?) and *supposition* (what if it were different?). Critical thinkers rely on inquisitive attitudes, utilize thinking strategies, access background knowledge, understand thinking vocabulary and apply relevant criteria when making thoughtful decisions.

Critical questioning based on The Carpet Boy's Gift (Deitz Shea, 2006)

Given that children may not have considered issues associated with child labour, the following set of questions has been devised using Meier's (2003) habit of mind frame:

Significance/Cause and effect: What happened? Why did it happen? Why is it significant? What does this story tell us about child labour?

Point of view/Perspective: Who is telling the story? What other perspectives are there? Who holds the power? How is power represented? How might the master's previous experiences have influenced his behavior in the story?

Evidence: What are the facts? Where did these facts come from? What story do the illustrations tell? How do they support the story? How might you have illustrated this book? How does the author's choice of words shape the message? How might the story be different if alternative words were used?

> *Connections:* How was child labour allowed to take place in this story? How is it connected to other events, e.g. poverty and power? How has the author represented literacy and freedom? Can you think of examples of child labour in the world today? How might you represent literacy and freedom in your own picturebook?
>
> *Suppose/wondering: Asking 'what if' questions:* How would you feel if you were one of the children in this story? Why are you able to go to school in this country?

The choice of challenging picturebooks is important for promoting critical thinking. Such picturebooks should be relatively open-ended and have a number of unanswered questions. Teachers need to research picturebook topics to communicate accurate information and facilitate new learning opportunities for children. Any stereotypical thinking or racist untruths need to be exposed. Stereotypical ideas need to be challenged immediately, effectively and clearly. Teachers should help children express why an image is unfair. Stereotyping can hurt people and it is generally misleading. If stereotypical images are evident in a book, it is a good idea to have a range of positive, accurate images ready for comparison.

Critical consciousness

To become critically conscious is to become aware of the historical, social and cultural ideologies that underpin acceptable or unacceptable behaviour in our society (Freire, 1973). We make decisions on the basis of our personal moral guidelines. There is a tendency to question the motivations of other people's actions rather than our own.

Becoming critically conscious also means developing an understanding about the conditions under which people live, some privileged and some disadvantaged. To promote critical literacy in class, teachers can discuss privilege and oppression locally, nationally and globally. Picturebooks provide an opportunity to open up these discussions. A skilful teacher will lead a discussion that allows children to link examples of privilege and disadvantage from children's literature to concrete examples from their own experiences. By using picturebooks as a platform for addressing assumptions, children are better able to articulate a critical consciousness in relation to their own lives (Johnson and Freedman, 2005).

Critical literacy

Commentators such as Comber (2001) argue that simple conceptions of *literacy*, so much promoted today, are inadequate. Being critically literate is essential for being literate in a media-saturated, diverse world. Today, children experience a constant stream of ideas and information online, in print and from electronic games and mass media. Therefore, in the twenty-first century the term *literacy* is changing and will continue to do so. The term *multiliteracies* immediately shifts us from the dominant written print text to the forms of literacy in the new millennium. Increasingly, knowledge is encountered in multiple forms, through print, images, video and combinations of forms in digital contexts. In response we are asked to represent our knowledge in an equally complex manner.

Critical literacy 'transcends conventional notions of reading and writing to incorporate critical thinking, questioning, and transformation of self or one's world' (McDaniel, 2004: 472). According to Keyes (2009: 48) critical literacy:

- widens the definition of literacy and encourages students to read with an inquiring stance
- prompts students to recognize connections between their lives and the lives of real or imagined story characters
- promotes exploration of text in order to reveal and discuss possible author bias and subtle messages
- guides reflection on how to take social action to create more compassion and equity in the world.

Critical literacy has been traced to the work of Paulo Freire, who taught adult learners to 'read the word' in order to 'read the world' and to engage in a cycle of reflection and action (Freire and Macedo, 1987). In *Pedagogy of the Oppressed* (1970), Freire provides an example of how critical literacy is developed in an educational context. He proposes a system of critiquing multiple forms of injustice through which students become more socially aware. Such awareness cannot be achieved if students are not given the opportunity to explore and construct knowledge.

According to Wolk (2003: 102), critical literacy is 'about how we see and interact with the world; it is about having as a regular part of one's life, the skills and desire to evaluate society and the world'. Critical literacy is the ability to read texts in an active and reflective manner that promotes deeper understanding of socially constructed concepts such as power, inequality and injustice in human relationships. It is more than just understanding what we are reading. It is about asking questions, looking at different points of view and ascertaining which perspective is presented. Educators, including parents and teachers, need to help children develop their own perspectives and understand the perspectives of others if they are to participate as citizens in our multicultural world.

The development of critical literacy skills enables people to interpret messages through a critical lens and challenge the power relations within those messages (Dolan, 2013). Educators who facilitate the development of critical literacy encourage children to interrogate societal issues such as poverty, education, equity and equality, and the role of institutions such as family and school. There is an explicit focus on socio-political issues, a commitment to social action and the promotion of social justice through disrupting and interrogating texts and cross-examining multiple viewpoints (Lewison *et al.*, 2002). Children's literature, including picturebooks, provides endless opportunities for teaching critical literacy and incorporating global and justice perspectives in the classroom.

Picturebooks have the potential to promote critical thinking through critical literacy in the classroom (Dolan, 2013). With higher order and imaginative thinking, children can grasp the meaning and significance of the core themes of picturebooks, and go well beyond what the author and illustrator suggest. More specifically, picturebooks 'can help them view themselves in a different and more informed manner than they did previously and introduce them to more complicated, mature and remote aspects of their real world (past, present and future) as well of the world of make believe' (Cianciolo, 1997: 3). Hence, picturebooks can provide a lens through which children can learn more about themselves, their opinions and their perspectives.

Critical questions

Questioning is a crucial aspect of good teaching. Who? What? When? Where? Why? How? Asking questions has always been fundamental to making sense of the world. Unless we are able to critically question what we see, hear and read, we cannot solve problems, create solutions, make informed decisions or enact change. In our information-laden age, it is more important than ever to decide what's relevant, legitimate and valuable. Asking questions can trigger various levels of cognition, from remembering, understanding and applying, to analysing, creating and evaluating (Godinho and Wilson, 2008).

Teachers need to be able to formulate critical questions, questions that enable critical thinking. Children need to learn how to ask 'good' questions – those which generate a deeper, critical, complex exploration of an issue.

Many quality picturebooks provide scope for generating critical questions. Harste (2000; cited in Meller *et al.*, 2009: 77) believes that in order to have conversations about social issues, teachers should select books that meet one or more of the following criteria:

- explore differences rather than make them invisible
- enrich understandings of history and life by giving voice to those traditionally silenced or marginalized
- show how people can begin to take action on important social issues
- explore dominant systems of meaning that operate in our society to position people and groups of people as 'other'
- don't provide happily ever after endings for complex social problems.

Critical questions interrogate text, illustrations, the central message and how this message is portrayed. Accepting any story as a given set of facts is not an option.

The development of philosophical and creative thinking through picturebooks

Development education and intercultural education require children to be able to think about complex topics and formulate their own ideas and opinions. Thinking skills need to be systematically developed with children. The Philosophy for Children (P4C) approach was originally developed by philosopher Matthew Lipman in the 1970s. Today, it is practised all over the world and in at least 16 languages. The aim of P4C is to engage children in philosophical enquiry in the context of a caring and collaborative community. It provides time during the day for the development of thinking skills. It taps into children's natural curiosity and assists them in their search for meaning. P4C encourages intellectual courage and rigour and helps children develop the qualities that make for good judgement in everyday life. Philosophical enquiry is a powerful practice, offering children the opportunity to question and explore issues, concepts and ideas that are important and relevant to their lives, whatever stage of life they may be at.

Haynes and Murris (2012: 22) argue that 'picturebooks open up a space between the real world and other possible worlds and encourage a free exploration of philosophical ideas'. Teachers can create a democratic space in which children are free to explore ideas provoked by contemporary picturebooks. Take, for instance, the beautifully illustrated story *The Three Questions* (Muth, 2002). A young boy named Nikolai searches for the answers to three questions in his quest to become a better person. He consults his friends and a wise old turtle. In the story, Nikolai is led to find the answers from within. The three questions are as follows:

- When is the best time to do things?
- Who is the most important one?
- What is the right thing to do?

Just imagine the responses children would generate to these questions. In *Zen Shorts* (Muth, 2005), the extraordinary picturebook based on Buddhist teachings, three siblings view the world differently when a giant panda moves into their neighbourhood and tells each of them an amazing tale. This unique and beautiful book offers real-life lessons in a gentle way and can foster thoughtful discussions about how we should treat ourselves and others. Zen 'shorts' are short meditations, ideas and concepts for children to contemplate according to their own cognitive and conceptual ability. Other books in this series include *Zen Ties* (Muth, 2008) and *Zen Ghosts* (Muth, 2010).

Picturebooks enhance creative thinking by showing children multiple creative interpretations of the world. Picturebooks are works of art in their own right. Potentially, they can inspire creativity in children through a range of written, illustrated and dramatic responses. Children can make their own picturebooks. They can retell traditional stories, create new stories and solve problems set out in picture story books by imagining a better future. Anthony Browne, renowned illustrator and author of several intriguing picturebooks, argues that as adults we lose a great deal of contact with our visual imagination. He uses a simple technique called the 'shape game' as a mechanism for inspiring creativity. According to Browne (2011: 9), 'the rules are very simple: the first person draws an abstract shape; the second person, ideally using a different coloured pen, transforms it into something'. This simple activity helps teachers and student teachers to rediscover their inner creative potential. Sadly, this potential too often remains undiscovered and dormant.

Thinking creatively about the future

Futures education is the term used to describe a form of education that helps young people think more critically and creatively about the future (Hicks, 2006). Today, creating education for empowering, hopeful and liveable futures is a fundamental challenge. The first step is to focus on the future and to consider our images of the future. Hicks maintains that it is as vital for children to understand the temporal interrelationships between past, present and future as it is for them to understand the spatial interrelationships between local, national and global dimensions. If education is a preparation for the future, children and teachers need to conceptualize their visions for a better future. I believe that picturebooks can be used to promote futures thinking in primary classrooms (Dolan, 2012a).

Stories told within European and North American traditions tend to have three stages: a beginning, middle and end. An additional dimension or a fourth stage can be added: what happens next? This stage can be created by each individual in terms of their perception of the story and their preferred and probable futures. By asking children to write the text and illustrate their ideas for the next page or the sequel to the picturebook, children are asked to think about an unknown scenario in the context of what has happened previously to predict the future. The illustration and presentation of possible future scenarios for the characters in a picturebook can provide us, whether as teacher educators, student teachers or children, with a gateway to our imaginations, which in turn allows us to share and contrast our emerging images in an accessible fashion.

The critical issues of power, agency and action

Power is a complex issue but its exploration is central to critical literacy. As humans, we possess power and have the capacity to make choices. People have varying levels of power depending on their self-esteem, personal finances and resources, personal satisfaction with their lives and levels of self-perception. Some types of power are legitimate, while others are illegitimate, inappropriate or abusive (Johnson and Freedman, 2005).

Reading picturebooks based on true biographies is an effective way of studying power and its abuse. Several picturebooks feature stories of people, such as Rosa Parks and Martin Luther King Jr, who used their positions of power or who created positions of power to make society more just.

Another force directly related to power is oppression – an abusive misuse of power. Oppression operates in different ways such as exploitation, bullying, exclusion, violence, peer pressure and cultural imperialism, with one group asserting its power over another.

Martin Waddell's *Farmer Duck* (2006) is a good book for discussing oppressive power and behaviour. It follows the unlikely premise of a duck running a farm on his own. The duck cuts wood, weeds the gardens, washes dishes, irons clothes and completes all other jobs. The farmer in charge is very lazy, lies in bed eating sweets and shouts out occasionally, 'How goes the work?'. When at long last the duck grows 'sleepy and weepy and tired', the other farm animals decide that enough is enough. Joining forces they run the lazy farmer out of town and set about doing the jobs equally, with the duck in charge. The book is useful for discussing the location of power, how it might be reclaimed and the responsibility associated with redistributed power.

Globally, experiences of colonization, war and greed have been underpinned by experiences of oppression, brutality and conflict. *The Rabbits* (Tan, 2010) tells the story about the invasion of 'rabbits' into a strange and foreign land. On a deeper level, the story is about politics and consequences of colonization, cultural assimilation and the effect of humans on our environment, and is a powerful allegory about colonization. Bandicoots (rabbit-like marsupials from Australia in danger of extinction) are used to represent indigenous peoples and rabbits to portray explorers. The design of the book cleverly integrates the words into the illustrations so that the two work as one. The sparse text is narrated from the bandicoots' point of view and is used to accentuate, rather than detract from, the illustrations, which tell elusive and multiple visual narratives (Mallan, 1999):

The rabbits came

Many grandparents ago

At first we didn't know what to think. They looked a bit like us. There weren't many of them. Some were friendly.

(Tan, 2010)

The text is concise and to-the-point yet its apparent simplicity conveys feelings of anger, hurt and grief: 'They ate our grass. They chopped down our trees and scared away our friends ... and stole our children'.

There are many picturebooks highlighted in this book which can be used to discuss oppression. Johnson and Freedman (2005: 119) make a number of suggestions about how such books can be used to promote critical engagement with children:

- teachers could use them to begin a unit on a particular type of oppression
- teachers can include them for read-aloud literacy lessons and invite the entire class to discuss the concepts
- children can compare different types of oppressive situations portrayed in different picturebooks
- children can use them as models for their own creative writing
- pairs of children can write reviews of the texts for a local paper
- children can refer to these picturebooks in individual enquiries about oppression

- children can use these picturebooks in small groups and discuss the evidence of oppression in the stories
- small groups can dramatize the stories for another class or age group.

Teachers who wish to explore issues of power with children ought to reflect on the location of power in their classrooms. Tiffany (2008) argues that the pedagogic functions of democracy are often overlooked, so teachers and children need to work together democratically. Democratic pedagogy occurs when good judgement and decision making are shared, and when children's suggestions are taken seriously by the school community (Haynes and Murris, 2012). Given teachers' latent power in the classroom, their disposition has a significant impact on the degree of freedom enjoyed by children as part of an enquiry.

Working with traditional literature

Traditional literature includes fairy tales, folk tales, legends, myths, trickster tales, Aesop's fables, creation stories and pourquoi tales. Such tales feature in many picturebooks. In most cases, fairy tales have a clear narrative structure. The setting, characters and problem are generally stated at the beginning of the story. As these stories have many layers of meaning, picturebooks with fairy tales can be adapted for a variety of developmental levels. Fairy tales provide a great opportunity to introduce critical thinking about texts because they are short. Their biases are often more overt and easier to identify than are those in longer works. The following is a suggested set of questions for critically exploring traditional fairy tales:

- What is the central message of the fairy tale?
- What happened in the story?
- What is the 'moral' of the story, if there is one?
- What ideas/values are important within this story?
- How are the characters stereotypical or unusual?
- Does the fairy tale remind you of any modern-day movies, television programmes, books, songs that you have seen or heard? If so, which?
- Do you have any problems with the story? Did you enjoy reading it?
- If you could ask the author two questions about any character or the plot itself, what would those questions be?
- If you could write this story from a different perspective, which perspective would you choose?

Working with *Cinderella*

Cinderella is one of the oldest, best-known and most valued fairy tales in the world. It has hundreds of cultural variants and retellings, from ancient Egypt and China to the present day. *Cinderella*'s origins are found in ninth-century China. Many multicultural variations on *Cinderella* have been turned into children's picturebooks (a full list is available in Appendix 1). Most versions include an ineffective father, the absence of a mother figure, some sort of gathering such as a ball or festival, a mutual attraction to a person of high status, a lost article and a search that ends with success. *Yeh-Shen: A Cinderella story from China* (Louie, 1996) presents the Chinese version of the tale, which is almost a thousand years older than the earliest known European version. The story contains many familiar details: a poor, overworked girl, a wicked stepmother and stepsister, a magical helper, a king in search of a wife and a lost shoe. But while Cinderella is simply handed gifts from her fairy godmother, Yeh-Shen earns her wishes through kindness to a magic fish. In contemporary Western culture, Cinderella has become synonymous with Perrault's *Cendrillon*. Originally published in 1697, this is the version on which the Disney animated movie (1950) was based. This version has been republished several times, most recently in both English and French (Perrault, 2011). With nearly every culture producing some variation of this tale, the study and comparison of Cinderella stories is a splendid way to foster cross-cultural comparisons in the classroom while teaching literacy and making connections across the curriculum.

There are two Mexican versions of the story: *Domítíla: A Cinderella tale from the Mexican tradition* (Coburn, 2000) and *Adelita: A Mexican Cinderella story* (DePaola, 2004). In the first, a young girl called Domítíla goes and cooks for the governor, and the governor is amazed by how good the girl's meals taste. However, **Domítíla's** mother dies and she must return home. The governor, who wishes to taste the wonderful food again, goes out and searches for the woman who can cook a feast out of weeds. After the governor encounters some hardships and dishonest people, he succeeds in finding and marrying **Domítíla**. In the second version from Mexico, Adelita's mother dies in childbirth. Her father remarries a mean woman with two cruel daughters. Once her father dies, Adelita is relegated to the kitchen where she works as a servant, cleaning and cooking. One day an invitation arrives for a fiesta at Senor Gordillo's hacienda to celebrate the homecoming of his son, Javier. Adelita's nanny takes on the role of fairy godmother, making certain that the girl has something to wear to the party. The text is interspersed with Spanish words and phrases and includes cultural references about Latin America, especially Mexican culture.

In *Mufaro's Beautiful Daughters* (Steptoe, 2001), Mufaro is a villager from Zimbabwe who has two beautiful daughters. Manyara has a bad temper and is selfish, whereas Nyasha is always kind and considerate to people and animals. When the Great King invites all worthy maidens to appear so that he might chose a wife, Mufaro sends both daughters. Though there is no fairy godmother and no slipper, the Great King does use magic and gets to know the girls' personalities before they appear before him. Thus, Nyasha is chosen to be queen, while her mean sister becomes a maid in the queen's household.

These books provide an invaluable resource for critically analysing and comparing similar accounts of a tale. In the classroom children can read a selection of Cinderella stories from around the world. By identifying plot elements that all Cinderella stories have in common, children can compare and contrast these different versions with a definite purpose. Similarities and differences can be recorded using a Venn diagram. Children can identify how Cinderella stories reflect information about a country's or a place's unique culture. Finally, children can make their own Cinderella stories based on their own cultural identity.

Fractured fairy tales

Fractured fairy tales are adaptations of traditional tales. They may show new points of view, role reversals, new characters and plot twists, sequels, and alternative settings or fairy tale combinations, and are very effective in allowing children to view multiple perspectives and construct their own. A full list of fractured fairy tales is available in Appendix 1.

Anthony Browne has retold the story of *Goldilocks and the Three Bears* in a picturebook called *Me and You* (2010). In the original story there is an assumption that Goldilocks trespasses on the bears' property, steals their food and breaks their possessions for no other reason than greed and mischievousness. Browne wondered why she broke into their cottage. Perhaps she was in distress and in need of food. In *Me and You* (2010) Browne presents two simultaneous interpretations of the story. Baby Bear's version on the right-hand page and Goldilocks' on the left. In wordless sepia-toned illustrations, Browne depicts Goldilocks' original story, now set in an inner city where she lives and is raised by her lone mother. Longing for Baby Bear's idyllic suburban life, the girl has no voice of her own and no colour in her existence. While standing in front of a shop window with her mum, she spots a balloon and runs off to catch it, not paying attention to where it's going. Before she knows it, she's lost and the balloon is way out of her reach. On the facing page, the Bears – in contemporary human attire – live a comfortable middle-class life. They arrive home one day to discover 'a horrible, dirty little child' fleeing their golden house, leaving a trail of broken chairs and empty porridge bowls.

Goldilocks wanders around and finds the Bears' impressively large and beautiful home. She roams through the house, sees how the other half live and revels in this colourful, desirable world. When the homeowners return and express their disapproval, Goldilocks flees, escaping their world and returning to hers, where she is greeted by her mother's open arms. Browne uses colour and sepia to convey voice and voicelessness, idealism and realism, to suggest the inner turmoil experienced by a little girl as she searches for her idea of a more fulfilling life.

Perspective

Fractured fairy tales and their construction provide a great opportunity to explore alternative perspectives. *Mirror Mirror* (Singer, 2010) is a collection of short poems that focus on various fairy tale characters, including, among others, Cinderella, Rapunzel and Red Riding Hood. One poem presents readers with the more traditional telling of the tale. The mirrored, or reversed, poem, however, tells the story from a different perspective. Author Jon Scieszka is a master of looking at things from an alternative perspective. *The True Story of The Three Little Pigs* (2009) presents it from the wolf's point of view. Other Scieszka stories include: *The Frog Prince Continued* (2009) and *The Stinky Cheese Man and Other Fairly Stupid Tales* (2007). Children can write traditional fairy tales from alternative perspectives and complete comparison charts between the traditional and alternative versions. Character profiles based on selected character quotes from these stories can also be constructed. By exploring some of the picturebooks mentioned in this chapter, children can identify which perspectives are represented and which perspectives are missing.

Voices in the Park (2008) by Anthony Browne is the story of a visit to the park. The story is told from the points of view of the four characters featured: a young boy, Charles; his mother; a young girl, Smudge; and her father. The storyline is very simple: the two children play together, their dogs do the same, while the adults keep to themselves. Browne reinvents and overlays the scene as one by one each parent and child describes their version of the events, altering light, colours and words and so creating a 'multi-layered reality' (Smidt, 2012: 151).

The mother, who is portrayed as upper middle class, considers the park to be full of 'frightful types'. She worries about her son playing with a 'rough looking' girl who is smiling, wearing her hair in pigtails and looks anything but rough. The unemployed father spends his time looking at job ads. The son has a great time playing with the girl and the girl herself appears to be the happiest of all the characters. While the voices are communicated through four individual characters, 'each voice is intricately connected to tell the story of how class, prejudice, control, hope and friendship determine the perspectives of the four characters' (Serafini, 2005: 50). Browne deliberately sets his story in a park because people from all social classes can be found walking their dogs in a park.

The four voices are represented by contrasting illustration styles, fonts, layouts and diction. The characters are depicted through surrealist illustrations as part-primate, part-human; the adults are gorillas and the children chimpanzees. Characteristically, Anthony Browne's visual text is rich in cultural allusion, making this a book that works on many levels and is open to interpretation. The real voices are located in the illustrations. In them, trees are oddly shaped, footsteps turn to flower petals and Santa Claus begs for change. In this picturebook Browne celebrates the redeeming power of connecting with another human being.

Woodson's *The Other Side* (2001) is told from Clover's perspective. It is about a young African American girl called Clover who is not supposed to play on the other side of the fence because 'that's the way things are'. A white girl called Annie lives on the other side. The two children study one another from afar until one day they meet on opposite sides of the fence. Though neither of them is allowed to climb over the fence, their friendship blossoms as they both sit on top of it. It offers a subtle way of showing children that friendship can overcome any barrier, even race. In 1964 the Civil Rights Act became law in the USA. Legally, segregation was over, but the remnants of racism remained in social, cultural and economic relations. Wiles's (2007) *Freedom Summer* is about two boys, one black, one white, and how they dared to be friends. The boys' perspective contrasts with that of the local community.

Our relationships with others are influenced both by personal perceptions and cultural values, which are reflected in a range of social structures. By examining one's perceptions and becoming aware of what affects them, we are in a better position to reflect on our relationships with others. The perspectives we hold are particularly significant in intercultural and multicultural settings.

A curriculum framework for teaching development and intercultural education through picturebooks

I have developed a curriculum framework based on three core development education and intercultural principles: *respect, understanding* and *action*. In Chapters 5, 6 and 7, respectively, I deal with each principle of the framework in turn. The framework is adapted from Picower's (2012) six elements of social justice curriculum design and informed by the work of Short (2009) and Banks and McGee Banks (2009).

Each component of the framework includes two elements as follows:

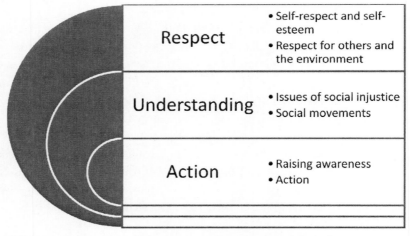

Figure 4.1: Components of the three-part framework and their elements

According to Picower, by addressing these six elements of social justice education in primary classrooms, 'teachers lead students to value themselves, respect the diversity of the world around them, understand how diverse people have been treated differently and often unjustly, recognize that ordinary people have worked to address such injustice and take action themselves' (2012: 2).

Part one: respect

ELEMENT ONE: SELF-RESPECT AND SELF-ESTEEM

In the classroom, teachers provide opportunities for children to learn about who they are and where they come from. A sense of dignity in their culture, heritage, ethnicity/race, religion and gender is nurtured in the classroom. Children learn about different aspects of their identity and the history associated with it.

ELEMENT TWO: RESPECT FOR OTHERS AND THE ENVIRONMENT

Teachers provide opportunities for children to share their knowledge about their own cultural background with their classmates. The goal is to create a climate of respect for diversity through children learning to listen with kindness and empathy to the experiences of their peers. Children deconstruct stereotypes about their peers' identities. I have added an environmental perspective to this component as I believe our environment frames our discussions, our livelihoods and ultimately our potential to survive.

Part two: understanding

ELEMENT THREE: EXPLORING ISSUES OF SOCIAL INJUSTICE

Teachers move from celebrating diversity to an exploration of how diversity has impacted on different groups of people. Children learn about the history of racism, sexism, classism, homophobia and religious intolerance and how these forms of oppression have affected different communities. Teachers demonstrate how the historical roots of oppression have had an impact on the lived experiences and material conditions of people today.

ELEMENT FOUR: SOCIAL MOVEMENTS AND SOCIAL CHANGE

Teachers share examples of iconic and heroic people standing together to address issues of social injustice. Rather than leaving children feeling overwhelmed and defeated, teachers help them understand that by working together, ordinary people have the power to create change.

Part three: action

ELEMENT FIVE: RAISING AWARENESS

Teachers provide opportunities for children to teach others about global and justice issues. This allows children to become advocates through raising awareness among peers, teachers and family and community members. It is important to recognize that while raising awareness is a necessary and important precursor for action, on its own it does not guarantee change in behaviour.

ELEMENT SIX: TAKING SOCIAL ACTION

Teachers provide opportunities for children to take action. Children identify issues they feel passionate about and learn the skills of creating change in their own lives, in their locality and in their community. While teachers are advised to work through the elements of respect, understanding and action sequentially, the elements may also be explored concurrently, particularly in the context of one story or issue. The elements are not mutually exclusive and they work best when they are seen as part of a three-part framework.

Conclusion

In this chapter, I have presented a number of key terms relating to critical literacy. Concepts of development and intercultural education – including culture, gender, class, race, ethnicity, fairness, justice or injustice and power – are often ambiguous and complex. Such issues, and by extension the actions they call for, demand that we, as teachers, become more reflective about the content we teach, the methods we use and the relationships we have with our children. Development education calls for critical thinking, critical consciousness and critical literacy. Critically reading the word and the world involves children in critical thinking, allowing them to question the way things are and the power relationships they observe and thus to consider different cultures, perspectives and ways of taking action. In the next three chapters I discuss in detail the three parts of the curriculum framework – *respect*, *understanding* and *action*.

Chapter 5

Learning about respect and how to develop respect through picturebooks

Introduction

Respect can be defined as a feeling of admiration for someone because of their abilities, qualities and achievements. The first part of my curriculum framework relates to the concept of respect, which is explored through two elements: self-respect and respect for others and the environment. Self-respect is a broad concept and related concepts include self-esteem and self-efficacy. Respect for others, which incorporates the ability to empathize, is a central aspect of intercultural education. Respect for the environment helps to nurture a holistic framework of respect, whereby children learn to appreciate the hidden treasures in their local and global environment. There is some crossover between the books that relate to elements one and two, and they can be used interchangeably to address the core theme of respect. Children need to feel good about themselves before they can learn to value other people. By reflecting on issues relating to self and identity, teachers can assist children in clarifying their feelings about themselves and others, and in learning to understand the rationale for such feelings. Thinking and feeling are natural everyday processes. Picture story books provide a useful platform for facilitating a discussion of children's thoughts and feelings, where issues relating to respect can be discussed.

In this chapter, I present a selection of picturebooks that deal with self-esteem, self-respect and identity. The issue of bullying is discussed using picturebooks that illustrate this controversial topic. I discuss teaching about respect and human rights with particular reference to some powerful stories about respect and hope. Finally, I consider picturebooks about environmental respect and Education for Sustainable Development (ESD).

Self-esteem and self-respect

The development of positive self-respect, self-esteem and the awareness of other aspects of child development are fundamental principles of elementary or primary education. Self-respect refers to a person's ability to like themselves, while self-esteem refers to their overall evaluation or opinion of who they are. People who have high self-esteem have a good self-image. They are generally self-assured and confident about their own personal strengths.

To work towards an inclusive society, teachers need to know about self-worth and equality. They also need to know how to promote such dimensions in the classroom (Buli-Holmberg, 2011). Self-efficacy and empathy are two dimensions of personal development and they influence how we live together collectively. Perceived self-efficacy is defined as people's beliefs about their capabilities in the areas that affect their lives (Bandura *et al.*, 2001). A strong sense of self-efficacy enhances well-being and a sense of personal achievement. People with high levels of self-efficacy approach difficult situations as challenges rather than threats.

To respect other people, one needs to be able to empathize. Empathy is the capability to share and understand another's emotions and feelings, and it is needed to develop solutions and diffuse conflict. Being able to step back and detach from our own emotions is essential for effective, constructive relationships. To show empathy is to identify with another's feelings and to virtually put oneself in the place of another. Empathy is literally empathizing with others, knowing how they are feeling in the moment and reacting to that knowledge.

Research indicates that empathy is basic for developing socially competent behaviour. Moreno *et al.* (2008: 613) argue that 'empathy is a critical part of a broader moral sense that leads generally to harmonious functioning between individuals on a day to day basis, as well as helping behaviours in times of distress'. Goleman (2006) refers to the importance of emotional intelligence (EI) and argues that success and successful relationships require the effective awareness, control and management of one's own emotions and those of other people. Goleman embraces two aspects of emotional intelligence: understanding oneself and understanding others. He identified the five domains of emotional intelligence as:

- knowing your emotions
- managing your own emotions
- motivating yourself
- recognizing and understanding other people's emotions
- managing relationships and the emotions of others

Several picturebooks presented in this book offer teachers an opportunity to explore emotions in the context of characters, plots and alternative plots. While emotional intelligence is important in its own right, it is also an important part of intercultural education. Buli-Holmberg (2011), who links Goleman's work to intercultural education, states that intercultural school programmes are based on two principles:

- development of increased awareness of self-efficacy and cultural identity
- development of increased empathy and awareness of the intrinsic value, equality and cultural diversity of others.

To understand who I am, who you are and who we are, teachers need to build intercultural competence by teaching children to value themselves and others. Their level of self-efficacy and empathy will influence the learning community in either a positive or negative way, so teachers have a central role in supporting children to develop high levels of self-efficacy and empathy.

Picturebooks about self-respect, identity and cultural diversity

Learning to value ourselves and others

Understanding and valuing ourselves is the first step to valuing others. If we have a positive sense of self, we are more likely to accept diversity. By exploring personal identity and cultural diversity, children learn about and connect their own cultural identity and heritage to those of others in different times and places. Cultural diversity concerns, but is not restricted to, language, race, ethnic background, country or region of origin, dress, values, religion and associated practices, social and community responsibilities, sexuality, disability, family and political views. Picturebooks provide several opportunities for exploring identity and diversity.

Only One You (Kranz, 2006) celebrates the uniqueness of each individual and the love shared by parents for their children. This beautifully illustrated picturebook explodes with colour and intuitive insights. Its message is simple: 'There's only one you in this great big world. Make it a better place.' Adri's mother and father share some of their wisdom with their eager son. Their simple and powerful words are intended to comfort and guide him as he goes about exploring the world. Kranz's uniquely painted rockfish, set against vibrant blue seas, make an unforgettable impression.

Learning about feelings of exclusion and inclusion

One of the most legendary stories that deals with self-esteem and self-respect is *The Ugly Duckling*. Created by Hans Christian Andersen, the story about a homely bird that blooms into a gorgeous swan has been translated into several languages, with many picturebook versions including those by Mitchell and Anderson (2007), Isadora (2009) and Pinkney (1999).

In Pinkney's edition, the mother duck knew from the start that one of her babies would be different from the rest, as the sixth egg was large and oddly shaped. When it finally hatches, she thinks the 'monstrous big duckling' must be a turkey chick! Other ducks are appalled by the ugly duckling, and he is chased, pecked and kicked aside. When he can't stand it anymore, he runs away from the pond, eventually taking refuge in the warm cottage of an old woman with a cat and a hen. Missing the delicious feeling of the water too much to stay, he heads out again into the wide, increasingly cold autumnal world:

> One day, he heard a sound of whirring wings, and up in the air he saw a flock of birds flying high. They were as bright as the snow that had fallen during the night, and their long necks were stretched southward. Oh, if only he could go with them! But what sort of companion could he be to those beautiful beings?
>
> (Pinkney, 1999)

At last, after a hard, cold winter, the duckling sees the same flock of birds he'd seen in the sky so many months before. He decides to follow them, somewhat dramatically preferring to be killed by them rather than suffer any more 'cold and hunger and cruelty'. Much to his surprise, they welcome him! And when he looks for his dull, awkward reflection in the water, he sees instead a beautiful swan.

The experience of arriving in a new, alien environment also features in *Beegu* (Deacon, 2004). Beegu is a beguiling character, with three eyes and long, floppy ears. Lost on Earth after her spaceship crashes, Beegu wanders a dark and lonely landscape looking for someone or something to understand and befriend her. Ignored by a sinisterly human-looking tree, by leaves that refuse to stop and listen, and by rabbits and humans alike, Beegu finally finds some schoolchildren who are willing to play, before a hostile teacher shoos her away. There is almost no text, but little is necessary. Alexis Deacon's illustrations, with their stark, empty backgrounds, allow the almost luminous Beegu to stand out. This gives the lost creature an authentically childlike appearance, making her rejection and isolation all the more telling. Other books about navigating new environments are discussed in Chapter 8.

Learning about diversity

Issues associated with the concept of identity feature in a range of picturebooks. According to Miller (2000), picturebooks help children become knowledgeable about cultural and diversity issues and allow them to make personal connections that lead to empathetic behaviour. *Welcome Dede: An*

African naming ceremony (Onyefulu, 2004) looks at the ritual of giving a child a name in Ghana. Picturebooks such as *My Name Is Yoon* (Recorvits, 2003), *The Name Jar* (Choi, 2001), *Hannah Is My Name* (Yang, 2004), *My Name Is Bilal* (Mobin-Uddin, 2005) and *My Name Was Hussein* (Kyuchukov, 2004) also feature stories about children's names, giving teachers a springboard to explore the experience of children settling into a new class, a new area and a new country. In *My Name Is Bilal*, the main character is not looking forward to his first day of school. He liked living in Chicago where there were many other Muslim children in the school. In his new school there are no other Muslim children. On the first day some boys run up to Bilal's sister and try to pull off her head scarf. Bilal is ashamed of himself for not coming to her aid. But he wants to fit in. When introduced to his classmates, he insists that his name is Bill.

My Name Was Hussein is an autobiographical account of Hristo Kyuchukov's early life story. It is about the way of life in a Roma family and is narrated in the voice of Hussein, a 10-year-old living with his parents in Bulgaria. Hussein belongs to the Roma. Roma were originally nomads, who migrated from India and settled in Eastern Europe. Their culture is a mix of Indian, Persian and European and they speak the Romani language. Hussein is a Muslim Roma. He introduces readers to the blend of many cultures and traditions that his family has incorporated over the centuries: the henna hand painting from India, the observance of Muslim religious ceremonies and an Arabic name passed down through generations. He loves his name: Hussein. In Arabic, Hussein means handsome. Life is good in Hussein's village, until the soldiers come with guns and tanks and dogs. Soon the mosques are closed. No one is allowed to enter and pray. Hussein and his family are forced to give up their names and ordered to choose Christian names. Hussein is now called Harry. The universal experience of wanting to fit in can be explored with children of all ages.

Books such as *The Blacker the Berry* (Thomas, 2008) and *I Love My Hair* (Tarpley, 2001) look at the issue of personal affirmation by highlighting the positive side of physical attributes. *I Love My Hair* is a children's picturebook about a young African American girl named Keyana. Every night her mother combs the tangles out of Keyana's hair, reminding her how unique and beautiful it is. Keyana experiences some doubt about this after she is teased at school one day, so her mother explains how lucky she is because her hair can be worn in any style she chooses. Through the rest of the book, Keyana shows the many different ways she wears her hair: in braids, a bun, a ponytail, pig tails, as an afro or with colourful beads. Keyana's mother and teacher reassure her that she should be proud of her hair because it represents her and her background. By the end of the book she happily declares that she loves her hair and its accompanying characteristics, textures and styles. This book is about self-acceptance and being proud of who you are.

The Blacker the Berry (Thomas, 2008) explains how beautiful and special each one of us is, by describing different skin colours in lyrical terms:

> The blacker the berry
> The sweeter the juice …
> Because I am dark the moon and stars
> shine brighter
> Because berries are dark the juice is sweeter

In *My Dadima Wears a Sari* (Sheth, 2007), two young sisters gain a better understanding of their cultural heritage as well as a deeper insight into the identity of their grandmother. Dadima's sari plays a central role in the story, and the sisters start to relate to their grandmother as they learn about the traditional Indian clothes she wears. In the story the sisters steadily acquire knowledge about where their family comes from, get excited about having a sari of their own and thus show the appreciation they feel for their culture and their family.

Celebrating universal experiences through picturebooks

Universal experiences and emotions can be explored comparatively through various picturebooks. People from all cultures experience emotions such as happiness, sadness, fear and anger. Special events such as the first day at school, making friends and traditional festivals are marked across cultures. No matter where in the world we live, children from every culture meet the challenges of growing up and celebrate their accomplishments with a little help from family and friends. Happiness features in *Anna Hibiscus' Song* (Atinuke and Tobia, 2012). In this story, Anna is so happy she is going to 'EXPLODE'. Her mother finally helps her channel her abundant happiness into songwriting. The 'Lulu' series of books by Anna McQuinn – *Lulu Reads to Zeki* (2013), *Lulu Loves the Library* (2011) and *Lulu Loves Stories* (2011) – describe a child's love of books and reading. In *Lulu Loves the Library*, Lulu loves Tuesdays because that's her library day. *Lulu Loves Stories* and *Lulu Loves the Library* are available in paperback with an accompanying CD that translates the story into 20 languages including English, Welsh, Irish, French, Polish, German, Dutch, Italian, Arabic, Swahili, Luganda, Somali, Tigrinya, Tamil, Urdu, Gujerati, Mandarin Chinese, Japanese and Spanish.

Losing one's first tooth is an important part of growing up. *Dave and the Tooth Fairy* (Wilkins, 2008) and *I Lost my Tooth in Africa* (Diakité, 2006) provide two multicultural perspectives of this important event. The former features a computer-literate, independently minded tooth fairy. The latter is about Amina, who wants to lose her loose tooth while visiting her family in Mali, West Africa. Only then can she put it under a gourd for the African tooth fairy, who will exchange it for two chickens! The illustrations by Baba Wagué Diakité are vibrant folk art paintings on white ceramic tiles. They depict daily life in the family compound in Bamako, where Amina eats from a big communal bowl, sleeps under a mosquito net and plays games with her cousins. When her wobbly tooth finally falls out, she receives two beautiful black and white chickens.

Bullying

Bullying is repeated verbal, psychological or physical aggression conducted by an individual or a group against others. It demonstrates lack of respect for oneself and for others. Bullying occurs in many forms: it can be verbal, physical or cyber-based. It can involve gesture, exclusion and extortion. For some children, bullying is a phenomenon they have observed, for others, something they have experienced either as victim or as perpetrator. Children tease one another from a very young age. They discover power by rejecting or ignoring a classmate or by taking another's toys. Bullying is a breach of the human rights of safety and inclusion. Anti-bullying programmes involve the development of healthy relationships, social skills such as understanding and respect, social responsibility and citizenship education. Many correlations can be drawn between children's experiences of bullying and universal stories of racism, oppression and abuses of power.

Picturebooks provide a thoughtful, provocative way to engage children in conversation and can be used to bring together disparate age groups to talk about the sensitive topic of bullying. From simply sharing a story about being different, to reading a book that directly addresses an ongoing bullying incident in a specific school, teachers and parents can challenge children to think creatively about how they treat one another and the daily events they observe.

For younger children, *The Three Bully Goats* (Kimmelman, 2011) is a twist on the traditional tale *The Three Billy Goats Gruff*. Gruff, Ruff and Tuff bully their way across a bridge. Frustrated with being friendly and polite, the ogre hatches a plan to teach the bully goats a lesson. In a more abstract representation, *One* (Otoshi, 2008) illustrates bullying beautifully by naming characters after a range of colours. Blue is quiet and passive and bullied by hot-headed Red. The other characters, also named by colours, are bystanders who do not agree with Red's behaviour but dare not say anything. Every time

Red says something mean and no one speaks up, he grows larger and more intimidating. Luckily, the number One shows the colours how to stand up to Red. All of the colours, including Red, learn that everyone counts. The final message of the book is that 'sometimes it just takes One'.

Two of a Kind (Robbins, 2009) is a thought-provoking depiction of how easily children can be lured by the desire to be popular and how difficult it is to be outcast. When Anna is first approached by Kayla and Melanie, she is flattered to be included in their exclusive friendship group and sits silently as the two malicious girls taunt her friend Julisa. Eventually, Anna realizes she doesn't like these popular but bossy and unkind classmates, and returns to her true friend. Written by a former teacher, this is a realistic look at friendship, loyalty and the powerful lure of popularity. It provides a good stimulus for discussing positive character traits, bullying and peer pressure.

The Recess Queen (O'Neill, 2002) is about a schoolyard bully who is enlightened by the new child in class. Powerful insights into playground bullying, school violence and poor self-esteem feature in the book. *The Worst Best Friend* (2008) by the same author demonstrates the mental and emotional forms of bullying. Other picturebooks that address this theme include: *Mr Lincoln's Way* (Polacco, 2003), *Stand Tall, Molly Lou Melon* (Lovell, 2001), *My Secret Bully* (Ludwig, 2003), *Just Kidding* (Ludwig, 2005) and *Bird Child* (Forler, 2009).

In *Goal* (Javaherbin, 2010) Ajani is excited to play a game with his friends, having just won a federation-sized soccer ball. He knows the streets of their South African town are dangerous, but the boys draw sticks and the loser takes up a position on the roof as duty guard. Preoccupied with the game, the boys do not notice the bullies until it is almost too late. Through some quick thinking, they are able to save the new ball and continue their soccer game. Highlighting universal themes of bullying and a love of sport, this book is about soccer's power to inspire and connect fans and players around the world.

Picturebooks that retell *The Ugly Duckling* can also be interpreted in terms of modern-day episodes of racist or bullying behaviour. The main character is discriminated against by other ducks because he does not look like them. Children who feel ostracized, or have experienced bullying, will be able to conceptualize their own experience through *The Ugly Duckling*. The story illustrates discrimination, a form of prejudice, which includes feelings of hostility, antipathy or indifference. The transformation to a beautiful swan provides a note of hope, and no doubt it was Andersen's wish to give children the hope of one day finding their own peaceful resolution to feeling excluded.

Teaching about respect and human rights

Teaching children about their human rights can reduce bullying and exclusions, improve relations with teachers and create a calmer atmosphere for learning (Osler and Starkey, 2010). On 10 December 1948 the United Nations proclaimed *The Universal Declaration of Human Rights* (UDHR), which states the reasons why it has become important to safeguard human rights all over the world, especially after the horrors of genocide in the Holocaust. Published by Frances Lincoln in association with Amnesty International, *We Are all Born Free: The Universal Declaration of Human Rights in pictures* (2008) is a beautiful picturebook celebrating the sixtieth anniversary of the UDHR. Each of the UDHR's 30 Articles has been simplified and illustrated by a renowned illustrator of children's picturebooks. It is sobering to be reminded of how few of the Articles are upheld, including: 'Nobody has any right to hurt us or to torture us'. The text is clearly valuable as a set of ideals for life and rules for the playground. The illustrations vary in tone, from comic to serious, childlike to sophisticated, fantastical to realistic. They are creative interpretations of the Articles and use a range of artistic styles from collage to screen prints. The South African illustrator Niki Daly depicts a statue of Nelson Mandela in a freedom park. Jane Ray's damaged rag doll portrays torture. Polly Dunbar communicates the idea of being innocent until proven guilty. Carrying thought-provoking messages, Alan Lee's paper planes caught on the barbed wire of a wall inspire readers to consider issues such as our freedom to travel.

Powerful stories of respect and hope

On 6 November 2012, Barack Obama was re-elected as the forty-fourth president of the United States of America. Obama's story is inspirational for all cultures today. In third grade (3rd or year two class), he wrote an essay titled 'I Want to Become President'. The first black president of America, his election marked a watershed in American history and is a symbol of hope for all black Americans. His story presents many opportunities for reflection and exploration in primary classrooms. His life story is presented in picturebook format in *Barack Obama: Son of promise, child of hope* (2009). Told by Nikki Grimes and illustrated by Bryan Collier, it is the story of an exceptional man.

Born to a white American mother and a black Kenyan father, Obama's unique origins and fascinating life experiences are retold for children in this picturebook format. *Son of promise, child of hope* (2009) sets out Barack's story from student, to organizer, to Senator, to Democratic Nominee for President of the United States of America. Bryan Collier's illustrations capture many important moments, including spearfishing with playmates in Hawaii, playing with pet gibbons in Djakarta and journeying to Kenya to meet his father's family. Obama has motivated Americans to believe that every one of us has the power to change ourselves and our world.

Obama has also written a picturebook. *Of Thee I Sing: A letter to my daughters* (2010) features a group of 13 American heroes and heroines whose traits he sees in his own children. The book, illustrated by children's artist Loren Long, begins by asking 'Have I told you lately how wonderful you are?' and goes on to offer repeated phrases of praise and encouragement to his daughters, while introducing them to the 13 great Americans who helped shape the nation – from Martin Luther King, who 'taught us unyielding compassion' and 'opened hearts', to Jackie Robinson, who 'swung his bat with the grace and strength of a lion and gave brave dreams to other dreamers'.

The list also includes George Washington – the first president, who 'believed in liberty and justice for all' and 'helped make an idea into a new country, strong and true' – and Mexican Labour activist César Chávez. Obama adapted Chávez's declaration '*Si, se puede!*' – 'Yes, you can!' – as his first election campaign slogan. The book is based on Americans from all walks of life and all periods of history, of all races, ethnicities and ages. Some might be familiar – like George Washington and Martin Luther King Jr – while others such as Maya Lin, who designed the Vietnam Veterans Memorial in Washington DC, are known for their great works rather than their names.

Barack Obama's election as the first black president of the United States of America has been a powerful source of inspiration for people all over the world. To explain the significance of Obama's election to her children, Rana DiOrio wrote a picturebook called *What Does it Mean to Be Global?* (2009). Her publishing company, Little Pickle Press, is dedicated to helping parents and educators to consciously explore the meaningful topics of their generation through a variety of media, technologies and techniques. Other books published by Little Pickle Press include *What Does it Mean to Be Green?* (DiOrio, 2010) and *What Does it Mean to Be Present?* (DiOrio, 2010).

Respect for the environment

Sustainability is an interdisciplinary concept with the potential to inform several cross-curricular themes in primary classrooms. There is widespread consensus in the literature that education has a key role to play in our attempts to realize ecologically sustainable development (Taylor *et al.*, 2003). Calls for more action from education have increased in the light of mounting anxiety over environmental problems. Education for Sustainable Development

(ESD) is defined as a 'concept that encompasses a new vision of education that seeks to empower people of all ages to be responsible for creating and enjoying a sustainable future' (UNESCO, 2002: 7). Spearman and Eckhoff (2012) differentiate 'big S' sustainability education for adults and adolescents and 'small s' sustainability education for young learners. Accordingly, young learners investigating 'little s' sustainability target activities in their own communities and establish connections with other communities. For instance, children could maintain a school garden and connect the project to the sustainable benefits of eating locally grown food.

Picturebooks about respecting the environment

Many picturebooks highlight our responsibility to protect our environment while generating an appreciation for the wonders of nature. These books feed children's immense curiosity about the world around them and present information in an imaginative, creative manner, imparting wisdom about our interrelationship with the planet and all living things. Picturebooks explore environmental issues in a number of ways, looking at, for example:

- spiritual aspects of the environment and environment as creation
- the relationship of people to the environment
- damage to the environment
- a celebration of the beauty of the environment
- actions that can be taken to enjoy and protect the environment.

SPIRITUAL ASPECTS OF THE ENVIRONMENT AND ENVIRONMENT AS CREATION

Certain picturebooks simply celebrate the world as creation. Some exquisitely illustrate the beauty of nature, while others document traditional myths, creation stories and metaphysical explanations for what makes up the world around us.

The Water Hole (Base, 2001) takes the reader on an exhilarating journey of discovery from the plains of Africa and the jungles of the Amazon to the woodlands of North America and the deserts of Australia. At first glance, this is a simple one-to-ten counting book featuring familiar animals as they gather at a water hole deep in the forest: *One Rhino, Two Tigers*, and so on. Page by page the number and diversity of animals increases, as representatives from different continents come to the water hole to drink. At the same time the water hole is shrinking until eventually it is nothing but cracked, dry mud. An interesting metaphor for world resources, a physical hole in the page, representing the water hole becomes increasingly smaller with each page turn. Younger readers will enjoy a simple counting book filled with familiar creatures. Older children will be challenged to discover a hundred hidden animals in the background. On each double spread, black silhouettes of the animals and their names are included in the border to indicate those hidden in the illustrations.

The picturebook *Enora and the Black Crane* (Meeks, 2010) is set in the rainforests of Queensland. Based on the traditional customs of Queensland's Kokoimudgji tribe and written by an aboriginal artist, the story is about Enora, who lives with his family in a tropical rainforest. The story follows Enora and his family as the natural world is created, and Enora's people are surrounded by delicious bush food and amazing animals. When Enora discovers a shimmering rainbow of colour flying through the rainforest, his curiosity overwhelms him and he sets out to discover its meaning. After encountering a flock of amazing birds, he accidentally kills a crane with dramatic consequences. Enora and his world lose their innocence for ever.

THE RELATIONSHIP OF PEOPLE TO THE ENVIRONMENT

Many picturebooks explore the relationship between humans and the environment. Books with an environmental theme can stimulate concern for the threats to our environment, provoke debate on solutions to environmental problems and arouse curiosity to discover more information on the topic (Miller, 1998). Australian illustrator Jeannie Baker creates wordless books for older readers. In *Window* (Baker, 2002), the reader looks both at and through the window simultaneously. Each page shows the same scene framed by a window. With the turning of every page the years pass and gradual changes can be deduced as nature gives way to an urbanized world, firstly through a building site, then through a village and finally through a fully developed city.

Window (2002) is based on a beautiful series of collage constructions that chronicle the changing world from the bedroom window during a boy's life. Baker's illustrations use several visual devices to indicate the passage of time as the child grows up – birthday cards on the window, different kinds of toys to mark different stages of his boyhood – and such changes beyond the window as environmental destruction through the felling of trees and an ever increasing number of houses. The book finishes with the young man, grown up and married, moving to another house in the middle of a wilderness. But there is a sign in the foreground reading 'House Blocks for Sale'. Baker's books demonstrate the complex concept of interdependence in a thought-provoking, challenging manner that children and teachers can use as a basis for further discussion and interrogation.

Window's story is reversed in the companion story *Belonging* (Baker, 2007), which begins with a window looking out into an urban scene. In a series of detailed collage illustrations, we watch as the view from the window transforms over a period of two years, as a young girl grows up and becomes a mother. As well as stimulating conversations about the environment, this inspiring book will also help children think about community, family and relationships.

DAMAGE TO THE ENVIRONMENT

Picturebooks reflect on the careless destruction of the environment because of greed and ignorance. *Where the Forest Meets the Sea* (Baker, 1998) tells the story of a boy and his father on a visit to a wonderful beach in northern Queensland, at a place where the ocean meets the edge of the Daintree Rainforest. This threatened landscape has been shrinking for decades. As the boy explores it, he imagines what it might have been like 100 million years before when dinosaurs roamed. He finishes the day cooking fish on the beach and contemplates coming again someday. But in the background we see a landscape overlain by ghostly images of what it might be like when he comes back again, should development do what it has done in many other parts of the Daintree Rainforest.

Picturebooks about controversial ecology issues provide wonderful inspiration for older children. The divisive subject matter stimulates children's interest and may serve as the impetus to work on related research projects (Miller, 1998). A book such as *Where the Forest Meets the Sea* (1998) can prompt a research project studying the effects of industrialization on nature, an interview with a nature conservationist or a debate on the pros and cons of industrialization.

Since its original publication in 1971, Dr Seuss's *The Lorax* (Seuss, 2009) has become a classic. For many children, the Lorax character has come to symbolize concern for the environment. In this story, a small boy notices a ramshackle house with a memorial to the Lorax at the end of a desolate street on the edge of town. He gazes at the home of the Once-ler and wonders about its significance. The Once-ler drops his Whisper-ma-Phone and for a small fee tells the boy the story of the Lorax and the once beautiful Truffula trees that covered the landscape, and the creatures that enjoyed the environment they helped sustain. The story of greed, excess and environmental destruction ends with the Once-ler giving the boy the last seed of a Truffula tree. Perhaps, just perhaps, in his young hands there may be hope for this place once more. What makes *The Lorax* so effective is the combination of a step-by-step look at cause and effect, how unfettered greed can destroy the environment, followed by an emphasis on positive change through individual responsibility. The story's end emphasizes the impact that one person can have, no matter how young.

The setting for Michael Foreman's *One World* (2011) is a tidal rock pool. This delicate story, with its beautiful illustrations, gently depicts deforestation, air pollution and the threat of global warming. After taking time to consider the diversity of animals on earth, a young girl visits a beach with her brother. Together, they explore a wondrous tidal pool, filled with seaweed, small fish, sea anemones and starfish. But it is not long before the children discover that the pool has been damaged by a rusty tin can and a blob of oil. As the day at the seashore progresses, the youngsters fill a bucket with water, add sand, pebbles, seaweed and shells, before deciding to catch some tiny live creatures. Equipped with a mini marine habitat, they revisit the rock pool and discover it is no longer beautiful. The discarded rusty can and oil are all that remain. Startled at what they see, the children set about returning the sand, pebbles, seaweed, shells and fish to the pool. They remove the tin can and draw the oil out of the water using a seabird feather. Satisfied with their progress, they decide to enlist the help of other children when checking the tidal pools the following day.

The picturebook *Varmints* (Ward, 2008) is about nature-loving creatures who take care of plants in the fields, before an industrial city is built over their peaceful landscape. 'There was once only the sound of bees and the wind in the wiry grass, the low murmuring of moles in the cool dark earth ... and the song of birds in the high blue sky.' So begins the story, a delicate, yet striking portrait of an idyllic world turned into a noisy dark hell, where the sound of bees is lost and no one can hear themselves think. Set over futuristic, dimly lit buildings and the scurrying shadows of residents – depicted as rabbit-like creatures with shiny black noses and eyes – the spidery lines of silver text are almost impossible to see. This book has been made into an animated film, an additional resource for exploring its environmental theme.

A CELEBRATION OF THE ENVIRONMENT, ITS BEAUTY AND WONDER

Many picturebooks capture the aesthetic beauty of the physical world through a variety of art forms. Trees are a popular subject in picturebooks. In *Are Trees Alive?* (2003), Miller explains how trees take in nutrients, grow and survive changes in their environment. Information is simply and effectively conveyed in a few sentences. Colourful illustrations show trees from regions around the world, which are identified in a picture glossary at the back of the book. One of the best illustrations captures the immensity of redwoods by angling the view downward from mid trunk and showing a tiny figure standing at the base of the tree. Work with this illustration can be used as a mechanism for generating discussion about the relationship between humans and trees. Other books about trees include Newell DePalma's *A Grand Old Tree* (2005), Muldrow and Staake's *We Planted a Tree* (2010) and Reid's *Picture a Tree* (2011). *There Was a Tree* (Isadora, 2012) is based on the song of the same name:

> There was a tree in the wood
> The prettiest little tree that you ever did see
> Well the tree was in a hole, and the hole was in the ground
> And the green grass grew all around, all around, the green grass
> grew all around

The East African savannah forms the backdrop for this picturebook and 'the prettiest tree that you ever did see' is a lovely acacia tree.

Two books present magnificent images of the baobab tree: *Tree of Life: The world of the African baobab* (Bash, 2002) and *This Is the Tree: A story of the baobab* (Moss, 2005). Often referred to as the Tree of Life, this tree may be one of the oldest life forms on the planet today. It can be found on the savannahs of Africa and the sunburned plains of Australia. Baobab trees are tremendous in size and have provided food, medicine and places of refuge for many. For most of the year the tree is leafless, and looks very much like it has its roots sticking up in the air, giving it its very distinctive appearance.

The tree is the source of much folklore and mythology and this features in Barbara Bash's book: *Tree of Life: The world of the African baobab*. According to African legend, each animal was given a tree to plant by the Great Spirit. When the hyena was assigned the baobab tree, the careless animal planted it upside down 'and that is why its branches look like gnarled roots'. Bash continues to present the life cycle of this majestic tree. Frequently measuring 60 feet tall and 40 feet wide, these giants 'outlive nearly everything on earth', their life span over a thousand years.

This Is the Tree: A story of the baobab (2000) by Miriam Moss presents an account of the baobab through a series of elegant three-line stanzas:

> This is the tree when the world was young,
> That pushed up through the earth

> As a small tender shoot.
> This is the tree, now old as a volcano,
> Standing alone
> On the African plain.

For anyone who has seen one, the illustrations in these books are a wonderful representation of the baobab and the wildlife in Africa.

The beautifully illustrated *All the World* (Scanlon, 2009) demonstrates the concept of interdependence, highlighting the connections between people and the world. It follows a family from morning until night through various places, activities and weather, all the while reaffirming that everything that happens is part of our world and yet part of a bigger world at the same time.

STEWARDSHIP: ACTIONS THAT CAN BE TAKEN TO ENJOY AND PROTECT THE ENVIRONMENT

Many picturebooks communicate the message that the time for action is now and that we all have a responsibility to make changes in our lives. *The Trouble with Dragons* (Gliori, 2009), written in rhyme, communicates the importance of sharing and caring, and of working together to protect the world we live in – or we will all be extinct just like the Dragons!

Other books that advocate action include: *S is for Save the Planet: A how-to-be green alphabet* (Herzog, 2009), *10 Things I Can Do to Help My World* (Walsh, 2008), *Don't Throw That Away* (Bergen, 2009), *The Three R's: Reuse, reduce, recycle* (Roca, 2007), *Big Earth, Little Me* (Wiley, 2009), *Why Should I Recycle?* (Green and Gordon, 2005), *George Saves the World by Lunchtime* (Roberts, 2007), *Compost Stew* (Siddals, 2010), *Sofia's Dream* (Wilson, 2010) and *Sandy's Incredible Shrinking Footprint* (Handy, 2010).

Kooser and Root's *Bag in the Wind* (2010) is a book about recycling. A woman driving a bulldozer pushing rubbish in a landfill sees an empty yellow plastic bag. The bag is a nameless, voiceless adventurer, the colour of the skin of a yellow onion, with two holes for handles. It is picked up by a puff of wind and blown over the fence. From there it is blown into the lives of several people: a girl collecting cans, a store owner with a draughty door and a homeless man. This picturebook teaches the reader the importance of recycling and thinking before throwing away an object that can be reused.

Children's experience of planting and growing seeds features in several picturebooks. *The Curious Garden* (Brown, 2009) is a magical story about a boy's dream and how the efforts of one small person can help change the world. Gradually the city is transformed as other citizens follow Liam's example and take up gardening. The illustrations are a veritable feast for the eyes, as the reader encounters the indomitable will of this little garden to go beyond the boundaries of the railway tracks and its bridge, to every nook and corner of a dreary city, livening up its landscape, spreading its curiosities and happiness to the local environment and community. The book focuses on the positive impact humans have had on the physical environment through gardening. Its central message could be usefully reinforced through a school garden.

The theme of regeneration or transformation also features in John Light's *The Flower* (2011). The main character, a sad-looking boy called Brigg, lives in a sad building in a sad city. He works in a library where dangerous books are kept. When he discovers a book that says 'Do Not Read', he can't help but have a look. Inside are pictures of beautifully coloured things called flowers. Brigg is filled with joy looking at the pictures but he is sad because there are no flowers in the city. He sets off in search of flowers in the old part of town. He looks everywhere until he arrives at the window of a junk shop where he sees the picture of a flower! In the shop he buys seeds, takes them home and waters them. One morning, the seeds blossom and Brigg's room is filled with wonderful colours until the room cleaning system sucks them away. The book is set in the future, where flowers have disappeared, probably sucked away by the cleaning system. The sad feeling of greyness is perfectly conveyed by the illustrations, so much so that when the picture of the flower appears, pink and bright, it lights up the whole page. The theme of planting and creating continues with *The Tin Forest* (Ward, 2001). An old man lives alone in the middle of nowhere, surrounded by other people's rubbish. He dreams of living in a beautiful place. One day he decides to use the rubbish around him to create his own forest, complete with tin flowers and animals. Then a real bird comes to the forest, and soon the old man's world is transformed.

Conclusion

In this chapter, I have examined the concept of respect in terms of self-respect, respect for others and respect for the environment. Respect is a key part of development and intercultural education, the first rung on the ladder of intercultural relations. It is essential for the development of empathetic connections and to motivate children to become involved in development education projects. An important aspiration for teachers using multicultural literature is to show children how to develop empathy (Miller, 2000). However, it is important for children not to be overwhelmed by negative feelings or a sense of powerlessness, so there needs to be a balance between the selection of stories and how they are discussed in class. The issue of respect can be extended into a whole-school philosophy, which informs school ethos, school practices and the kinds of relationships that children experience in school.

According to the NCCA:

> Children are citizens with rights and responsibilities. They have opinions that are worth listening to, and have the right to be involved in making decisions about matters which affect them. In this way, they have a right to experience democracy. From this experience they learn that, as well as having rights, they also have a responsibility to respect and help others, and to care for their environment.

(2009: 8)

In a framework of development and intercultural education, the development of respect is fundamental. It needs to be revisited constantly throughout the primary school. Picturebooks can assist teachers in introducing the concept of respect, in reinforcing important messages about respect and in exploring the implications of respect and its antithesis, lack of respect.

Chapter 6

Understanding

Introduction

Development education deals with a range of social justice issues: injustice, trade, unequal distribution of resources and poverty. Picturebooks can help children engage with development issues and learn about the historical global movements that developed in response. These development education issues are at the heart of the second part of my curriculum framework: *understanding*. The concept of understanding is explored in element three (issues) and element four (global movements) of my framework, which is outlined in Chapter 4. There is considerable crossover between elements three and four, and picture story books from both can be used.

In this chapter, I look at developing understanding in the context of contemporary issues – for example, the 2010 earthquake in Haiti. Other topics included are the unequal distribution of resources in the world, dealing with statistics and important development issues such as gender inequality, climate change, deforestation, slavery, apartheid and the Holocaust. Development education helps make sense of the complexity of our world. The picturebooks I discuss in this chapter highlight specific development issues, stimulate debate, encourage creativity and provide fresh perspectives for children.

Historical and recent contemporary events

To help children understand how the world works, teachers only have to discuss with them a number of significant events that have taken place long ago and recently. Many are nervous about their personal knowledge and, in some instances, avoid teaching contemporary events. However, certain picturebooks will assist teachers in exploring these important issues.

The Khmer Rouge and the Killing Fields

During the reign of the genocidal Khmer Rouge regime in Cambodia from 1975 to 1979, an estimated 1.7 million Cambodians died of starvation, torture or execution. The death toll represented approximately one quarter of the Cambodian population.

The picturebook *Half Spoon of Rice: A survival story of the Cambodian genocide* (Smith, 2010) was inspired by the true stories of those who survived four years of horror. The dark history of the Cambodian genocide is largely untold in schools around the world. The book is intended to help ensure that Cambodia's killing fields will not be forgotten.

Smith's narrator is 9-year-old Nat, celebrating the New Year in Phnom Penh. Soldiers force people to leave their homes because Americans are supposedly about to bomb the city. Nat and his parents can only grab a little food and a few belongings. As the march begins, they join Malis, a girl separated from her parents. For three days they march at gunpoint, not allowed to stop or eat. Nat's father correctly guesses that everyone is being ordered to the countryside to grow rice. Finally, they reach a place where Nat can soak his aching feet in the cool mud. Along the way they have seen the bodies of those too weak to march, and more horrors await them.

Eventually, the children are separated from parents and boys from girls. In Nat's clear, simple language, readers learn what he endures – cruel forced labour and severe hunger:

> Our food ration is now only about half a spoon of rice a day. I sneak out into the forest behind our tent to try to catch something to eat. I know I'm taking a chance and might get caught, but I'm so hungry. I find a frog and pull its legs off and eat them. It tastes horrible, but it satisfies my stomach.
>
> (Smith, 2010)

Nat and Malis eventually find each other. When soldiers abandon their posts after four long years, the children go to a camp in Thailand. Nat's parents survive too. They adopt Malis, and the family emigrates to San Francisco.

A Path of Stars (O'Brien, 2012) and *A Song for Cambodia* (Lord, 2008) also deal with the war in Cambodia. Other books dealing with Cambodian culture include *Running Shoes* (Lipp, 2009), *Angkat: The Cambodian Cinderella* (Coburn and Flotte, 1998), *The Caged Birds of Phnom Penh* (Lipp, 2001) and *Little Sap and Monsieur Rodin* (Lord, 2006).

The 2010 Haitian earthquake

On 12 January 2010, an earthquake with a magnitude of 7.0 on the Richter scale struck Haiti. More than 300,000 people were killed, an estimated 300,000 were injured and more than one million were rendered homeless. The capital city, Port-au-Prince, was devastated. The Presidential Palace, Parliament and many other important structures were destroyed, along with countless homes, businesses, hospitals, schools and shanty towns. Many watched loved ones die. Some citizens were stuck in the rubble of their homes and rescued several days later. In the aftermath of the earthquake, teachers faced the dilemma of teaching the issue in a humanitarian fashion, while respecting the dignity of the Haitian people. One option was to raise funds and send the money to Haiti. Another was to conduct an enquiry in the classroom, asking such key questions as:

- What is it like to live in Haiti?
- Why did the Earthquake take place?
- How were people affected?
- Why were so many people injured and killed?
- What is the most useful way for us to respond?

There are now picturebooks that deal with Haiti in its own right as well as the Haitian earthquake (Dolan, 2012b). *Eight Days: A story of Haiti* (Danticat, 2010) is one account of the Haitian earthquake, carefully crafted in a picturebook by Haitian-born author Edwidge Danticat. Instead of focusing on loss, Danticat writes about a boy who is saved, thanks in part to his imagination. This is a story about survival and hope. It begins with 7-year-old Junior being pulled from the rubble, eight days after the earthquake. Though Junior's body was trapped, his mind was free, and each day he did something new, including flying a kite with his friend, Oscar, who was with him when the earthquake took place.

Watson's book *Hope for Haiti* (2010) is another post-earthquake publication. The young boy who narrates the story lives in an area that was destroyed by it. His family joins several others to set up makeshift housing in a soccer stadium. Before long, the children start playing soccer with a ball made of rags. In this story, a soccer ball signed by Manno Sanon, a famous Haitian player, inspires a small but powerful link between a heartbroken country's past and its hopes for the future.

I Came from the Water: One Haitian boy's incredible tale of survival (Oelschlager, 2012) is based on the true story of Moses, a young Haitian boy. He survived the earthquake because his relatives placed him in a basket and sent him down the river. The book includes an interview with Moses, and provides a brief history of the earthquake and pictures of the church, orphanage and hospitals mentioned in the story.

It is important not to romanticize disasters such as earthquakes. Reading quality non-fiction books about earthquakes together – such as Simon (2006) and Branley (2005) – might aid a broader discussion about where earthquakes can occur, where Haiti is in relationship to the child's home, the history of the Haitian people and how we can help.

The earthquake had a devastating social, physical and economic impact. Haiti sits on the boundary between the Caribbean and North

American tectonic plates, creating a fault line across the country. This was the largest earthquake to strike Haiti in more than two hundred years. It was a relatively shallow earthquake, thus exacerbating the physical impact. With 80 per cent of the Haitian population living below the poverty line, Haiti is one of the poorest and least developed countries in the world and struggles with political upheaval, social and health problems and a series of hurricanes and destructive earthquakes. One reason for the higher death tolls in Haiti compared to other earthquake-prone areas is the high number of people living in urban areas in unsound housing. The poorest people in Haiti were worst affected by the earthquake.

Haitian history is characterized by colonization and exploitation. The island of Hispaniola (*La Isla Española*), today occupied by the nations of Haiti and the Dominican Republic, was initially invaded or discovered (depending on one's political perspective) by Christopher Columbus in 1492. The Taino Indian (or *Arawak*) inhabitants referred to their homeland by many names but most commonly used *Ayti* or *Hayti* (mountainous). In less than ten years after Columbus arrived in Haiti, the majority of the Taino population had died as a result of slavery, abuse and murder. The story of Columbus's arrival in Central America as told from the Taino perspective is available in the picturebook *Encounter* (Yolen, 1996).

At the end of the seventeenth century, Spain ceded the western portion of Hispaniola (Haiti) to France. Sugar, coffee, cotton and indigo plantations made Saint-Domingue France's most lucrative colony by far and it became known as La Petite France or Little France. Saint-Domingue's black population quickly increased as the slave trade flourished following the need to manage the large agricultural plantations. Under French rule the colony prospered. Wealth was created alongside brutal slavery and corrupt administrations. Many slaves died within a few years of arriving, but were quickly replaced. The last French troops withdrew in late 1803, and in 1804 the territory gained independence as the Republic of Haiti after a decade of slave revolts. France recognized Haiti as an independent country in exchange for a large financial settlement, which placed the country in crippling debt. Haiti was the first independent nation of Latin America and the Caribbean, the first black-led republic in the world and the second republic in the Americas.

Over a hundred years later the country was colonized by the United States of America. When the US departed in 1934, Haiti was left with a US military force, the Haitian National Guard, which supported the corrupt Duvalier regime. Haiti under the Duvaliers was marked by extremes of poverty and wealth. Government officials, army officers, coffee exporters and landowners lived in luxurious hillside villas with fountains and swimming pools. Poor people lived in the slums below. This unequal income distribution still exists today between the impoverished Creole-speaking majority and the affluent French-speaking minority.

The unequal distribution of wealth has contributed to environmental destruction. Rich land owners, the state and foreign companies control the best land. So the low-income farmers have had to clear land on steep mountain slopes to plant their crops. As trees were uprooted, erosion stripped the soil away. Trees were cut to make charcoal, the only fuel poor families could afford. The hills became barren and dusty. Poverty forced hundreds of thousands of rural Haitians to migrate to Port-au-Prince in search of work. When the earthquake occurred, these people could not escape.

Teachers need to know this background to teach the Haitian earthquake as a development issue and to maximize learning potential from the many excellent picturebooks about Haiti. *Selavi, That Is Life: A Haitian story of hope* (Landowne, 2005), about a homeless child befriended by other street children living in Haiti, is a complex true story of hardship and resourcefulness, persecution and triumph. Together the children find a caring community and create a radio station run by and for children. A story with a positive message, it vividly presents the poignant difficulties that street children face in daily life. The book is particularly good for introducing the concept of human rights to young readers. While the issues of political instability and chaos of revolution are not mentioned directly, their evidence is present for the older child and more discerning readers.

Josias, Hold the Book (Elvgren, 2006) is the story of a Haitian boy whose family depends on him to tend the garden. When the beans in Josias's garden do not grow, he must find a solution or his family will not have enough to eat. He asks a friend who is lucky enough to hold the book (attend school) if the answer might be found in a book. When the garden doesn't thrive, Josias and his family realize learning is vital to success with the garden and with life.

In *Circles of Hope* (Williams, 2011), readers are introduced to the realities of rural life in the mountains of Haiti. The story is about a boy named Facile whose father has taught him the value of trees. He has planted a mango tree in honour of Facile's birth, and this tree is now generously yielding fruit and shade as well as preventing landslides, but Facile's father had to leave to find work. After the birth of his sister Lucia, Facile decides to plant his own tree as a gift to her, but the task is difficult without his father's assistance. Facile tries to plant a mango tree three times. The first twig is eaten by a rambling goat. The second is swept away by rains. And the third is scorched by scrub fires. After each failed attempt Facile asks an adult in the family, 'How can I plant a tree that would grow strong?'. Every time he asks, he receives an answer that reveals the local Haitian techniques for handling the challenge of reforestation. Deforestation is a conspicuous yet subtle issue throughout the book, illuminating the current environmental crisis in Haiti. Close to the end, the boy learns from his uncle that he needed *éspéré* (hope) to make the tree grow. Facile himself has the brilliant idea of using the plentiful stones to build protective walls around the sprouting trees.

Picturebooks such as the four described above are timely and timeless resources to encourage children to make a connection with the people and places portrayed. They build upon the news and facts by providing a context for understanding people who are affected. With the guidance of a teacher, picturebooks can be used to develop understanding and empathy and perhaps the will to help. Certain contemporary issues such as the Haitian earthquake bring together dimensions of development, culture and sustainability, which can be explored effectively through picturebooks. However, it is important to develop pedagogical approaches and to offer interpretive frameworks that will help children critically engage with the core themes and messages of each picturebook.

The 2004 tsunami and Hurricane Katrina

Recent natural disasters, which are becoming more commonplace, remind us of the infinite power of the earth. Tsunamis are huge waves of water usually caused by earthquakes or volcanic eruptions. The Japanese word 'tsunami' literally means 'harbour wave'. On 26 December 2004, an earthquake with a magnitude of 9.0 on the Richter scale caused a tsunami off the west coast of Sumatra, Indonesia, that killed over 200,000 people. The tsunami affected 12 countries in south and south-east Asia and the north-eastern coast of Africa. It received extensive global media coverage and prompted exceptional expressions of human solidarity and an international aid response. From a development perspective the poorest people were worst affected. The aftermath of the earthquake affected Indonesia, Sri Lanka, India and Thailand to differing degrees. In addition to the disaster's immediate consequences, it created long-term challenges of resettlement and reconstruction. In Aceh, Indonesia, and Sri Lanka, the response was affected by ongoing conflict. The event also highlighted the fragility of the earth and the power of natural disasters. People were able to witness the event as it unfolded due to mass access to video and recording equipment, and it generated far more media attention than other natural disasters, as the region is popular with international tourists.

There are three excellent picturebooks for teaching about tsunamis in general and remembering the 2004 disaster in particular. *Mama* (Winter, 2006) is told entirely through illustrations, except for the words 'mama' and 'baby'. On the last page of the book is a brief synopsis of what occurred when a baby hippo became separated from his mother when the great waves hit following the 2004 tsunami. After struggling alone for several days, the baby hippo was rescued by Kenyan wildlife officers and brought to live in an animal refuge. There, it adopted a new 'mama', a 130-year-old giant male tortoise and they've been inseparable ever since.

Tsunami! (2009) by Kimiko Kajikawa is based not on the 2004 event but on a famous Japanese legend, and powerfully conveys the force of a tsunami. Ojiisan lived in Japan long, long ago. The word *Ojiisan* means grandfather. When the rice harvest festival is underway, all the villagers except Ojiisan and his grandson gather on the beach at the foot of a mountain to celebrate. The wealthiest man in the village, Ojiisan lives simply and humbly on the top of the mountain with his beautiful fields of rice. On the day of the festival, however, something doesn't feel right to him. An earthquake occurs, but though he's felt many before, this one seems different. And when he looks at the sea he realizes to his horror that the sea is running away from the land. A tsunami is coming, and all those people down below will be killed if he doesn't do something. By setting fire to his precious rice fields, Ojiisan lures the villagers up the mountain just in time to escape the imminent vicious inhuman disaster. The illustrations are mixed media and combine natural textures, bold colours and abstract shapes to convey compelling images of chaos and disaster as the rice fields burn and the wave rushes in. There is a particularly strong bird's-eye view of the village after the tsunami has crashed ashore.

Elephants of the Tsunami (Laiz, 2006) is a pictorial retelling of an extraordinary true event that occurred on Khao Lak Beach, Thailand, on the morning of the devastating South Asian tsunami. The book gives a different perspective of the tsunami through the elephants that saved the lives of 50 people. An elephant's power to recognize danger signals from nature gives us much to consider socially, scientifically and ecologically.

Over the past 35 years the number of category four and category five hurricanes worldwide has nearly doubled and global sea surface temperatures have increased. Are recent increases in the number and strength of hurricanes due to the greenhouse effect and a warmer climate? Or are they the result of a natural cycle? Scientists continue to research what is causing this trend; however, there is no doubt that such storms have a huge impact on coastal communities. In 2005, Hurricane Katrina was one of the deadliest and most expensive hurricanes ever to hit the United States, killing over 1,500 people and causing an estimated $80 to $100 billion in damages. The storm's destruction spread along the US central Gulf Coast, from central Florida to Texas. Coastal cities such as New Orleans, Louisiana, Mobile, Alabama and Gulfport, Mississippi were hit badly. Much of the damage was caused by the storm surge and levee breaks between New Orleans and Lake Pontchartrain.

The devastating event has inspired a number of picturebooks. *Two Bobbies: A true story of Hurricane Katrina, friendship, and survival* (Larson, 2008) features a cat and a dog that form a special bond when they are left by their owners after Hurricane Katrina hit New Orleans. *A Storm Called Katrina* (Uhlberg, 2011) is a fictional but realistic account of a 10-year-old boy living in New Orleans during the hurricane and its aftermath.

In *A Place where Hurricanes Happen* (Watson, 2010) four friends describe their lives before, during and after the storm through poetic verse. Adrienne, Keesha, Michael and Tommy have been friends for *forever*. They live on the same street in New Orleans where everybody knows everybody. They play together all day long, every chance they get. It's *always* been that way. But then people start talking about a storm headed straight for New Orleans. The children must part ways, since each family deals with Hurricane Katrina in a different manner. And suddenly everything that felt like home is gone:

> I look out the window
> And I see the whole block swimming in water
> Furniture, clothes and toys are swirling in the flood
> Roofs are crumbling and windows are shattering
> Big winds have come and trees are breaking
> And all I can see is more water rising
> So I look away and I squeeze Jasmine's hand
> Real tight because now I am scared too.

Two picturebooks were initiated by teachers. The pictures and stories by children were collected in an attempt to help them deal with their own experiences of the hurricane. *Story of a Storm: A book about Hurricane Katrina* (Visser, 2006) tells a story through pictures created by 30 young children, who collaborated on collages to create a beautiful account of a terrible day in August 2005. The story is told through creative and collaborative collage art with simple messages that express profound emotions and describe the devastating effects of the storm. It starts with preparation and evacuation, moves through the stresses of being displaced and not knowing the whereabouts of loved ones or the condition of one's home and belongings, and ends with a message of the persistence of hope.

The Storm: Students of Biloxi, Mississippi, remember Hurricane Katrina (McGrath, 2006) is a compilation of stories and artwork by 91 children. The book is divided into four sections that parallel the disaster's timeline and effects: evacuation, storm, aftermath and hope. The children's work ranges from single-sentence descriptions and short paragraphs, to poems, black and white pencil sketches and paintings. The impact of the storm on the families of Biloxi and their struggles to rebuild their lives are vividly portrayed. Ultimately, the book emphasizes the resilience of children and the healing powers of art.

It is important for teachers to critically interrogate these topics, to ask who was worst affected by the disaster and why. According to Hartman and Squires (2006), the impact of Hurricane Katrina was uneven, and race and class were deeply implicated in the unevenness. It was not by accident that the poorest neighbourhoods, with the highest proportions of black residents, were the ones that were buried underwater. Privileged rich people have the means to escape and rebuild their lives in another area. The poor are not so fortunate.

Unequal distribution of resources

Unequal distribution of resources in the world is a challenging concept for children. The story *Angus Rides the Goods Train* (Durant, 2004) describes a small boy's dreamtime journey into a land where he encounters the starving and destitute, the rich and greedy. The story is short and simple, making the theme of social justice and unequal distribution of resources accessible to young children. Unequal distribution of wealth is a fact of life today, affecting people in many ways. This message can be explored in greater depth through *If the World Were a Village* (Smith, 2011). The world population as of 11 October 2012 was 7,044,996,963, or for simplicity's sake just over seven billion people. *If the World Were a Village* encourages the reader, regardless of age, to consider the world's population as if it were a village with a population of 100 people.

If the World Were a Village

Before reading the book with children, the following is a useful exercise. If the world were a village made up of only 100 people, how many of those people do you think:

	Estimate	Actual
Speak English		
Are 9 years of age or younger		
Go to school		
Have electricity		
Have access to a safe source of water		
Are from Europe		

Each double-page spread relays interesting information about topics such as nationalities, food, language and religion. With the aid of a calculator, even younger children can work out the statistics based on today's population of seven billion people.

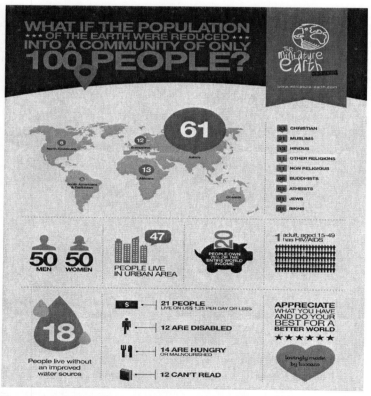

Figure 6.1: This infographic chart, available as a full-sized poster, illustrates the idea of reducing the world's population to a community of only 100 people. It visually communicates some of the statistics from *If the World Were a Village*.

Source: The Miniature Earth Project (2013)

Dealing with statistics

Understanding statistics about the unequal distribution of global resources can be challenging. *This Child, Every Child* (Smith, 2011) compares the lives of children around the world in a way that simplifies statistics. Every second of every day, four more children are added to the world's population of over two billion children. Some of these two billion children will be cared for and will have enough to eat and a place to call home. Many others will not be so fortunate. *This Child, Every Child* uses statistics and stories to draw children into the world beyond their own borders and provides a window into the lives of fellow children. The book is packed with relevant and timely facts and lessons not only about economic concepts but the worldwide population, cultural differences and, more importantly, children's rights in a global society. The author notes early on that:

> Children who live in poverty, generally speaking, have shorter life spans than children elsewhere because they do not have adequate food supplies, medical care or access to schools and clean water. Other more fortunate children don't have to worry about these things.

Other useful information is provided. Family sizes and structures are affected by monetary resources. In some homes, children contribute to the family income; in others, homes are shared with extended family to save money. Fewer educational opportunities for girls means that more women live in poverty. There are 220 million children who work full time, for little or no pay and often in hazardous jobs with a high risk of accidents. Such information places the numbers in context and explains why the current situation is disastrous for some children. These explanations also help illustrate economic concepts such as scarcity and wants versus needs. The book makes the concept of money more tangible to children and shows the far-reaching effects of poverty.

Development issues and global responses

While development education issues are complex, there are a myriad of cross-curricular approaches through which they can be discussed in the classroom. In this section, I examine the issues of gender, climate change, deforestation, slavery, apartheid and the Holocaust, as well as looking at some of the global responses that such issues have generated.

Table 6.1: Development issues and global movements to which they have given rise

Issue	Global movement
Gender	International Feminist Movement
Climate change	Education for Sustainable Development
Deforestation	Green Belt Movement
Slavery	Civil Rights Movement
Apartheid	First free election in South Africa
The Holocaust	Human Rights Movement

Gender and the International Feminist Movement

Teachers should ensure that children have access to picturebooks that show diversity in families and gender roles. More and more children live in mixed families – that is, families in which the children live and grow up with single fathers or mothers, with stepmothers or stepfathers, with lesbian mothers or gay fathers.

Teachers should give children an opportunity to respond to texts and to deconstruct their implicit and explicit gender messages about being a girl or a boy. Picturebooks in which strong, cool, mischievous, brave, daring, fearful, sad, shy, cuddly girls and boys live in relationships with thoughtful, caring, unemployed, achievement-oriented, professionally successful fathers and mothers show the children how diverse and colourful the various lives led by girls, boys, men and women can be. The stereotypical portrayal of gender needs to be challenged. For example, Mary Hoffman and Caroline Binch's heroine in *Amazing Grace* (2007) proves there is no reason why a black girl cannot play Peter Pan in the class play.

While restrictive stereotypical gender images are still commonplace in picturebooks, many do feature characters who display non-stereotypical male or female traits. In *The Best Beekeeper of Lalibela: A tale from Africa* (Kessler, 2006), Almaz overcomes gender discrimination and becomes the best beekeeper in her village, inventing a new hive and a way to keep it safe from ants.

When Grace in *Princess Grace* (Hoffman, 2008) wants to be chosen as one of the princesses for the school's upcoming parade, her grandmother asks her a thought-provoking question: 'What kind of princess would you like to be?'. Grace and her friends are only thinking about the European images of princesses they are accustomed to seeing in the media. Her grandmother introduces the idea of different princesses such as princess Amina of Nigeria, princess Pin-Yang of China and other princesses who are scientists, artists and sports women:

> Even the story princesses the teacher had found were not like the ones Grace thought she knew. There were Cinderellas from Egypt, Cambodia and the Philippines – a Zimbabwean girl called Nyasha who was kind to a snake that turned into a prince.
>
> Grace felt less and less like being the pink and floaty kind of princess. She couldn't imagine making friends with a big snake and wearing a sort of fairy costume at the same time.

The story presents a diverse spectrum of what princesses can and do look like, providing children with images of princesses and beauty beyond the Eurocentric/American view perpetuated through, for instance, Disney merchandise. In this book, children learn about princesses of different cultures, as well as the importance of accepting oneself for who one is and not simply accepting mainstream views. Princesses come in all shapes and sizes and from many different cultures. The end pages contain some information for teachers about contemporary princesses, together with a note about kente cloth 'the cloth of kings' made by the Asante people of Ghana and the Ewe peoples of Ghana and Togo.

Piggybook (1986) by Anthony Browne is about constructions of gender roles within a family. The story begins in traditional fashion with Mummy, Daddy and their two sons typically exemplifying the perfect family. Daddy has a very important job, the boys go to their very important school and Mummy stays at home and does the ironing, washing and cooking. Then she goes to her not-so-important job. But then something happens. One day Mummy isn't there. What follows is a slow metamorphosis of the remaining family into pigs. Daddy and the boys have no time for cleaning the house or washing clothes. As the family changes, the house becomes a pigsty, making *Piggybook* interesting for older readers too.

Fairy tales are a wonderful genre to explore how gender is portrayed historically and in current times. Traditional fairy tales and fractured variations (modern-day fairy tales with a twist) allow primary schoolchildren to think critically about how men and women are portrayed and compare these portrayals to their own families and communities. By comparing the picturebooks listed in Table 6.2, children can examine the socially constructed nature of gender in fairy tales.

Table 6.2: Picturebooks exploring constructions of gender

Traditional fairy tales	Fractured fairy tales
Cinderella (Disney, 2005)	*Prince Cinders* (Cole, 2009)
Snow White and the Seven Dwarfs (Baker, 2009)	*Snow White in New York* (French, 2009)
The Ugly Duckling Mitchell and Anderson (2007), Isadora (2009) and Pinkney (1999)	*The Sissy Duckling* (Fierstein, 2005)
Rapunzel (Gibb, 2011)	*Princess Smartypants* (Cole, 2009)
The Princess and the Pea (Child, 2006)	*The Paper Bag Princess* (Munsch, 2009)

Originally published in 1980, *The Paper Bag Princess* (Munsch, 2009) is a classic fairy tale with a twist: the roles of the damsel in distress and the prince are reversed. The book reverses traditional gender roles and challenges definitions of beauty. Typical fairy tales often portray women as weak characters waiting to be rescued by handsome princes. Here Princess Elizabeth is a strong and wise young woman, conquering a fire-breathing dragon and rescuing a prince. The ending provides a different happily-ever-after scenario, in which Princess Elizabeth is able to take care of herself and does not need to marry Prince Ronald to find her happiness.

Others books that are useful for addressing gender include: *Ballerino Nate* (Bradley, 2006), *The Basket Ball* (Codell, 2011), *10,000 Dresses* (Ewert, 2008), *The Princess Knight* (Meyer, 2004), *Elena's Serenade* (Geeslin, 2011), *My Princess Boy* (Kilodavis, 2011), *Dogs Don't Do Ballet* (Kemp, 2010), *A Princess, A Pirate and One Wild Brother* (Funke, 2008), *Red Rockets and Rainbow Jelly* (Heap and Sharratt, 2007), *The Boy with Pink Hair* (Hilton, 2011) and *The Odd Egg* (Gravett, 2011).

For slightly older children (over 8 years of age), *Amelia to Zora: 26 women who changed the world* (Chin Lee, 2008) celebrates the achievements of 26 brave women from all over the world who refused to take no for an answer. The first name of each begins with a letter from A for Amelia, pilot Amelia Earhart, to Z for Zora, writer Zora Neale Hurston. Each woman has made a difference in one of a great variety of fields – the arts, sports, journalism, science and entertainment. At the end of the book, the author explains why she has chosen to use the given (rather than family) names for each woman:

Family names are usually based on a father's or husband's name. Using a woman's name seemed more personal to me ... I followed this strategy with Asian names, in which the given name comes after the family name. For Daw Aung San Suu Kyi, 'S is for Suu Kyi.' In Burmese, Daw is an honorary title, meaning aunt, Aung San is the family name and Suu Kyi is the given name.

Since 2002, as part of the International Feminist Movement, the Amelia Bloomer Project has published a bibliography of feminist books for young readers. The list recognizes the positive portrayal of female roles in children's literature. Books that have won this award confront traditional female roles, showing girls and women exploring exciting ways to solve practical dilemmas through the courage of their convictions. Set anywhere from prehistoric times to the present, and covering both fiction and non-fiction, they feature role models of strong, capable, creative women. They introduce children growing up in the southern states of America during the Civil Rights Movement, photographers on the cutting edge of their time, young women surviving in today's Afghanistan and pioneers in the fields of flying and space exploration. Books included in the recommended titles for this award are *Seeds of Change* (Cullerton Johnson, 2010) and *Mama Miti* (Napoli, 2010), both based on the life story of Wangari Maathai, who is discussed in the section on deforestation (see page 111).

Gender continues to be an important development issue. Internationally, sex trafficking of girls and young women has multiplied. Increasing poverty on a global scale has disproportionately affected women and the children for whom they care. In general, sexism results in preference for male babies and higher rates of female infanticide. On a global level, girls and women disproportionately face a lack of educational and economic opportunities and health care, and higher levels of malnutrition.

Climate change and Education for Sustainable Development (ESD)

Climate change and global warming are pressing challenges of our time. The United Nations declared the years 2005–14 as the Decade of Education for Sustainable Development. Education for sustainable development emphasizes a holistic, interdisciplinary approach to developing the knowledge and skills needed for a sustainable future, and argues for changes in the values, behaviour and lifestyles affecting the planet. Due to global warming, the sea ice on which polar bears live melts earlier every year, leaving them with a smaller area in which to find food. Their plight is a direct result of climate change. Although well adapted to water and able to swim several miles to land, their commuting distances are increasing as the Arctic ice diminishes.

Though pollution and hunting are other threats to polar bears, climate change is their biggest risk. Several picturebooks address the plight of the polar bear – otherwise known as the Ice King, Sea Bear, Great White Bear or 'Nanuq' – and its interdependent relationship with humans.

In Olive O'Brien's picturebook *Perry the Polar Bear Goes Green* (2010), Perry discovers that he has to leave home because the ice is melting. Courageously, he goes on a mission to save the polar bears and their home. Along the way he meets a killer whale, a family of seals and the King of the Polar Bears. The animals all gather for a special meeting to discuss climate change and ideas for preventing the ice from melting further. Perry asks 'but how does global warming affect us?' and is told:

> Well with all the extra heat, winters are becoming shorter here. There is less ice. More and more polar bears have to swim for longer to go from one patch of ice to another. This makes them very tired and weak. Less ice means that it is also harder for polar bears to hunt for food.

Perry meets a little boy called Tommy and explains his predicament. This is the first time Tommy has ever heard of global warming and he promises to return with a television crew to transmit the important message to reduce carbon emissions. This eco-friendly book teaches children about climate change and reminds us that everyone can make a difference. Another book in this series is *Perry the Playful Polar Bear* (2009).

Kyoto: A big story about a boy and a little bear, and a little story about global warming (Melrose, 2010) also addresses global warming. The first scenes feature a bear and a boy playing together until their iceberg breaks away and floats into the sea. They begin a long journey that takes them to another land. The illustrations and text show us a land that is dirty and strange, full of factory machines, coal trucks and dumping diggers. Once they locate a wooden pallet, they begin their journey home. The contrast between the illustrations of their homeland and new land is stark and the implicit message about climate change is clearly communicated. The name of the book, *Kyoto*, plays on the name of the Kyoto Protocol to the United Nations' *Convention on Climate Change* (1997).

Winner of the 2008 Green Earth Award, Okimoto's *Winston of Churchill: One bear's battle against global warming* (2007) brings a Canadian perspective to the issue of climate change. As the British Prime Minister Winston Churchill rallied his countrymen against the Nazis, this is a call to battle against global warming. Because the earth is getting warmer, the ice in Hudson Bay breaks up earlier and the polar bears don't have as much time to hunt for their food. They have become thinner and female bears are having fewer cubs. Winston, a 'fierce and brave bear', writes a book to explain global warming and distributes it to all his fellow polar bears. He galvanizes them to protest about the human beings' polluting behaviour.

Such stories convey hope. The relationships between Perry the Polar Bear and Tommy, and a boy and a little bear, are characterized by mutual respect, love and admiration and underline how we depend on each other. The books illustrate the interdependent relationship between earth and all its inhabitants. While the topic of climate change is complex and challenging to teach, a good place to start is with an engaging story about a polar bear.

Trishna and the Dream of Water (Douglis, 2006) is a children's environmental storybook dealing with water in dry land areas. Written by Carole Douglis, it is part of the United Nations Environment Programme's (UNEP) Tunza Environmental Series for Children. *Tunza* means 'to treat with care or affection' in Kiswahili. 'I wish our village stayed green so we could have more of a harvest,' says Trishna, as she goes to collect water. Passing an abandoned borehole pump and a diminished stream, Trishna guides the reader through lessons about deserts and desertification. This picturebook is designed to create awareness of environmental problems and provides information about how to stop such problems as desertification. Other books in the series include: *Tore and the Town on Thin Ice* (Douglis, 2006), *Tessa and the Fishy Mystery* (Douglis, 2004), *Theo and the Giant Plastic Ball* (Douglis, 2005) and *Tina and the Green City* (Douglis, 2005).

Deforestation and the Green Belt Movement

Several picturebooks highlight the importance of trees in a global context. Beautiful illustrations represent the aesthetic value of trees and underline the delicate relationship between humans and nature. The story of Wangari Maathai demonstrates the interrelations between gender, development and the environment. The first African woman to win the Nobel Peace Prize, Maathai's personal story of working in veterinary medicine, then founding the Green Belt Movement, then inhibiting deforestation in Kenya, is inspirational. Four excellent picturebooks have been written based on her life: *Mama Miti: Wangari Maathai and the Trees of Kenya* (Napoli, 2010), *Wangari's Trees of Peace: A true story from Africa* (Winter, 2008), *Planting the Trees of Kenya: The story of Wangari Maathai* (Nivola, 2008) and *Seeds of Change* (Cullerton Johnson, 2010).

A brief synopsis of Maathai's story is set out on the dust jacket of Nivola's book:

> Wangari Maathai, winner of the 2004 Nobel Peace Prize and
> founder of the Green Belt Movement, grew up in the highlands of
> Kenya, where fig trees cloaked the hills, fish filled the streams, and
> the people tended their bountiful gardens. But over many years, as
> more and more land was cleared, Kenya was transformed. When
> Wangari returned home from college in America, she found the
> village gardens dry, the people malnourished, and the trees gone.
> How could she alone bring back the trees and restore the gardens
> and the people?

When Maathai returned from her studies in America, she discovered the
landscape of Kenya had changed dramatically. Fields were heavily cultivated,
and with no trees as protection against sun and rain, the soil was washed
away. Maathai planted seven trees in her backyard, and in 1976 began
to show people how to plant trees in what would become the Green Belt
Movement.

Maathai began to urge Kenyan farmers, 70 per cent of whom were
women, to plant trees as a protective belt around fields. She toured schools to
urge students to ask their parents to plant native species of trees – baobabs,
acacias, paw paws, crotons, cedars, citrus trees and figs. In recruiting women
and children, Maathai's Green Belt Movement has grown into a major force in
Kenya. Today it has over fifteen hundred tree nurseries that produce 30 million
trees. In 1986, Kenyan Green Belt members began to teach their methods to
people from different African countries, an initiative that became known as
the Pan African Green Belt Movement. There are active groups in Tanzania,
Uganda, Malawi, Lesotho, Ethiopia and Zimbabwe. In 2002, Maathai was
elected to parliament, where she worked tirelessly to raise awareness of
environmental issues and to have the terrible burden of international debts
lifted from impoverished African countries. In 2004, she was awarded the
Nobel Peace Prize for her work with the Green Belt Movement.

Planting the Trees of Kenya (Nivola, 2008) tells the story in both its
scope and detail. Nivola's panoramic landscapes show Kenyan farmland,
dotted with women in colourful outfits, with men, women and children
nurturing seedlings. The author explains: 'They did not need schooling to
plant trees. They did not have to wait for the government to help them. They
could begin to change their own lives.' With its blocky illustrations and bright
colours, Jeanette Winter's book *Wangari's Trees of Peace* (2008) is suitable
for younger children. As a child, Maathai harvests sweet potatoes with her
mother, and after college she gets her knees dirty with the first seedlings

of her own. She's a role model who makes gardening look like serious, if backbreaking, fun, a heroine children can relate to.

Jeanette Winter does not hide from some of the sociopolitical elements of Maathai's story. Men laugh at the women planting trees: 'Women can't do this,' they say. 'It takes trained foresters to plant trees.' Later, a policeman beats Maathai with a billy club at a demonstration against tree cutting, with bloody results. Such episodes, absent from *Planting the Trees of Kenya*, suggest that activism, like planting, is difficult and challenging. We see Maathai in jail: 'And still she stands tall. *Right is right, even if you're alone.*' She is not alone, as the sequence of women planting trees on the next page suggests. Based on a true story, the book presents a message of hope and demonstrates the power of one. Through one plant, one woman inspires a lifelong, worldwide change. 'We are planting the seeds of hope,' Maathai tells the village women. 'The trick is to turn those seeds into a revitalized earth.'

Cullerton Johnson's book *Seeds of Change: Planting a path to peace* (2010) also presents some of the political aspects of the story, first highlighting the lack of access to education for girls. This award-winning book brings to light lessons about the importance of educating girls and protecting the environment, offering information about Maathai's life for older children. Johnson includes an account of her training for a doctorate in biology and the political obstacles she faces. An image of the Kikuyu people's sacred mugumo tree, the source of Maathai's tree planting project, runs throughout the book.

Mama Miti (the mother of trees) (Napoli, 2010) tells Maathai's story with the aid of Kadir Nelson's stunning collage illustrations. Under the stewardship of her tribal elders, the young Mama Miti learned the significance of caring for the natural environment and for trees especially. As trees were removed, the foundation of a community was destroyed. Maathai carried this message into adulthood. She grew up in the shadow of Mount Kenya, listening to stories about the people and land around her. As she became involved with local community groups, she encouraged women to plant trees with her. Soon the countryside was filled with trees. Kenya was strong once more. Maathai had changed her country 'tree by tree'.

Slavery and the Civil Rights Movement

Among the universal stories of the world are accounts of oppression, racism, protest and successful resolution. Specific examples include the struggle of black slaves in America. Black History Month, celebrated in February in the US and November in the UK, observes the history of the African diaspora. A number of picture story books deal with the struggle of black people in America – for example, *The Listeners* (Whelan, 2009) and *Henry's Freedom*

Box (Levine, 2007) – while the themes of segregation, struggle and hope are continued through stories about the Civil Rights Movement. These liberation movement stories include *Coretta Scott* (Shange, 2009), *Martin's Big Words* (Rappaport, 2007), *Rosa* (Giovanni, 2005) and *Moses: When Harriet Tubman led her people to freedom* (Weatherford, 2006).

Gloria Whelan's *The Listeners* (2009) provides a wonderful introduction to the topic of slavery in a manner that is authentic yet appropriate for young children. Young Ella May and her friends, Bobby and Sue, pick cotton all day. Their most important work, however, begins at night, when they hide under their master's window, listen for news and information and run back to the slaves' quarters to report it. In this way, the adults know what to expect and how to deal with it. The book has no scenes of horror, although clearly the slaves are not free. There are even happy moments at the slave cabins – the joy of family, food and community, dancing to music heard from the master's house and the news that Abraham Lincoln, who abolished slavery in the US, has been elected president.

From the early 1600s, before the establishment of the United States of America and until the abolition of slavery in 1865, people could lawfully own, buy and sell a fellow human being. For today's teachers and children this is a difficult scenario to imagine. Throughout the course of slavery, there were always people who ran towards freedom. Early in the 1800s, a group of courageous men and women formed a network which became known as the Underground Railroad. Workers of the Underground Railroad came from all walks of life. Most were ordinary people, shopkeepers and farmers, who quietly did what they thought was right. Informally organized, the Underground Railroad grew out of people's concern for each other, and was made up of black people and white, many of them Quakers, working closely together. Runaway slaves could carry little food and had to make their journey weakened by hunger.

By 1830 the Underground Railroad was well established, yet no one knew the entire system because it had to operate in secret. Records were never kept because of the dangers involved. The Railroad was most active in the 60 years before the Civil War, when there were over 3,200 workers on the Railroad. An estimated 500 escaped slaves returned south each year to conduct other black people to freedom. No one is certain of the origin of the Railroad, but it extended to every home that welcomed runaways and every individual who offered food, clothing or other assistance. Such pilots gave directions and spread details about the Railroad. Conductors undertook the most dangerous work, leading slaves, whom the law designated as property, north, often to Canada. Conductors led passengers on foot or hid runaways in wagonloads of straw or vegetables. Homes, churches and schoolhouses served as hiding places, otherwise known as stations, depots or safe houses, operated by station masters. Escaped slaves were hidden underground in cellars or tunnels, as well as in attics, fake presses or secret rooms. In addition to shelter, the Railroad's cargo was given food and clothing, and if needed, care for broken bones, cuts and sometimes bullet wounds.

The Underground Railroad has inspired several picturebooks for children. One of the most famous women associated with it was Harriet Tubman. *Minty: A story of young Harriet Tubman* (Schroeder, 2008) presents a fictionalized account of her childhood on a Maryland plantation and the cruelty shown to slaves. Carole Weatherford's *Moses* (2006) is about the older Harriet Tubman and begins with Tubman addressing God on a summer night as she is about to be sold south from the Maryland plantation where she and her husband live. She says 'I am your child, Lord; yet Master owns me, drives me like a mule'. In bold text, God tells her he means her to be free. The story continues as a dialogue between Harriet and God, showing her escape from slavery and her role in the Underground Railroad helping hundreds of other slaves to escape.

In *Underground: Finding the light to freedom* (2011), Evans explores the emotional *and* physical journey of fugitive slaves running to freedom in pre-emancipation America. The author pairs 19 short, direct sentences with bold pictures in contrasting colours, dark blue with white and yellow, orange with brown and green. Minimalist phrases like 'the darkness', 'the fear' and 'some don't make it' portray the trials of escaped slaves in addition to their gratitude for the help of others.

Henry's Freedom Box (Levine, 2007) is based on the true story of Henry 'Box' Brown. Taken from his mother as a young boy, Henry goes to work in a tobacco factory. He marries another slave and has children, but all the members of his family are sold. Left with nothing to lose, Henry asks a white abolitionist to nail him in a box and ship him to Philadelphia to freedom. The illustrations are wonderful and the book gives the dimensions of the box so children and teachers can make and crouch inside a similar box to experience the confinement Henry would have felt. In *Almost to Freedom* (Nelson, 2003), the story of escape from slavery is told from the viewpoint of Sally, a rag doll made by Lindy's mother, Miz Rachel. When life on the plantation becomes intolerable and Lindy's father is sold, Lindy and her mother take flight in the middle of the night. They find a safe house on the Underground Railroad and are reunited with Lindy's father, but as they flee during the night, Sally is accidently left behind. In an author's note, Nelson tells how she was inspired to write this story by a folk art museum's exhibit of black rag dolls, a few of which were discovered in Underground Railroad hideouts.

Cole's (2012) *Unspoken: A story from the Underground Railroad* begins with an illustration of a star-patterned quilt hanging over a fence, signifying a safe house. This wordless picturebook is about a white girl who discovers a black slave hiding in the barn. The author shows the fear and questioning of the girl, who ultimately chooses to remain silent. She helps the runaway slave and receives a beautiful thank you gift, a corn husk doll.

The wordlessness of the book affords opportunities to discuss concepts relative to slavery as well as bravery, privilege, race, culture and identity. While the grand narrative of slavery highlights the cruelty of white people and the submissiveness of black people, *Unspoken* reminds us that the brave people who risked their lives to do the right thing were both black and white.

COMMUNICATION THROUGH QUILTS

In their fight for (and flight to) freedom, African American slaves used an ingenious communication method called *the quilt system*. During the process of designing an escape plan, a quilt would be stitched with a quilt code and hung on the clothes line each day to communicate crucial secret messages during the escape. One pattern, called the Monkey Wrench, meant *gather your stuff for the journey*, another, Tumbling Blocks, was code for *time to go!* There were even quilts with directions to safe destinations. Crossroads, for example, showed the way to Cleveland. Triangles in quilt design signified a way of offering prayer, while individual colours held a similar significance. The colour black, for instance, indicated that someone might die, while blue was believed to protect the maker. To the slaves, these quilts were a lifeline to a better life. To the plantation owners, they were just pretty blankets, a common sight on plantations. Slaves could not read or write as it was illegal to teach a slave to do so. Codes, therefore, were part of their route to freedom.

There is still controversy among historians and scholars over the quilt code theory, and whether or not escaping slaves actually used codes concealed within quilt patterns to follow the escape routes of the Underground Railroad. However, stories about quilts have inspired many picturebooks. *Sweet Clara and the Freedom Quilt* (Hopkinson, 1993) features a quilt of a map of the local area. *Under the Quilt of Night* (Hopkinson, 2005) is narrated by a young girl in a family of five as her family flees slavery. As they run, the young daughter watches for a safe house on the Underground Railroad and is finally rewarded by the sight of a log cabin quilt with a blue centrepiece hanging by a simple farmhouse. She musters all her courage to knock on the door and say the password, 'a friend of a friend'. In *Most Loved in all the World* (2009), Hegamin tackles difficult concepts of slavery, courage and sacrifice in a poignant book about a mother who sends her daughter on the Underground Railroad, armed with a quilt she has made for her. The mother, identifying herself as an agent, stays behind to help other slaves escape. The quilt's centrepiece depicts a smiling girl, as her mother wants her daughter to always remember that she is 'the most loved in all the world'. The illustrations mirror the beauty of quilting through unique textile collaging and expressive acrylic paintings.

Quilt making has also been associated with storytelling, identity and the process of recording history. In *Stitchin' and Pullin': A Gee's Bend quilt* (McKissack, 2008) a young girl in Gee's Bend, Alabama, makes her first quilt. As the young girl says when she completes her quilt, 'quilts are about me, where I live, and the people who have been here for generations'. The book also includes numerous references to African American history.

I Lay my Stitches Down: Poems of American slavery (Grady, 2011) contains illustrated poems that chronicle the story of American slaves. Using imagery from quilting and fibre arts, each poem is narrated from a different perspective: a house slave, a mother losing her daughter to the auction block, a blacksmith and a slave fleeing on the Underground Railroad. Through poetry, the author tells stories of slaves learning to write in the dirt, toiling in kitchens, escaping at night and working in the blacksmith shop. The titles originate from quilt designs and each one is made up of ten lines of ten syllables to represent quilt squares.

THE CIVIL RIGHTS MOVEMENT

Until recently, most picturebooks about the Civil Rights Movement focused on leaders such as Martin Luther King Jr. Now, authors and illustrators are using multiple lenses, choosing to illuminate the inner workings of a populist revolution in which many people, with differing beliefs, made difficult choices. Such books about the Civil Rights era contain universal themes: How do we recognize and address our own prejudices? How do we make social change happen? How do we find the strength to overcome adversity? How can one person change the world?

Courageously defying the 'whites only' edict of the era, four young black men took a stand against the injustice of segregation in America by sitting down at the lunch counter of a Woolworth's department store. Countless others of all races soon joined in, following Martin Luther King Jr's powerful words of peaceful protest. By sitting down together, they stood up for civil rights and created the perfect recipe for integration not only at the Woolworth's counter but also on buses and in communities throughout the South. The story is carefully documented in Pinkney's (2010) *Sit-In: How four friends stood up by sitting down*. Eight-year-old Connie presents the story from her perspective in *Freedom on the Menu: The Greensboro sit-ins* (Weatherford, 2007). The experiences of other ordinary people during the Civil Rights Movement are addressed in: *This is the Dream* (Alexander, 2009), *Child of the Civil Rights Movement* (Young Shelton, 2009), *We Troubled the Waters* (Shange, 2009), *Finding Lincoln* (Malaspina, 2009), *A Sweet Smell of Roses* (Johnson, 2008), *We March* (Evans, 2012) and *Ruth and the Green Book* (Ramsey, 2010). As president, Abraham Lincoln guided the nation through a long and bitter civil war and penned the document that would lead to the end of slavery in the United States. *Abe's Honest Words: The life of Abraham Lincoln* (Rappaport, 2008) is a biographical picturebook featuring lines from his most famous speeches.

Climbing Lincoln's Steps: The African American journey (Slade, 2010) outlines the history of the Civil Rights struggle and its leaders. The story begins with Lincoln's signing of the Emancipation Proclamation in 1863. Completed in 1922, the enormous marble sculpture of Abraham Lincoln has been the site of key moments in African American history. Denied a place in Constitution Hall because she was black, Marian Anderson sang instead at the Lincoln Memorial in 1939. On Lincoln's steps in 1963, Dr Martin Luther King Jr delivered his powerful 'I have a dream' speech. In 2009, the first African American president and his family made a pilgrimage to the spot. Further information on picturebooks detailing leaders of the Civil Rights Movement – including Dr Martin Luther King Jr and Rosa Parks – are provided in Chapter 7.

Apartheid and the first free election in South Africa

Every now and then we are afforded opportunities to celebrate figures of great importance in our societies. Nelson Mandela was a true hero of our times. In 2009, the twentieth anniversary of Mandela's release from prison, Macmillan published the official picturebook edition of his bestselling autobiography. *Nelson Mandela: Long walk to freedom* (van Wyk, 2009) tells the story of a long-term activist who herded sheep when he was young and fought for democracy in South Africa. Mandela was born in the village of Mvezo in 1918, went to school there, began a career as a lawyer and was a member of the African National Congress. The book covers his 27 years in prison, his release and finally his election as South Africa's first black president.

Mandela's constant quest for equality was evident at the launch of the book in September 2009, when his grandson conveyed this message to the audience on his behalf:

Our children are our greatest treasure. They are our future. The system of apartheid robbed many children of their right to a decent education and of the joy of reading. This joy is one that I have treasured all my life, and it is one I wish for all South Africans. We are happy that all children are now able to read in the language of their choice, the story of the long road we travelled for freedom in South Africa. The children of South Africa need to know this history.

(South African Government News Agency, 2009)

As well as the English edition, Macmillan has published the book in all 11 official South African languages to ensure Mandela's request is reached.

Kadir Nelson's *Nelson Mandela* (2013) tells the story of this global icon. It is the story of a young boy's determination to change South Africa and details the struggles of a man who eventually becomes the president of his country by believing in equality for all colours. Every illustration is a beautiful tribute to Mandela. The two final pages provide biographical information that enriches the story.

Nelson Mandela has had a profound influence on the population of South Africa. *The Day Gogo Went to Vote* (Sisulu, 2009) is a book about the first time black South Africans were allowed to vote. It is written from the perspective of a young girl named Thembi, who describes her great-grandmother's first voting experience. Thembi's great-grandmother, or Gogo as she calls her, is 100 years old and has not left her house in years. Once it is announced that black South Africans can vote, Gogo is determined to, despite her family's anxiety. She takes her young great-granddaughter with her to show her how important this moment is for all South Africans. Gogo catches the attention of others so fervently that people come out to see her vote. She even features on the front page of the local newspaper.

On the occasion of Mandela's death on 5 December 2013, there was an intense reaction from around the world. Nelson Mandela led a Rainbow Nation out of strife and into democratic freedom with moral authority. He forgave his persecutors and brought inspiration and hope to all ethnic groups in South Africa. Recognized as a global icon and an international advocate for human rights, tributes were recorded all over the world. Archbishop Desmond Tutu said, 'the sun will rise tomorrow, and the next day and the next. It may not appear as bright as yesterday, but life will carry on'. In his speech, US President Barack Obama said:

We've lost one of the most influential, courageous and profoundly good human beings that any of us will share time with on this earth. Through his fierce dignity and unbending will to sacrifice his own freedom for the freedom of others, Madiba transformed South Africa and moved all of us. His journey from a prisoner to a president embodied the promise that human beings and countries can change for the better.

(BBC News, 2013)

World leaders, including presidents, former presidents, prime ministers and monarchs, went to South Africa to pay homage to this outstanding and transformative leader. They paid tribute to South Africa's first black president and anti-apartheid icon at his state memorial service in Johannesburg. His life will continue to inspire children all over the world through the legacy of his story, recorded in a number of inspirational picturebooks.

The Holocaust and the Human Rights Movement

A watershed event in world history, the Holocaust is the name given to one specific case of genocide, the attempt by the Nazis and their collaborators to wipe out the Jewish people. It resulted in the mass murder of six million Jews. Over a million Gypsies and Roma were also murdered, along with innumerable communists, gay people, Jehovah's Witnesses and people deemed to be mentally or physically deficient. There have been other examples of genocide since the Holocaust, such as the 1994 Rwandan genocide and the genocide of 1993–95 in the former Yugoslavia (Supple, 2007). The United States Holocaust Memorial Museum's website (2013) sets out the learning opportunities:

- the Holocaust provides a context for exploring the dangers of remaining silent, apathetic and indifferent in the face of the oppression of others. Silence and indifference to the suffering of others, or to the infringement of civil rights in any society can, however unintentionally, perpetuate the problems
- the Holocaust was not an accident in history, it occurred because individuals, organizations, and governments made choices that not only legalized discrimination but also allowed prejudice, hatred, and ultimately mass murder to occur
- study of the Holocaust assists students in developing an understanding of the roots and ramifications of prejudice, racism, and stereotyping in any society
- a study of these topics helps students to think about the use and abuse of power, and the roles and responsibilities of individuals, organizations and nations when confronted with civil rights violations and/or policies of genocide.

Picturebooks about the Holocaust raise difficult questions that teachers need to anticipate: why were the Jews and others treated in this way? Why were they removed from their jobs in hospitals, schools and universities? Using the viewpoint of a fictional cat, *Benno and the Night of Broken Glass* (Wiviott, 2010) shows what happened to families in one Berlin community. Benno feels welcome in many homes and stores, and every day he likes to follow a Jewish girl, Sophie, and her Christian friend to school. Then everything changes, and the neighbourhood is no longer friendly. Benno cowers as terrifying men in brown shirts light bonfires. Then there is *Krystalnacht*, a night 'like no other', during which Benno hears screams and shattering glass and watches apartments being ravaged and the Synagogue burn. The next day, life continues for some, but Benno never sees Sophie and her family again.

Keeping the Promise: A Torah's journey (Lehman-Wilzig, 2003) is an inspirational true story about a Dutch rabbi named Simon Dasberg who carried a tiny Torah scroll – the books of the Old Testament – to the concentration camp of Bergen-Belsen. There, he carried out a Bar Mitzvah for a 13-year-old, giving him the little Torah and commanding him to keep it and always tell the story. It was this very scroll that was taken into space by Israeli astronaut Ilan Ramon aboard the ill-fated *Columbia*. In 2003, the spacecraft exploded upon re-entering the earth's surface. All crew members died and the Torah scroll was never recovered. Ramon's inspiring words were: 'this little *Sefer* (book) Torah in particular shows the ability of the Jewish people to survive everything, even the darkest of times, and to always look forward with hope and faith for the future'.

Other picturebooks that deal with the suffering and endurance of the Jewish people are: *Star of Fear, Star of Hope* (Hoestlandt, 2000), *The Cats in Krasinski Square* (Hesse, 2008), *Rebekkah's Journey: A World War II refugee story* (Burg, 2006), *The Harmonica* (Johnston, 2008), *The Butterfly* (Polacco, 2009), *The Yellow Star: The legend of King Christian X of Denmark* (Deedy, 2002), *Willy and Max: A Holocaust story* (Littlesugar, 2006), *Luba: The angel of Bergen-Belsen* (McCann, 2003) and *Rose Blanche* (Gallaz, 2011).

During the atrocities, several individuals risked their own lives to save Jewish people. *The Grand Mosque of Paris: A story of how Muslims rescued Jews during the Holocaust* (Ruelle, 2009) and *Passage to Freedom: The Sugihara story* (Mochizuki, 1997) highlight bravery, moral courage and a sense of working for justice. One person who dedicated his life to Jewish children was Janusz Korczak. A Polish Jewish children's writer and educator, he developed the concept of progressive orphanages, founded the first national children's newspaper, trained teachers in what we now call moral education, and worked in juvenile courts defending children's rights.

The ideas he implemented in his orphanage were ahead of his time: care and love were emphasized, older children acted as mentors to younger children and a democratic system of governance was put into place.

Historical events put an end to Korczak's well-run orphanage. When the Nazis conquered Poland in 1939, life became bleak for the Jews, and when they were ordered to move into the Warsaw Ghetto, Korczak and his orphans were compelled to move there. The book portrays the resilience displayed by Korczak in those dark days. He continued to provide unwavering love and care for his beloved orphans and tried his best to see to their needs, though people were starving in the ghetto. Finally, in 1942, the order for deportation came. Korczak's orphans were asked to report for deportation to Treblinka, a notorious extermination centre. Though he could have saved himself with the help of willing friends beyond the ghetto walls, Korczak refused and went with his orphans to their death. Korczak is an inspiration to child advocates everywhere. He continues to be a beacon of hope and inspiration to those who believe in the rights of a child to a decent quality of life.

Two picturebooks deal with Korczak's inspirational life: *Janusz Korczak's Children* (Spielman, 2007) and *The Champion of Children: The story of Janusz Korczak* (Bogacki, 2009). The Janusz Korczak's International Literary Prize was established in 1979 to honour the memory of an outstanding humanist, paediatrician and writer. The prize was given every two years (until 2000) to living writers for outstanding books, both for children and about children, that promote understanding and friendship among children all over the world. Korczak's stated and lived-by beliefs – that children should be loved, educated and protected – continue to inspire many in the present day, including those who facilitated the United Nations International Year of the Child (1979) and the *Convention on the Rights of the Child* (1989).

Ideas about human rights have evolved over many centuries, achieving strong international support following the Holocaust and the Second World War. To protect future generations from such horrors happening again, the United Nations adopted *The Universal Declaration of Human Rights* (UDHR) in 1948 and invited states to sign and ratify it. For the first time, *The Universal Declaration* set out the fundamental rights and freedoms shared by all human beings. In 1947, the UN established the Human Rights Commission to draft the UDHR, with representatives from a range of countries involved in the process. On 10 December 1948, the Declaration was adopted by the UN. The preamble to the UDHR sets out the aims of the Declaration, namely to contribute to 'freedom, justice and peace in the world', and states that such aims will be achieved by universal recognition and respect for human rights.

Such rights are then defined in 30 Articles, which address civil, political, economic, social and cultural rights.

The main innovation of the UDHR is its recognition that a universal entitlement to rights applies to 'all members of the human family'. Before this the rights and freedoms of individuals were regarded as the domestic affair of the state within whose jurisdiction they fell. The traumatic events of the Second World War prompted the strong belief that this situation was no longer tenable, that universal protection was needed for all people and that the international community should monitor what happens inside states.

In 1989, world leaders decided that children needed a special set of rights. The *Convention on the Rights of the Child* was written by the United Nations and has since been ratified by 193 countries around the world. Comprising 54 Articles, the *Convention* is a legally binding international agreement, incorporating all the minimum human rights all children are entitled to, and that all governments should respect. *I Have the Right to Be a Child* (Serres, 2012) translates some of the Articles of the *Convention* into accessible language accompanied by beautiful illustrations. The book *For Every Child: The UN Convention on the Rights of the Child in words and pictures* (Castle, 2001) features 14 Articles that are most relevant to children's everyday lives. Such books are excellent resources for teachers who would like to introduce children to the topic of human rights.

Children can be asked to discuss the following picturebooks and identify which Article applies to the scenario presented in each book: *As Good as Anybody* (Michelson, 2008), *Waiting for the Biblioburro* (Brown, 2011), *Let There Be Peace on Earth: And let it begin with me* (Jackson, 2009), *The Long March: The Choctaw's gift to Irish Famine Relief* (Fitzpatrick, 2001), *We Planted a Tree* (Muldrow, 2011), *Brothers in Hope: The story of the lost boys of Sudan* (Williams, 2005), *Beatrice's Goat* (McBrier, 2001), *Listen to the Wind: The story of Dr. Greg and three cups of tea* (Mortenson, 2009) and *If the World Were a Village* (Smith, 2010). Alternatively, children can be invited to make a picturebook bibliography that best represents each of the 30 Articles of the UDHR, or to illustrate their ideas about Articles in the UN *Convention on the Rights of the Child*.

Conclusion

In this chapter, I have presented the second part of the curriculum framework – *understanding* – by looking at issues and social movements. This part of the framework is about learning to appreciate and understand certain complex development education issues and the intercultural context in which they are located. The framework is presented through a range of picturebooks that mediate these complex issues for children and tell important stories all people should hear. Due to curriculum overload, classroom pressure and unaware teachers, however, many children are never given the chance to read and interact with such stories. In today's world, genocide still occurs, poverty continues to destroy the lives of millions and racism remains a destructive force. I believe that the important picturebooks in this chapter need to be introduced to children and young people as a matter of urgency. While the issues are central to development and intercultural education, they are sometimes perceived as too complex for children. Through text and illustrations, however, picturebooks have the ability to communicate difficult and complicated issues in a coherent way that connects children to the issues cognitively, conceptually and emotionally.

Chapter 7

Raising awareness and taking action

Introduction

Taking action to make the world a better place is at the heart of development education. After raising awareness and developing understanding comes the final part of the curriculum framework: *action*. Picturebooks are chosen that build upon work covered through the earlier parts of the curriculum framework, *respect* and *understanding*. This is the opportunity for children to learn about a person, issue or topic and those who have taken various actions. Children can design their own actions according to their age, talents and interests and the resources available to their class, but they need to be kept within appropriate limits.

Children engage in a range of actions in the classroom every day. They speak, debate, write and illustrate their ideas and develop the imagination, self-belief and confidence that enable taking action. *The Dot* (Reynolds, 2005) is a striking picturebook about children expressing themselves in painting and drawing. 'Just make a mark and see where it takes you,' advises the teacher. The book conveys a gentle but powerful message about how children can find greatness and freedom of expression within themselves.

Action and development education

Citizenship education and development education have 'transformative potential' (Osler, 1994: 3) for young people to move from awareness, through deeper understandings to informed involvement, as they are taken through the steps of informing, understanding, reflecting and acting (Irish Aid, 2006).

Many schools engage in fundraising and charitable projects, but often without engaging in enquiry about the social and global context of the problem or considering possible strategies for action. If children engage in charitable actions, it should be in the full knowledge that charity represents a short-term action, where justice approaches are more long term, political and in some cases controversial. Picturebooks can raise awareness about the need for action, demonstrate the possible options for action and motivate children to determine their own actions. Children can also determine whether actions in picturebooks are charity-based or justice-based.

Short (2011) presents a number of guidelines (discussed below) for adopting authentic action in the classroom.

Authentic action develops through enquiry and experience

Any action the children take should be grounded in their lived experiences and informed by investigation. A study of any social issue can begin with picturebooks that allow children to explore an issue from a distance. For instance, an investigation into hunger should begin by differentiating needs and wants. *Lola: I really, really need actual ice skates* (Child, 2010) and *Those Shoes* (Boelts, 2009) help children understand that financial restrictions affect people in different ways. More global examples of financial constraints are *Four Feet, Two Sandals* (Williams, 2007), *The Hard-Times Jar* (Smothers, 2003) and *Mia's Story: A sketchbook of hopes and dreams* (Foreman, 2007). These stories show poverty and hardship but they also offer hope and highlight children's agency. In *Mia's Story*, Mia is portrayed as an intelligent, imaginative, caring, courageous girl who demonstrates strength, resourcefulness and resilience in the face of adversity and brings hope to her family.

Authentic action meets genuine needs

Any need and action has to be identified by children themselves through enquiry-based learning. Children who would like to take action on behalf of children in Haiti can learn about life in Haiti through books such as *Circles of Hope* (Williams, 2011) and *Selavi: A Haitian story of hope* (Landowne, 2005).

Authentic action builds collaborative relationships

Action is more effective when children work collaboratively. Cooperation is illustrated in picturebooks such as *Stone Soup* (Muth, 2003). Muth blends a traditional European folktale with elements of Chinese folklore and the Buddhist story tradition, in an inventive retelling of the Stone Soup story. The three monks, Hok, Lok and Siew – deities from Chinese folklore – wander into a village where hard times have closed the doors of trust, even between neighbours. Only one brave little girl is willing to approach them. The monks describe their plan to make stone soup, and the child is happy to help. Curiosity draws villagers out of their homes, and soon one person after another is bringing something to add to the pot – carrots and spices, pea pods and ginger root, beans and taro root. The monks are not only helping the villagers make soup, they are helping them open their hearts to one another and build a sense of community. In an author's note, Muth notes that tricksters, in the

Buddhist tradition, seek to spread enlightenment rather than gain anything for themselves. He invites children to find the symbols from Asian culture that he has incorporated into the illustrations of this inspiring tale.

Many books feature members of a family working collaboratively towards a common goal. *A Castle on Viola Street* (DiSalvo-Ryan, 2001) is the story of a family dreaming and working together to move from their tiny apartment into a house of their own. *Babu's Song* (Stuve-Bodeen, 2003) and *Beatrice's Goat* (McBrier, 2001) describe children selling wares in the market and eventually earning enough to attend school, as the children long to do.

To foster collaborative working, literature circles, group projects and group research activities can be initiated to discuss picturebooks. Children need to learn the rules for effective group work to be able to work well together.

Authentic action results in mutual exchanges

Many action initiatives tend to be adult-led, charity-based activities where children raise money for the poor but learn little about the recipients of their charity. Through human rights initiatives in a school, children can identify projects whereby the people involved could share their experiences with the class. Children learning about Fair Trade through such picturebooks as Ingrid Hess's *Think Fair Trade First* (2010) have an opportunity to hear from locally based groups who promote the practice. This enables a mutual exchange of ideas, information and skills. If children raise funds for Dafur after learning about Sudan and reading *Brothers in Hope: The story of the lost boys of Sudan* (Williams, 2005), they might like to hear the story of a locally based refugee or asylum seeker. In any case, it is important for children to obtain feedback about how their money is spent.

Authentic action includes action and reflection

A direct link between action and reflection is imperative. Children should have opportunities to witness the outcome of their action as this can encourage further reflection. Children may be involved in many different types of action within one project such as investigating the types of organizations involved in hunger campaigns or raising money for international projects that support sustainability. *Beatrice's Goat* (McBrier, 2001) is based on the true story of how one family was helped by Heifer Project International, an organization that donates livestock to poor communities. Beatrice lives in the village of Kisinga, Uganda, with her mother and five younger brothers and sisters. Life is difficult and her family is very poor. Beatrice dreams of going to school but knows her family will never have the money for books and a uniform. One day everything changes when the family receives a goat. Beatrice names the goat Mugisa, meaning lucky. When the goat gives birth to two kids, the family have milk to drink and some to sell. In time, they are able to sell one of the kids to improve their lives even more. They build a new hut with a steel roof that won't leak and make Beatrice's dream of going to school a reality. Dan West, founder of Heifers for Relief, is the father of the author of *Give a Goat* (2008), Jan West Schrock. Its first shipment of heifers was sent to Puerto Rico in 1944. Jan herself is now a senior advisor for Heifer International, an organization that has grown to serve over 8.5 million people in more than 125 countries. Children can debate and critique the advantages and disadvantages of sending goats or other livestock overseas.

Authentic action invites children's voice and choice
Ideally, children should have an active role in deciding which issues to investigate and what actions to take. They need the opportunity to research and understand an issue from several perspectives (Vasquez, 2004). Literature, and picturebooks in particular, help children develop an emotional connection to the issue under review (Short, 2011).

Civic/global responsibility for social justice
Civic engagement from a social justice perspective (Freire, 1970) focuses on the location of power in the context of social conditions, locally and globally. A useful framework for classroom teachers is the notion of *critique, hope and action*. Critiquing an issue involves asking deep questions about the nature, cause and dimensions of the issue. Hope is about imagining positive solutions. Action involves taking action for social change and justice.

Reflecting on different kinds of environmental action
People have been motivated to take actions which either destroy or protect the environment for various economic, cultural, environmental and social reasons. Picturebooks can help teachers and children reflect on the current actions being taken in school, how effective such actions are and the possibility of designing new actions.

Al Gore's Oscar-winning film *An Inconvenient Truth*, based on his book (Gore, 2006), helped bring the issue of climate change to an international audience. He compared the battle against climate change to the fight against Hitler. In an address to an audience at Oxford University he said that future generations would pose one of two questions: 'What were you thinking? Didn't you see the North Pole melting before your eyes, didn't you hear what the scientists were saying?' or 'How is it you were able to find the moral courage to solve the crisis which so many said couldn't be solved?'

Mick Manning's book *Planet Patrol* (2011) offers factual information about climate change but, more importantly, indicates what children all around the world can do to combat it. The accompanying website provides additional resources and information for teachers. The summary of the book provided on the back cover reads as follows:

> Freya was so cross about global warming and all the damage it was doing to wildlife, that she formed her own group to do something about it – Planet Patrol – and now she's got members all around the world. Meet the Planet Patrollers and find out why they joined and what they are doing to fight climate change.

The book urges children to play their part: 'Don't just wait for grown-ups to act, it's our world too! We can all do something now to fight climate change.'

Many schools promote recycling schemes. In *We Are Extremely Very Good Recyclers* (Child, 2009), Charlie convinces Lola to recycle her old toys instead of throwing them away. Lola discovers a recycling competition. If she can recycle one hundred plastic, metal and paper items, she can plant her own tree. As she only has two weeks, Lola asks her classmates to help. They turn out to be extremely very good recyclers indeed. Oliver Jeffers' book *The Great Paper Caper* (2009) appeals to children who like to solve a mystery. It shows that paper comes from trees and highlights the serious issue of deforestation and its impact on a range of species.

The Mangrove Tree: Planting trees to feed families (Roth, 2011) is based on the work of Dr Gordon Sato. This Japanese American cell biologist made saltwater and desert land productive. He developed an interest in gardening while confined in Manzanar, a Japanese internment camp. In the village of Hargigo in Eritrea, he showed local women how to plant mangrove trees, which supplied them with much needed income. The trees turn carbon dioxide into oxygen, attract fish and feed goats and sheep, and therefore also feed children. The project has been replicated in Morocco.

Discussing the political nature of action

One form of action is discussion, available for all classes and teachers. Doreen Cronin's *Click, Clack, Moo: Cows that type* (2000) and *Duck for President* (2006) are not associated with development education, but they provide a humorous stimulus for discussing action, politics and agency.

Click, Clack, Moo: Cows that type has an understated message about the power of words. Farmer Brown has problems when his cows send him notes requesting electric blankets because the barn is cold at night. All communication between Farmer Brown and his animals is done through notes on the typewriter. A battle ensues between the farmer and the cows. The hens decide to join in and also demand electric blankets. The battle escalates when the cows and hens go on strike. Farmer Brown and the animals reach an agreement: the cows and hens get their electric blankets in exchange for the typewriter, so they can no longer write notes to Farmer Brown. The duck is used as the go-between, but rather than returning the typewriter, they send a typed note to Farmer Brown demanding a diving board for their pond. The story ends with an image of a duck diving into a pond from a diving board.

Doreen Cronin's *Duck for President* (2006) displays the levels of governmental power achieved by the book's protagonist, Duck. Duck is unhappy with his lot. Rather than staging a *coup d'état*, going on strike or otherwise halting production, Duck begins to campaign, sure that he can do a better job than Farmer Brown. His decision sets him on the road to a political career with unexpected results. Duck goes from being voted farmer to governor to eventually becoming President of the United States. But he constantly laments the difficult work that every job involves and eventually decides to move on to something else. At the end of the story, he returns to the farm and begins working on an autobiography.

In *Grace for President* (DiPucchio, 2008), Grace discovers that no women have ever been president, and decides she will be one day. Picking up on this, the teacher decides to run a school-wide election to teach the children about presidential politics. Initially, Grace is not challenged, and she thinks that 'becoming president will be easy'. But then a white boy from another class is recruited as her rival. The usual campaign issues ensue, until Grace is victorious by a narrow margin. Children can discuss these stories in the context of modern-day politics and the present decision makers in our society. Many politicians are visible during campaigns but what happens when they come into office? How accountable are they? These books provoke political discussion and can inspire children to think about changes they would make if they became leader of their country.

Reflecting on people who have taken action

One Hen: How one small loan made a big difference (Milway, 2008) promotes a powerful concept that everyone can be an agent of change. Kojo, a young boy from Ghana, uses a small loan to purchase a single hen. The hen makes a significant contribution not only to Kojo and his mother, but ultimately to the entire country. She lays enough eggs for Kojo and his mother to enrich their diets and for Kojo to sell the extra eggs at the market. Kojo uses the money earned to purchase another hen and after a year has a flock of 25. Selling all their eggs yields Kojo enough money to pay his school fees, where, after many years, he gains the qualifications needed to become a commercial farmer. Another loan after his graduation helps him start a new poultry farm that grows to become Ghana's largest, creating not only a job but export earnings and tax revenues.

The story is based on the life of Kwabena Darko, a Ghanaian who built the largest poultry farm in West Africa from one microloan. *One Hen* shows the power of individuals and the importance of helping others, and teaches children about the work of Dr Muhammad Yunus, a banker and economist who won the Nobel Peace Prize in 2006 for developing the idea of microfinance, granting modest loans to low-income people to start their own businesses.

The Boy who Harnessed the Wind by W. Kamkwamba (2012) is a true story set in Malawi, based on the author's autobiography of 2010 (Kamkwamba, 2010). William's family and country were devastated by a famine caused by drought. When William can no longer afford school and his family eat only one meal a day, he seeks solutions in the local library, which was enhanced by an international aid organization. There he reads science books with the help of a dictionary, and discovers how to make a windmill that can create electricity. Using items from the junkyard, he and his friends build a successful windmill that generates electricity for his home. This is an uplifting story of a young boy who embodies courage, determination, energy and hope.

Ryan and Jimmy: And the well in Africa that brought them together (Shoveller, 2006) is a story about action, brotherhood and determination. When Ryan Hreljac's first-grade teacher explains that it would cost only $70 to build a well to supply clean water for an entire village in Africa, Ryan, with his parents' encouragement, decides to raise the money himself by doing household chores. Undeterred by setbacks, he gradually gains media attention, receives donations from individuals and organizations throughout Canada and eventually travels to Uganda for the unveiling of the well. There, Ryan meets Akana Jimmy, a young Ugandan orphan who had been his pen pal. Jimmy is kidnapped by rebels and though he manages to escape, his life is still at risk. The Hreljacs help bring him to Canada, where he is granted asylum, becomes a member of their family and successfully adjusts to an entirely new way of life.

Picturebooks feature people who have campaigned for social justice issues such as Nelson Mandela and Wangari Maathai. By providing a selection about one character, teachers can enable children to compare the perspectives, stories and illustrations presented in each book. They can conduct further research to write their own picturebook about these characters. Picturebooks about Rosa Parks and Martin Luther King Jr are described here to illustrate the possibilities for biographical study.

Known as the 'Mother of the Civil Rights Movement', Rosa Louise McCauley Parks (1913–2005) was an African American civil rights activist. On 1 December 1955 in Montgomery, Alabama, Rosa Parks, aged 42, refused to obey bus driver James Blake's order that she give up her seat to make room for a white passenger. Her action sparked the Montgomery Bus Boycott. Parks' act of defiance became an important symbol of the modern Civil Rights Movement and she became an international icon of resistance to racial segregation. She collaborated with civil rights leaders, including boycott leader Martin Luther King Jr, helping to launch him to national prominence in the Civil Rights Movement. Her story features in several picture story books for children. Nikki Giovanni and Bryan Collier's book *Rosa* (2005) was written to mark the fiftieth anniversary of her refusal to give up her seat on a bus.

Two books present Rosa's story from the perspective of the bus. Faith Ringgold's book *If a Bus Could Talk: The story of Rosa Parks* (2003) sees a talking bus narrate Rosa's story. Marcie, who is expecting to travel to school as usual, finds out that something is amiss: the bus has no driver, the passengers are unfamiliar and the bus can talk. The bus tells Marcie the story, beginning with Rosa as a child and describes her life up to the infamous moment when she refused to give up her seat. In Jo S. Kittinger's book *Rosa's Bus* (2010), the creative narrative explains the history of Bus #2857 – from the streets of Montgomery to its present home in the Henry Ford Museum – and describes the injustice of segregation to new generations.

Back of the Bus (Reynolds, 2010) retells the story from the perspective of a young boy, a fellow passenger on the bus. A boardbook version, *The Story of Rosa Parks* (Pingry, 2007), is available for early childhood educators.

Martin Luther King Jr's sister, Christine King Farris, has written two books about her brother's life. *My Brother Martin: A sister remembers growing up with the Rev. Dr. Martin Luther King* (2003) deals with his childhood experiences. *March On: The day my brother Martin changed the world!* (2008) is an account of how her brother wrote the landmark 'I Have a Dream' speech. Another more contemporary family perspective is provided by her daughter and Martin Luther King Jr's niece, Angela Farris Watkins, in her books *My Uncle Martin's Words for America* (2011) and *My Uncle Martin's Big Heart* (2010). The author emphasizes that Uncle Martin Luther King Jr's big heart was full of love. In an author's note, Watkins writes:

I wrote this book so that children could get to know Martin Luther King Jr. the way I knew him when I was a child, through his love ... I want them to see how much love he really had – enough to share with his family and his friends, enough to encourage his church, enough to strengthen his community, and enough to change the world.

Martin's Big Words: The life of Dr. Martin Luther King, Jr. (Rappaport, 2007) tells the life story of Dr Martin Luther King Jr in simple words and beautiful pictures, which incorporate words from his teachings and introduce children to his lessons about non-violence. It begins with young Martin reading a 'Whites Only' sign in his hometown. Martin grows up, becomes a preacher and studies the writing of Mahatma Gandhi. He puts his ideas into practice at the Montgomery Bus Boycott and other civil rights demonstrations. He speaks to the nation, and more and more people listen to him. The book ends with some of the 'big words' for which Dr King is remembered: peace, love, freedom and dream. *The Story of Martin Luther King, Jr.* (2001) by Johnny Ray Moore provides an accessible introduction to Martin Luther King Jr for younger children.

On 28 August 1963, Martin Luther King Jr gave his powerful and memorable speech on the steps of the Lincoln Memorial, Washington. In *I Have a Dream* (2012) Kadir Nelson illustrates his words with magnificent paintings. The themes of equality and freedom for all are relevant 50 years later, and the book introduces young readers to experiences of oppression, slavery and a vision for change. Included with the book is an audio CD of the speech. This is a picturebook to be enjoyed by children and adults. Further information about picturebooks featuring the Civil Rights Movement are included in Chapter 6.

The Indian Independence leader, Mohandas Karamchand Gandhi, commonly known as Mahatma Gandhi, is renowned internationally as an activist and a pacifist. On 12 March 1930, he began a defiant march to the sea in protest of the British monopoly on salt, his boldest act of civil disobedience yet against British rule in India. With over 70 marchers, Gandhi walked from his hometown near Ahmedabad to the seacoast by the village of Dandi. The march was a non-violent means to protest against the taxes that Great Britain had imposed on the purchase of salt. Gandhi believed that peaceful protests were an effective way to challenge British law, and his peaceful but ultimately successful movement became known as Satyagraha. McGinty's (2013) *Gandhi: A march to the sea*, beautifully illustrated by Thomas Gonzalez, recreates this famous march and captures the spirit of the

Indian people in their pursuit of freedom. Presented in verse format, the lines echo the marching rhythm of Gandhi's historic journey.

Designing and taking action

Several picturebooks may inspire children and broaden their concepts of action. The award-winning poetry collection *Dare to Dream: Change the world* (Corcoran, 2012) pairs biographical and inspirational poems about people who invented something, stood for something, said something, defied the sceptics, and changed not only their own lives but the lives of people all over the world. Inspired by coverage of the uprising in Egypt in 2011, Corcoran was committed to including themes of social justice and possibility. Many poems pay tribute to activists, artists and iconoclasts, from Anne Frank and Jonas Salk to Steven Spielberg and the founders of YouTube.

Karen Lynn Williams focuses on the struggles and dreams of children in global settings, including Pakistan, Sudan, Haiti, Malawi and Afghanistan. Her award-winning picturebooks, based on her experiences of living and working in these countries, include *Four Feet, Two Sandals* (2007), *My Name Is Sangoel* (2009), *Circles of Hope* (2011) and *Galimoto* (1991). Picturebooks from the publishing company Kids Can Press inform children about complex global issues. Books in the collection address such topics as water conservation, food security, micro-lending and citizenship, and include *If the World Were a Village* (Smith, 2011), *One Hen* (Milway, 2008), *Ryan and Jimmy: And the well in Africa that brought them together* (Shoveller, 2006) and *The Good Garden* (Milway, 2010).

Once children have studied an issue and conducted an enquiry, they are in a better position to decide if they wish to take action, and can discuss and design feasible options. They can advocate for action by designing posters supporting initiatives such as Fair Trade. Once children complete these actions, continuous reflections will inform the design of future actions.

It is important for children to appreciate their own agency and to realize that they have a voice. The picturebook *Olivia's Birds: Saving the Gulf* (Bouler, 2011) is a good example of an action taken by one girl in response to the oil spill in the Gulf of Mexico. Olivia designed a book about what she loves most, birds. Written in her words and illustrated with her own palette of colours, this book features 50 beautifully drawn birds. When Olivia saw the devastation caused by the oil spill, she 'just sat down and sobbed' and then set out to make a difference. Olivia created and donated 500 original watercolour illustrations for her fundraiser, many of which are showcased in her book. She painted a bird for every person who made a donation. To date she has made over 500 paintings of 120 different birds.

The Good Garden: How one family went from hunger to having enough (Milway, 2010) is about food security. It is based on the true story of a teacher, Don Elías Sanchez, who helped thousands of Honduran families adopt more productive farming practices and sell cash crops at local markets. Poor farmers around the world are generally not food secure – they do not grow enough to feed their families and buy other necessities in life. The book and its interactive website provide children with tools and information to help them make a difference locally and globally.

It is important for children and teachers to believe they can make a difference, however small. Although teachers may never hear about the impact they have on the children, their influence is immeasurable. Children need to be able to imagine the kinds of actions they can take, such as planning a campaign to win an election or the next Nobel Peace Prize for Children. They need a creative space to think big and the guidance of an innovative teacher. *26 Big Things Small Hands Do* (Paratore, 2008) is a wonderful A-to-Z book celebrating the way children make our world a better place:

> Your hands are small
> But they do BIG
> Things that make this
> A wonderful world

Fair Trade and thinking about how we spend our money

Many schools are involved in fundraising activities such as No-Uniform Days. However, children can learn principles in trading when they make and sell something as part of a school initiative. First, they decide what they can make, or what services they can offer, such as special calendars or school magazines. They investigate their potential market, agree the price and work out a marketing, promotion and sales strategy.

After studying trade and Fair Trade practices, children may find Ingrid Hess's *Think Fair Trade First* (2010) a stimulus for action. Younger children will be most interested in the fictional story about two children in search of a birthday gift for their mother. Older children and adults will appreciate the non-fiction sidebars explaining Fair Trade.

Children can investigate products such as tea, coffee and cocoa to identify their origin and journey from source to shop. In doing so, they will uncover who benefits from these products and the role multinational companies play. In *Cloud Tea Monkeys* (Peet, 2010), Tashi lives with her mother, a tea picker, in a small village in the shadows of the Himalayas. Tashi's mother works long days on the tea plantation, under the watchful eyes of the bad-tempered Overseer. Although Tashi comes along, she is too young to pick tea and instead spends her time playing and resting in the shade with a group of friendly monkeys. When her mother becomes gravely ill and cannot work, Tashi manages to carry the heavy tea basket to the plantation to earn money to pay for a doctor, but the angry Overseer mocks her attempts to pick tea. Even worse, after she retreats to her private spot in the shade, some of the adult monkeys grab the basket and run off with it towards the mountain. Although all seems lost, Tashi learns that small acts of kindness can be reciprocated in unusual and unexpected ways. The book addresses a number of important development topics, including the vulnerability of the working poor and the incidence of child labour in developing countries.

While children may think individual actions are pointless, mathematical investigations into the purchasing power of the children in one class show otherwise. In *Grandpa's Corner Store* (DiSalvo-Ryan, 2000) the store is under threat from the large neighbouring supermarket but the owner's granddaughter, Lucy, rallies the local community to shop locally and together they manage to save the store. Correlations can be drawn with contemporary examples of struggling stores and local supermarkets.

Conclusion

In this chapter, I have addressed the issue of action. I have indicated how children can learn about different kinds of action and design and deliver their own action component as part of their experience of development education. Picturebooks allow authors and illustrators to dream and, importantly, to share their dreams with a wider audience. Children need the opportunity to dream and create a vision for a better society. When they take actions and reflect on their implications, children appreciate that everyone has a political voice and their sense of self-esteem, confidence and agency develops accordingly.

Chapter 8

Exploring the journey of refugees through picturebooks

Introduction

Children's literature about seeking asylum in a foreign country proliferates (Hope, 2008). Refugees are defined according to the UN *Convention Relating to the Status of Refugees* (UN Economic and Social Council, 1951) as those who have fled their country and are unable to return due to a 'well-founded fear of being persecuted for reasons of race, religion, nationality, membership of a particular social group, or political opinion'. An asylum seeker is someone who is seeking protection but whose claim for refugee status has not yet been assessed.

While it is important for asylum seekers and refugees to see their stories feature in classrooms, it is equally important for indigenous children to hear these stories, learn about the experiences refugees face and understand that refugee children are ordinary children in extraordinary circumstances (Hope, 2008). For this to happen they need access to these stories. In this chapter, I discuss the experience of seeking refuge as a development education concept and explore a range of relevant picturebooks about refugees and the themes they share.

Refugees: an important topic in development education and intercultural education

Today there are refugees in countries all over the world as more and more people are denied the protection of their state and have to seek the protection of the global community.

Refugees are a reminder of the failure of societies to exist in peace. Those forced to flee are often escaping human rights abuses and violations or social breakdown and war. The media generally misrepresents migrants, refugees and asylum seekers, creating stereotypes and fuelling myths and misunderstandings, rather than applying such concepts as justice, equality, tolerance, freedom and minority rights. At a time where one in every 100 people in the world has been forced to flee persecution, violence or war, it is important for all citizens to understand why people are driven to seek refuge. However, issues pertaining to refugees are complex and difficult to understand.

The UN Convention Relating to the Status of Refugees – the Geneva Convention – is the international human rights treaty, drafted in 1951 to provide rights to millions of people displaced as a result of war in Europe. The *Convention* defines a refugee, outlines their rights and explains what governments should do to protect refugees in their territory. In countries that have not signed the *Convention*, the UN High Commissioner for Refugees (UNHCR) is responsible for protecting refugees and, where possible, arranging for them to either return home safely, integrate into society or be resettled in another country. Article 14 of *The Universal Declaration of Human Rights* states that everyone has the right to seek asylum from persecution.

Over the past 60 years, *The Convention Relating to the Status of Refugees* and the countries that have signed it have protected millions of people. The *Convention* and the accompanying UNHCR guidelines are not always followed but when they are, people can be protected, crises can be averted and people's lives can be improved.

Refugees and picturebooks

Picturebooks about refugees and asylum seekers address the universal emotions of fear, grief and confusion, and pay homage to the resilience of children in difficult situations. They provide opportunities for exploring issues such as compassion, empathy, tolerance, justice, conflict resolution and human rights.

Mary Hoffman's *The Colour of Home* (2002) tells in simple language the story of Hassan, a refugee from Somalia who has witnessed things no child should ever see. When he arrives in England, everything is so different and it is very difficult for him to respond to friendliness from his new classmates. His teacher invites him to paint a picture, and this allows Hassan to communicate his experiences in Somalia when his home was burnt and his uncle shot. Through his picture, his teacher and classmates slowly come to understand what he went through and why he must try to build a new life far from home. The clever use of colour, bright and happy for his home, red and black for anger and war, tones of grey for his sadness and loss, elucidate Hassan's moods and feelings where words would fail. Towards the end of the book, colour and hope begin to return to Hassan's life.

Another perspective on asylum seekers is provided by Ben Morley. His book *The Silence Seeker* (2009) tells the story of Joe and his quest to find a quiet place for his new neighbour, an asylum seeker, according to Joe's mother. Joe misunderstands and thinks the boy is *a silence seeker*, especially when Mum adds that he needs peace and quiet. The story shows friendship developing between the two boys, but Joe also comes to realize that he can't find a peaceful and quiet place for his friend, and readers are introduced to the threats and tensions that lie in their environment.

Endorsed by Amnesty International, *Azzi in Between* (2012) was written by Sarah Garland after she had spent time with refugees in New Zealand. Told from a child's perspective, *Azzi in Between* is a sensitive story about Azzi and her family, who are forced to flee their country to survive. Presented in a graphic format, this picturebook is suitable for children from 8 years onwards. Its central message about the plight of refugees is also informative for adolescents and adults.

The cover image for *Azzi in Between* shows a little girl clutching her teddy bear as she looks cautiously behind her while walking through a war-torn landscape. It sets the scene for what is to come, as Azzi and her family flee their unspecified Middle Eastern country and arrive as refugees in the Western city that will gradually become their home. War is depicted in shades of grey that contrast with the bright colours in Azzi's home life. The impact of the war on the family gradually erupts and Azzi's father, a doctor, receives a phone call warning the family that they must leave. There follow the hurried departure, a terrifying journey and the bewildering newness of everything at their destination: food, language, school and so forth. Azzi desperately misses her grandmother who has stayed behind, and worries that she may never see her again.

Azzi's parents manage to shield her from the brunt of their worries, as revealed by the shadows under Mother's eyes, and the fact that Father is too tired when he comes home in the evening to share the new words he has learned that day. There are many nuanced messages in the book for more mature readers. When Azzi asks her father if he is now happy, he responds 'I think you are making me happier, Azzi'. This conversation provides inspiration for further interrogation in the classroom.

Why Are People Refugees? (Senker, 2007) explains the differences between being a refugee, an internally displaced person and an economic migrant. Readers can find out about the experience of being forced from home and understand how many people in the world are treated in this way. The author uses illuminating statistics to summarize the plight of individuals in various geographic areas and times. Issues such as war, natural disasters, abuse of human rights and economics are discussed as causative factors. Case studies quoting refugees create additional impact. Colour and black and white photographs amplify the nature of the circumstances of those affected.

The metaphorical portrayal of refugees in picturebooks

Hans Christian Andersen's story *The Ugly Duckling* can be interpreted as a metaphor – a refugee swan in a pond of ducks. Like refugees everywhere, the swan is different. He is ridiculed, shunned, excluded and bullied. When he becomes a swan, even the ducks can see his beauty. David Miller's book *Refugees* uses the metaphor of a pair of wild blue-billed ducks whose home is destroyed when their swamp is dug up and they have to find a safe place to live. Their difficult and dangerous journey seems doomed to failure. They struggle to settle in different environments, first an ocean, then a busy river port and then a swamp where duck shooting is allowed. They are close to exhaustion when the intervention of an unknown person changes their fate.

David Miller's colourful and detailed paper sculptures add a three-dimensional quality to the story that captures the reader's interest and expands on the text. The scenes are presented from the ducks' perspectives. Although the language and illustrations in the book are easy for young readers to engage with, there are hidden depths to intrigue and challenge older readers.

In *The Island* (Greder, 2007) a man is washed up on the shores of a remote and fortress-like island. The Islanders grudgingly accommodate him but are not kind. Soon their irrational fear of the stranger/other leads them to send the man back to sea. Appropriate black and white illustrations accompany this frightening depiction of the treatment of refugees. This metaphorical account of how prejudice and fear create artificial barriers between people, which they use to exclude others in order to protect themselves, explains why there are refugees and why detention centres and refugee camps proliferate.

Emergent themes

Certain themes have emerged in picturebooks about refugees: personal testimonies, loss and loneliness, identity, resilience, the journey, upheaval and chaos during departure, the process of settling into a new country, challenges, experiences in a new country and important artefacts.

Personal testimonies

Anthony Robinson and Annemarie Young's excellent 'Refugee Diary' books, based on the real-life experiences of four children, give a voice to refugee children. The books follow the journeys undertaken by: Gervelie, escaping from the war in the Republic of Congo; Hamzat, who steps on a landmine in Chechnya: an Iraqi Kurd, Mohammed, who sees his parents beaten; and Meltem from eastern Turkey, who experiences racism as he waits to find out if he can stay in Britain. The books are supported by real photographs and sensitive illustrations.

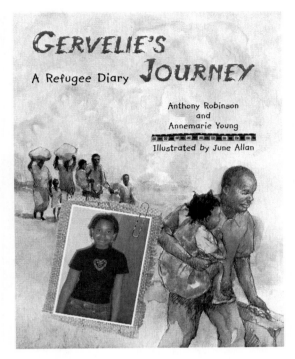

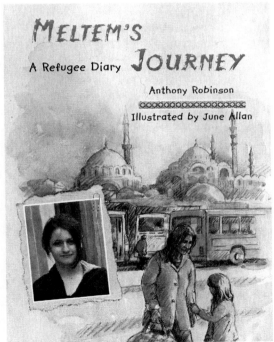

Book covers reproduced with permission from Frances Lincoln Publishers.

Anh Do is a well-known Australian comedian and author of *The Happiest Refugee: A memoir* (2011) and subsequent picturebook *The Little Refugee* (2011). When he was a toddler, he travelled with his family to Australia, as 'boat people' after the Vietnam War:

> Giant waves crashed down on our little boat. I was terrified but my mum hugged me tight and told me, 'Everything will be okay. Don't worry, it will be okay.'

In the aftermath of the Vietnam War and childhood poverty, Anh, his family and friends flee their country by fishing vessel. They battle heat, storms, hunger, thirst, attack, loneliness and fear before they find a safe haven and a new life in Australia. But they have to adapt and learn new skills in order to survive. Life is difficult for the small Vietnamese boy with no English and whose parents have to work all the time to make ends meet. While the war and the dangerous journey in a smelly boat are illustrated in sombre tones, the family's arrival in Australia is signified by a change to vibrant colour. Even though life is difficult and there are significant obstacles to overcome, including poverty and the challenge of settling into a new school with a new language, the book strongly conveys optimism and hope.

In *Mali under the Night Sky: A Lao story of home* (2010) Youme Landowne tells the true story of artist Mali Jai Dee, whose family was forced to flee Laos when she was 5. Before the war began, Mali lived in a community where she felt safe and was much loved. She loved to sit in front of her house and ask everyone who passed by, 'Where are you going?'. She herself went everywhere too, climbing on the flowering trees, catching tiny fish in a rice field, looking for pale bamboo shoots in the dark forest. Mali's idyllic life is shattered when war breaks out, driving her and her family through a dangerous journey across the Mekong River. The family lands 'in the worst place [Mali] had ever been, a crowded jail'. In spite of war and imprisonment, Mali 'grew up to be an artist and an activist so that all people may celebrate their own creativity even in the most difficult situations'. Mali's story reveals the strength of family and culture to carry a child through unthinkable hardship.

Loss and loneliness

Loss and loneliness feature in several picturebooks about refugees. It may be advisable to discuss this emotive and challenging theme in abstract terms first. Several picturebook versions of the Hans Christian Andersen classic *The Little Mermaid* (2011) tell how the little mermaid gave up her sea world, her family, even her voice to move to an unfamiliar place.

Oliver Jeffers' *Lost and Found* (2006) features a boy who finds a penguin on his doorstep. He decides the penguin must be lost and tries to return him. But no one seems to be missing a penguin. So the boy decides to take the penguin home himself and they set out in his rowing boat. When they arrive at the South Pole, however, the boy discovers that maybe home wasn't what the penguin was looking for after all.

Refugees often leave their homes in traumatic circumstances. They undertake difficult journeys and experience long periods of uncertainty in temporary accommodation in refugee camps or detention centres before they can settle and be accepted in a new home. Their efforts to survive are underpinned by severe feelings of loss for their home, family, friends, country and sense of familiarity. *Muktar and the Camels* (Graber, 2009) brings to life the plight of child refugees from Somalia and the challenges in adjusting to a new way of life away from home. Muktar lives in an orphanage on the border between Kenya and Somalia, longing deeply for his parents and his former nomadic lifestyle:

> 'Stop dreaming lazy fellow!' Mr Hassan claps his hands. 'Don't cause trouble,' whispers Muktar's best friend, Ismail. Muktar stirs his posho with sticky fingers. 'My mother and father rest in graves

beneath piles of stones.' He scoops the porridge into his mouth. 'I miss my parents. I miss wandering.' He stares at the acacia trees dotting the scrubby land. 'And I miss camels.'

The beautiful illustrations are slightly out of focus, capturing the dreamlike quality and personality of the young boy. The book has a brief note about Somalian nomads and the camel caravan of the Kenya National Library Service. In a region characterized by harsh climate, bad terrain, and poor transport infrastructure, the camels carry books to children, adults and community health workers who otherwise could not access a library.

Identity

Refugee children have to move between the worlds of home, unfamiliar classrooms and a new, unfamiliar culture. Kenner and Kress (2003) describe how children live in 'simultaneous worlds'. Throughout this process children reinvent themselves and re-establish their identities. Shaun Tan, author of *The Lost Thing* (2000), *The Red Tree* (2010) and *The Arrival* (2007), talks about the notion of belonging and 'the problem of belonging', which he considers an existential question that surfaces for everyone when we are in new situations like starting a new job or relationship, facing a crisis or settling into a new country.

My Name Is Sangoel (Williams, 2009) is told from the perspective of a young Sudanese Dinka boy who with his family leaves a refugee camp to be resettled in the United States. Sangoel is sad because people cannot pronounce his name properly. This can be seen as a metaphor for the need for identity and heritage to be respected and the difficulty all refugees face when settling into a new country. Sangoel finally asserts his identity and teaches his classmates and teacher to pronounce his name correctly.

As refugees settle into new homes, their children develop new identities that encompass the values and culture of their parents along with the ideals and aspirations of their friends, schools and the host society. Sociological literature refers to the idea of a 'third culture' perspective. When individuals who have integrated aspects of the other culture into their personal psychology begin working with each other, they may evolve entirely new ways of doing things (Evanoff, 2006).

People who move from one culture to another experience a sense of displacement. Even though they are happy in their new culture, they miss aspects of their former culture. *Grandfather's Journey* (Say, 2008) is inspired by the author's grandfather's journey from Japan to the United States. The text and illustrations describe the love he and his grandson have for both countries. The grandfather's internal struggle is also felt by Say, who writes that he too misses the places of his childhood and periodically returns to them. The last line tells us: 'The funny thing is, the moment I am in one country, I am homesick for the other.'

The resilience of refugees

Children are resilient, but the refugee experience pushes resilience to the limit. Many of the picturebooks in this chapter illustrate the hardships refugees face and their resilience as they await acceptance in a new country. Some of the stories show how children find strength and support in the most unusual ways. John Heffernan's picturebook *My Dog* (2001) is about the plight of a young boy from the former Yugoslavia. Alija's village is torn apart by fighting and tensions between neighbours of different ethnic backgrounds. The terrible suffering caused by ethnic cleansing in the former Yugoslavia is presented through the eyes of a young boy. Alijia loses his mother, father, sister, aunt and grandmother but is comforted by the companionship of a dog, another refugee.

Thousands of orphaned boys fled Sudan's civil war and forced military service by walking 3,000 kilometres to Camp Kakuma in Kenya. The boys' strength and persistence through adversity is celebrated in *Brothers in Hope: The story of the lost boys of Sudan* (Williams, 2005). Based on true events, this moving picturebook tells the story of Garang, an 8-year-old Sudanese boy, whose family and village are overtaken by war while he is away tending cattle. Garang is forced to embark on an epic journey across deserts and mountains, to Ethiopia and eventually Kenya. He joins a band of over 1,000 boys, some as young as 5, who share his predicament. Despite the hardships of a perilous journey and years spent in refugee camps, Garang occupies himself with the welfare of younger boys, seizes any educational opportunity and never loses hope of a new life in a permanent place of safety. In *Four Feet, Two Sandals* (Williams, 2007), two girls living in a refugee camp in Kenya, both with calloused feet, each find one sandal of a pair. The girls resolve to take turns wearing the sandals. Friendship is shown to be an important strategy for survival.

The journey

Many picturebooks feature the story of the journey itself. *Ziba Came on a Boat* (Lofthouse, 2012) tells the story of a young girl and her mother escaping by boat to Australia. The author was inspired by stories told to her by people from the Hazara community in Australia who are refugees from Afghanistan. *When I Left my Village* (Schur, 1996) follows a family of Ethiopian Jews in their escape from drought and persecution. Travelling through plains, mountains and deserts, 12-year-old Menelik, his parents and young brother head for a Sudanese refugee camp from where people are airlifted to Israel, where they are given homes, clothing and food, and offered freedom, safety and equality. The boy tells the story of the perilous journey, the hunger, fear of discovery and death, of a furtive border crossing, of weeks of unsanitary living in the crowded camp and, finally, of resettlement in a small white hut in the hills near Jerusalem. A map of the Middle East shows the family's escape route, and an author's note adds historical information.

Upheaval and chaos during departure

It is difficult for children to imagine what it would be like if they had to pack suddenly and leave their family, home, friends and country. Few can imagine what it is like to be displaced, our lives threatened and dreams shattered. John Marsden and Matt Ottley have produced the powerful *Home and Away* (2008) about the disintegration of one happy, loving family due to war. It says on the dust jacket:

> Everyone wants a place of safety, a place to share with the people they love. A place to relax. A home. Right now, more than a billion people don't have a home, that's one in seven of the world's population. There are only two places you can be in life: home or away.

This picturebook for readers aged over 10 challenges us to imagine that we are sailing the world in search of refuge. An ordinary family living in the suburbs of Sydney has to flee because of a sudden disastrous war. They have a harrowing journey and the children are finally taken to a detention camp. The front cover depicts a small boy trapped behind a tall wire fence topped with barbed wire. The word *home* in the title is crossed with barbed wire. This bleak picturebook provokes discussion on the plight of refugees throughout the world.

Settling into a new country

Shaun Tan's *The Arrival* (2007) tells the story entirely in pictures of a young husband and father who emigrates to a new land to build a better life for his family. It explores arriving in a new country from the perspective of the immigrant, the almost never-ending possibilities for linguistic and cultural confusion, and the need to relearn even simple things such as preparing the native fruit and vegetables, buying a bus ticket or posting a letter. With just a suitcase and some money, the immigrant must find a place to live, food to eat and some kind of employment. He is helped along the way by sympathetic strangers, each carrying their own unspoken history, stories of struggle and survival in a world of incomprehensible violence, upheaval and hope.

Helped by the kindness of others, the immigrant gradually settles in, finds a job and is able to save enough to pay for his wife and daughter to join him.

One day his daughter goes shopping and helps another new arrival and thus one immigrant's journey comes full circle as a new one begins. Although *The Arrival* does not shy away from the darker sides of humanity, it is ultimately a wonderful exposition of human kindness, warmth and generosity, demonstrating how braveness of spirit can conquer fear, terror and sorrow. Eight hundred stunning drawings look like an album of old photographs, worn around the edges, gently creased through years of handling. Tan brilliantly captures the strangeness of everything. Objects, like a car, that appear familiar are, on closer examination, quite strange. Just as the book is wordless, so too is the immigrant. The essence of the book is captured in its presentation: a hardback publication which has the look and feel of an old but much loved leather notebook.

Emily and Laura study some of the illustrations from *The Arrival* (Tan, 2007)

Challenging experiences in a new country

Having escaped from conflict and survived an arduous journey, an asylum seeker's troubles have only just begun. Simply told from the perspective of a young girl, *A True Person* (Gabiann, 2008) illustrates some of the challenges asylum seekers face on arrival in a new country. Zallah and her mother, who have escaped from a war-torn country, find themselves in a refugee detention centre in Australia while their application for admission to the country is being processed. The illustrations are powerful: in the picture of her mother talking to two officials, the reader shares Zallah's perspective as she looks up at the towering adults. Zallah and her mother ultimately move to a less restrictive environment, closer to a 'new life', where mother has promised she will be able to go to school. Meanwhile, Zallah has made some friends at the detention centre. One, an African called Mwalo, has been waiting for two years but is confident of being admitted – he is a 'true person' because his papers are in order. Such logic causes Zallah to worry about her own situation, but her mother reassures her that being a true person comes from having 'eyes that see you and hearts that love you'. The story calls for respect and understanding.

Gifted young writer Czenya Cavouras created *Rainbow Bird* (2007) between the ages of 12 and 14. Her inspiration came from talking to her grandfather about his visits to an immigration detention centre and then imagining what it must be like to be a refugee. *Rainbow Bird* is a striking picturebook of few words that conveys a strong message. Readers are invited to explore the likely emotions of young refugees, forced to flee the home they love and to endure the uncertainty and indignity of a detention centre in a new country – in this case, Australia – awaiting a decision that will affect their lives. The book ends on a note of hope, as the Rainbow Bird flies past the window.

Artefacts

For some migrants, memories of home are closely associated with a treasured artefact that they have brought with them. For centuries, needlework has been part of the Hmong culture. Since the war in Vietnam and Laos, a new narrative form of 'story cloths' has emerged. *Dia's Story Cloth: The Hmong people's journey of freedom* (Cha, 2009) is autobiographical and for older children, while *The Whispering Cloth: A refugee's story* (Deitz Shea, 1995) is fictional and suitable for younger children. Both books include detailed information about the historical and geographical background of the story cloth.

The Lotus Seed (Garland, 1997) reflects the large number of Vietnamese people who fled a long war and settled in America. The narrator's grandmother keeps a lotus seed from the emperor's palace garden as the old regime falls. When the lotus seed is planted, it flowers – a metaphor for the adaptation and hope for the future, embodied in the young children of the family. Artefacts such as sweet grass baskets in *Circle Unbroken* (Raven, 2007) and quilts in *Under the Quilt of Night* (Hopkinson, 2005) feature in picturebooks about the slave trade from Africa to America. Also featuring cultural artefacts are *This Is the Rope: A story from the Great Migration* (Woodson, 2013), *The Matchbox Diary* (Fleischman, 2013), *Grandma's Humongous Suitcase: A tale of Ethiopian history and culture in a child's voice* (Abebe, 2011), *The Harmonica* (Johnston, 2008) and *The Memory Coat* (Woodruff, 1999).

Eve Bunting's book *Gleam and Glow* (2005) is based on the true story of the Malkoc family, who fled the Jezero village during the Bosnian war. Two goldfish, Gleam and Glow, are placed in the care of two little girls by a refugee who left the village days before them. As they too leave, the elder girl places the fish in the pond. After many months of war, the family returns to their village. Everything has been destroyed by the bombs, except the pond full of thriving goldfish. The following is a list of books about refugees according to the region they have departed:

Table 8.1: Picturebooks about refugees according to the region they have departed

Region of origin	*Title*
General	*The Arrival* (Tan, 2007) *The Island* (Greder, 2007) *Why Are People Refugees?* (Senker, 2007)
Africa	*Brothers of Hope: The story of the lost boys of Sudan* (Williams, 2005) *The Colour of Home* (Hoffman, 2002) *Four Feet, Two Sandals* (Williams, 2007) *My Name Is Sengoel* (Williams, 2009)
Asia and the Middle East	*Chachaji's Cup* (Krishnaswami, 2003) *Dia's Story Cloth: The Hmong people's journey of freedom* (Cha, 2009) *Gleam and Glow* (Bunting, 2005) *Home and Away* (Marsden, 2008) *How I Learned Geography* (Shulevitz, 2008) *The Journey that Saved Curious George: The true wartime escape of Margret and H.A. Rey* (Drummond, 2005) *The Lotus Seed* (Garland, 1997) *My Dog* (Heffernan, 2001) *My Freedom Trip: A child's escape from North Korea* (Park, 2010) *Rainbow Bird* (Cavouras, 2007) *Sitti's Secrets* (Nye, 2009) *The Wishing Cupboard* (Hathorn, 2002) *Ziba Came on a Boat* (Lofthouse, 2012)
Central America	*Alfredito Flies Home* (Argueta, 2007) *The Long Road* (Garay, 1997)

Children can critically interrogate how picturebooks depict refugee issues by comparing them. *Home and Away* (Marsden, 2008) and *Ziba Came on a Boat* (Lofthouse, 2012) provide differing perspectives of the refugee experience. Based on actual accounts of Afghani refugees living in Australia, *Ziba Came on a Boat* tells how a girl and her family experience the desperately high social and economic costs of war and conflict. *Home and Away*, on the other hand, uses a fictional account of an Australian family forced to flee from war to illustrate that it could be us who are forced to flee our homes for an uncertain future, so safety and security should never be taken for granted. Shaun Tan's magnificent wordless picturebook, *The Arrival* (2007), can deepen children's understanding of an immigrant's experience.

Conclusion

I have argued that children's literature, including picturebooks, provides endless opportunities for teaching critical literacy and incorporating global and justice perspectives in the classroom (Dolan, 2013). Hope (2008) asserts that although children's literature about the experience of refugees gives an ideal context for sharing the stories, feelings and fears undergone by such children, literature remains marginal in school libraries and classroom reading lists. In this chapter, I have discussed picturebooks that embrace the refugee experience, enlightening children about persecution, flight and resettlement, while also reassuring readers who are refugees that there is new life and hope for the future in an adopted country. Books on this sensitive topic must be well written, properly researched and convincingly illustrated. They must depict refugees in a positive and factually accurate way. Realistic characterization is essential if the books are to develop empathy and broaden the understanding of non-refugee readers while affirming the experiences of refugee children.

Development education and intercultural themes are complex, but picturebooks can make such issues accessible to children. Teachers need to familiarize themselves with the best picturebooks available before they explore development and intercultural themes. Student teachers and teachers alike need opportunities to engage in critical thinking about the sociopolitical aspects of children's literature because using multicultural literature with children is not without difficulties. Mendoza and Reese (2001) have identified four problems: the availability of suitable books, the time required to locate and evaluate materials, beliefs in the adequacy of a single book and the use of books that are not accurate nor authentic.

As this book shows, picturebooks have been published that together offer a comprehensive picture of development and intercultural themes.

But excellent as they are, they are useless if teachers do not use them. The study by Cremin *et al.* (2008) highlights the lack of professional knowledge about children's fiction, teachers' over-dependence on a small selection of writers and their inadequate knowledge of global literature. They are right to be worried and to maintain that teachers cannot be effective if they have no knowledge of children's literature. This is an important issue for teacher educators, librarians and schools.

Clearly, teachers cannot expect the picturebook alone to teach a theme. Careful consideration is needed to select and plan the most appropriate methodologies in light of the age of the children, the nature and theme of the picturebook and the potential of the book to stimulate critical engagement and reflection. I hope *You, Me and Diversity* will assist student teachers and teachers to select picturebooks that will enhance their teaching and help them design methodological approaches that maximize the learning opportunities afforded by the books they use in the classroom.

I close with an extract from a poem by Bruce Coville.

Ripples

No one acts in isolation
And no act leaves the world the same.
Words and gestures ripple outward,
What shores they reach we cannot name.

(Corcoran, 2012)

References

Agosto, D.E. (1999) 'One and inseparable: Interdependent storytelling in picture storybooks'. *Children's Literature in Education* 30 (4), 267–80.

Allan, C. (2012) *Playing with Picturebooks: Postmodernism and the postmodernesque.* London: Palgrave Macmillan.

Arizpe, E. and Styles, M. (2003) *Children Reading Pictures: Interpreting visual texts.* London: RoutledgeFalmer.

Arnove, R.F. and Torres, C.A. (2003) *Comparative Education: The dialectic of the global and the local.* Lanham, MD: Rowman and Littlefield.

Aveling, N. (2006) 'Hacking at our very roots': Rearticulating white racial identity within the context of teacher education'. *Race, Ethnicity and Education* 9 (3), 261–74.

Bader, B. (1976) *American Picturebooks from Noah's Ark to The Beast Within.* New York: Macmillan.

Bandura, A., Barbaranelli, C., Caprara, G.V. and Pastorelli, C. (2001) 'Self-efficacy beliefs as shapers of children's aspirations and career trajectories'. *Child Development* 72 (1), 187–206.

Banks, J.A. (2008) *An Introduction to Multicultural Education.* 4th edn. Boston: Pearson/Allyn and Bacon.

Banks, J.A. and McGee Banks, C.A. (2009) *Multicultural Education: Issues and perspectives.* 7th edn. Hoboken, NJ: Wiley.

Banyard, K. (2010) *The Equality Illusion: The truth about women and men today.* London: Faber and Faber.

BBC News (2013) 'Nelson Mandela death: World reaction'. Online. www.bbc.co.uk/world-africa-25250082 (Accessed 28 December 2013).

Benson, C. (1986) 'Art and language in middle childhood: A question of translation'. *Word and Image* 2 (2), 123–40.

Berman, S. (1997) *Children's Social Consciousness and the Development of Social Responsibility.* Albany: SUNY.

Bishop, R.S. (1990) 'Mirrors, windows, and sliding glass doors'. *Perspectives* 6 (3).

— (1997) 'Selecting literature for a multicultural curriculum'. In Harris, V. (ed.) *Using Multiethnic Literature in the K-8 Classroom.* Norwood, MA: Christopher-Gordon.

— (2007) *Free within Ourselves: The development of African American children's literature.* Westport, CT: Greenwood.

Blumer, H. (1969) 'The methodological position of symbolic interactionism'. *Symbolic Interactionism: Perspective and method.* Berkeley, CA: University of California Press.

Browne, A. (2011) *The Shape Game: A life in picture books with the Children's Laureate.* London: Random House.

Buli-Holmberg, J. (2011) 'How to improve cultural identity and equality: Experiences from intercultural dialogues in a school for all'. *Dedica Revista de Educação e Humanidades* (1), 137–46. Online. http://hum742.ugr.es/media/grupos/HUM742/cms/DEDiCA%20HUM742.pdf#page=139 (Accessed July 4 2013).

Cai, M. (2006) *Multicultural Literature for Children and Young Adults: Reflections on critical issues.* London: Greenwood.

Chafel, J.A., Flint, A.S., Hammel, J. and Pomeroy, K.H. (2007) 'Young children, social issues, and critical literacy: Stories of teachers and researchers'. *Young Children* 62 (1), 73–81.

Cianciolo, P.J. (1997) *Picture Books for Children.* Chicago: American Library Association.

Colby, S.A. and Lyon, A.F. (2004) 'Heightening awareness about the importance of using multicultural literature'. *Multicultural Education* 11 (3), 24–8.

Comber, B. (2001) 'Critical literacies and local action: Teacher knowledge and a "new" research agenda'. In Comber, B. and Simpson, A. (eds) *Negotiating Critical Literacies in Classrooms.* Mahwah, NJ: Lawrence Erlbaum.

Courtney, A. and Gleeson, M. (2010) *Building Bridges of Understanding.* Limerick: Mary Immaculate College.

Cremin, T., Mottram, M., Bearne, E. and Goodwin, P. (2008) 'Exploring teachers' knowledge of children's literature'. *Cambridge Journal of Education* 38 (4), 449–64.

Daly, N. (2011) 'Website'. Online. http://mysite.mweb.co.za/residents/njdaly/home.htm (Accessed 4 June 2011).

Derman-Sparks, L. and the Anti-Bias Curriculum (ABC) Task Force (1989) *Anti-bias Curriculum: Tools for empowering young children.* California: National Association for the Education of Young Children.

Dinesen, I. (2001) *Out of Africa.* London: Penguin.

Do, A. (2011) *The Happiest Refugee: My journey from tragedy to comedy.* Sydney: Allen & Unwin.

Dolan, A.M. (2012a) 'Futures talk over story time'. *Primary Geography* 78 (2), 17–26.

— (2012b) 'Making a connection'. *Primary Geography* 79 (3), 16–17.

— (2013) 'Critically reading the world through picture story books'. In O'Riordan, J., Horgan, D. and Martin, S. (eds) *Early Childhood in a Global Context.* Oxford: Peter Lang.

Dowd, F.S. (1992) 'We're not in Kansas anymore: Evaluating children's books portraying Native American and Asian cultures'. *Childhood Education* 68 (4), 219–24.

Evanoff, R. (2006) 'Integration in intercultural ethics'. *International Journal of Intercultural Relations* 30 (4), 421–37.

Evans, J. (ed.) (2009) *Talking Beyond the Page: Reading and responding to picturebooks.* London and New York: Routledge.

Fecho, B. and Allen, J. (2003) 'Teacher inquiry into literacy, social justice and power'. In Flood, J., Lapp, D., Squire, J. and Jensen, J. (eds) *Handbook of Research on Teaching the English Language Arts.* Mahwah, NJ: Lawrence Erlbaum.

Fiedler, M. (2008) 'Teaching and learning about the world in the classroom: Development education in culturally diverse settings'. In *Policy and Practice: A development education review* 7, 5–17. Online. www.developmenteducationreview.com/issue7-focus1 (Accessed 7 May 2013).

Fitzgerald, H. (2007) *The Relationship between Development Education and Intercultural Education in Initial Teacher Education*. Dublin: DICE. Online. www.diceproject.ie/docs/relationshipbetweenDEandICE.pdf (Accessed 7 May 2013).

Fountas, I.C. and Pinnell, G.S. (2006) *Teaching for Comprehending and Fluency: Thinking, talking, and writing about reading, K–8*. Portsmouth, NH: Heinemann.

Fox, D.L. and Short, K.G. (2003) *Stories Matter: The complexity of cultural authenticity in children's literature*. Urbana, IL: National Council of Teachers of English.

Freire, P. (1970) *Pedagogy of the Oppressed*. New York: Continuum.

— (1973) *Education for Critical Consciousness*. New York: Continuum.

— (1987) *Literacy: Reading the word and the world*. London: Routledge.

Freire, P. and Macedo, D.P. (1987) *Literacy: Reading the word and the world*. London: Routledge and Kegan Paul.

Galda, L. (1998) 'Mirrors and windows: Reading as transformation'. In Raphael, T. and Au, K.H. (eds) *Literature-based Instruction: Reshaping the curriculum*. Norwood, MA: Christopher-Gordon.

Galda, L., Sipe, L.R., Liang, L.A. and Cullinan, B.E. (2013) *Literature and the Child*. 8th edn. Belmont, CA: Wadsworth.

Gamble, N. and Yates, S. (2008) *Exploring Children's Literature*. London and Thousand Oaks, CA: SAGE.

Gates, P.S. and Mark, D.L.H. (2006) *Cultural Journeys: Multicultural literature for children and young adults*. Lanham, MD: Scarecrow Press.

Genette, G. (1997) *Paratexts*. Cambridge: Cambridge University Press.

Glasgow, J. and Rice, L.J. (2007) *Exploring African Life and Literature: Novel guides to promote socially responsive learning*. Newark, DE: International Reading Association.

Glazier, J.A. (2003) 'Moving closer to speaking the unspeakable: White teachers talking about race'. *Teacher Education Quarterly* 30 (1), 73–94.

Glazier, J. and Seo, J.A. (2005) 'Multicultural literature and discussion as mirror and window?' *Journal of Adolescent and Adult Literacy* 48 (8), 686–700.

Godinho, S. and Wilson, J. (2008) *Helping your Pupils to Ask Questions*. London: Routledge.

Goleman, D. (2006) *Emotional Intelligence: Why it can matter more than IQ*. New York: Bantam.

Goodwin, P. (2008) *Understanding Children's Books: A guide for education professionals*. London: SAGE.

Gopalakrishnan, A. (2011) *Multicultural Children's Literature: A critical issues approach*. Thousand Oaks, CA: SAGE.

Gore, A. (2006) *An Inconvenient Truth: The planetary emergency of global warming and what we can do about it*. Emmaus, PA: Rodale Books.

Graham, J. (1990) *Pictures on the Page*. Sheffield: National Association for the Teaching of English.

Grant, C.A. and Ladson-Billings, G. (1997) *Dictionary of Multicultural Education.* Phoenix, AZ: Oryx.

Greene, M. (1995) *Releasing the Imagination: Essays on education, the arts, and social change.* San Francisco: Jossey-Bass.

Griffith, H. and Allbut, G. (2011) 'The danger of the single image'. *Primary Geography,* Summer (75) 16.

Hamilton, M.C., Anderson, D., Broaddus, M. and Young, K. (2006) 'Gender stereotyping and under-representation of female characters in 200 popular children's picture books: A twenty-first century update'. *Sex Roles* 55 (11), 757–65.

Hancock, M.R. (2008) *A Celebration of Literature and Response: Children, books, and teachers in K-8 Classrooms.* Upper Saddle River, NJ: Pearson/ Prentice Hall.

Haran, N. and Tormey, R. (2002) *Celebrating Difference, Promoting Equality: Towards a framework for intercultural education in Irish classrooms.* Limerick: Centre for Educational Disadvantage Research and Curriculum Development Unit, Mary Immaculate College.

Harris, T. and Hodges, R. (1995) *The Literary Dictionary: The vocabulary of reading and writing.* Newark, DE: International Reading Association.

Harste, J. (2000) 'Supporting critical conversations in classrooms'. In *Adventuring with Books: A booklist for pre-K–grade 6.* Urbana, IL: National Council of Teachers of English.

Hartman, C. and Squires, G.D. (2006) *There Is No Such Thing as a Natural Disaster: Race, class, and Hurricane Katrina.* New York: Routledge.

Haynes, J. and Murris, K. (2012) *Picturebooks, Pedagogy, and Philosophy.* New York and London: Routledge.

Hicks, D. (2006) *Lessons for the Future: The missing dimension in education.* London: RoutledgeFalmer.

Hiemer, E. (1938) *Der Giftpilz* (The Poisonous Mushroom). Nuremberg: Der Stürmer.

Ho, M. (2002) 'Ask the author: Minfong Ho'. In Temple, C., Martinez, M., Yokota, J., Naylor, A., Freeman, E. and Naylor, E. (2010) *Children's Books in Children's Hands: An introduction to their literature.* 4th edn. New York: Pearson.

Hope, J. (2008) '"One day we had to run": The development of the refugee identity in children's literature and its function in education'. *Children's Literature in Education* 39 (4), 295–304.

Irish Aid (2006) *Irish Aid and Development Education... describing... understanding... challenging the story of human development in today's world.* Dublin: Irish Aid.

Jenkins, E.C. and Austin, M.C. (1987) *Literature for Children about Asian and Asian Americans: Analysis and annotated bibliography, with additional readings for adults.* New York: Greenwood.

Johnson, H. and Freedman, L. (2005) *Developing Critical Awareness at the Middle Level.* Newark, DE: International Reading Association.

Kamkwamba, W. and Mealer, B. (2010) *The Boy who Harnessed the Wind: Creating currents of electricity and hope.* New York: William Morrow.

Kenner, C. and Kress, G. (2003) 'The multisemiotic resources of biliterate children'. *Journal of Early Childhood Literacy* 3 (2), 179–202.

Keyes, D.K. (2009) 'Narratives of critical literacy: Critical consciousness and curriculum making at the middle level'. *Critical Literacy: Theories and Practices* 3 (2), 42–55.

Khan, R. (2006) 'Muslims in children's books: An author looks back and at the ongoing publishing challenges'. *School Library Journal* 52 (9), 36–7.

Kiefer, B. (1993) 'Children's responses to picture books: A developmental perspective'. In Holland, K., Hungerford, R. and Ernst, S. (eds) *Journeying: Children responding to literature*. Portsmouth, NH: Heinemann.

Kuykendall, L. and Sturn, B. (2007) 'We said feminist fairy tales, not fractured fairy tales!' *Children and Libraries: The Journal of the Association for Library Service to Children* 5 (3), 38–41.

Ladson-Billings, G. (1994) *The Dreamkeepers: Successful teachers of African American children*. San Francisco, CA: Jossey-Bass.

Lewis, D. (2001) *Reading Contemporary Picturebooks: Picturing text*. London: RoutledgeFalmer.

Lewison, M., Flint, A.S. and Van Sluys, K. (2002) 'Taking on critical literacy: The journey of newcomers and novices'. *Language Arts* 79 (5), 382–92.

Lipman, M. (1988) 'Critical thinking: What can it be?' *Educational Leadership* 46 (1), 38–43.

Mallan, K.M. (1999) 'Reading(s) beneath the surface: Using picture books to develop a critical aesthetics'. *Australian Journal of Language and Literacy* 23 (1), 11–21.

Marriott, S. (2002) 'Red in tooth and claw? Images of nature in modern picture books'. *Children's Literature in Education* 33 (3), 175–83.

Martinez, M., Yokota, J., Naylor, A., Temple, C., Freeman, E. and Naylor, E. (2001) *Children's Books in Children's Hands: An introduction to their literature*. New York: Allyn and Bacon.

McCabe, J., Fairchild, E., Grauerholz, L., Pescosolido, B.A. and Tope, D. (2011) 'Gender in twentieth-century children's books: Patterns of disparity in titles and central characters'. *Gender and Society* 25 (2), 197–226.

McDaniel, C. (2004) 'Critical literacy: A questioning stance and the possibility for change'. *The Reading Teacher*, 57 (5), 472–81.

McGinley, W., Kamberelis, G., Mahoney, T., Madigan, D., Rybicki, V. and Oliver, J. (1997) 'Re-visiting reading and teaching literature through the lens of narrative theory'. In Rogers, T. and Soter, A.O. (eds) *Reading across Cultures: Teaching literature in a diverse society*. New York: Teachers College.

Meier, D. (2003) 'Becoming educated: The power of ideas'. *Principal Leadership* 3 (7), 16–9.

Meller, W.B., Richardson, D. and Hatch, J.A. (2009) 'Using Read-Alouds with Critical Literacy Literature in K–3 Classrooms'. *Young Children* 64 (6), 76–8.

Mendoza, J. and Reese, D. (2001) 'Examining multicultural picture books for the early childhood classroom: Possibilities and pitfalls'. *Early Childhood Research and Practice* 3 (2), 1–31.

Miller, H.M. (2000) 'Teaching and learning about cultural diversity: A dose of empathy'. *The Reading Teacher*, 54 (4), 380–1.

Miller, T. (1998) 'The place of picture books in middle-level classrooms'. *Journal of Adolescent and Adult Literacy* 41 (5), 376.

Miniature Earth Project (2013) *What if the Population of the Earth Were Reduced into a Village of only 100 People.* Online. www.miniature-earth.com/ (Accessed 9 June 2013).

Moreno, A.J., Klute, M.M. and Robinson, J.A.L. (2008) 'Relational and individual resources as predictors of empathy in early childhood'. *Social Development* 17 (3), 613–37.

Morris, L. and Coughlan, S. (2005) *Cross-currents: A guide to multicultural books for young people.* Dublin: iBbY Ireland.

Mourão, S. (2013) 'Response to the *The Lost Thing*: Notes from a secondary classroom'. *Children's Literature in English Language Education* 1 (1), 81–104.

NCCA (National Council for Curriculum and Assessment) (2005) *Intercultural Education in the Primary School: Guidelines for schools.* Dublin: NCCA.

— (2009) *Aistear: The early childhood curriculum framework.* Dublin: NCCA.

Nieto, S. (2010) *The Light in their Eyes: Creating multicultural learning communities.* New York: Teachers College.

Nikolajeva, M. and Scott, C. (2001) *How Picturebooks Work.* London and New York: Routledge.

O'Neil, K. (2010) 'Once upon today: Teaching for social justice with postmodern picturebooks'. *Children's Literature in Education* 41 (1), 40–51.

Osler, A. (1994) 'Introduction'. In Osler, A. (ed.) *Development Education: Global perspectives in the curriculum.* London: Cassell.

— (2000) 'Children's rights, responsibilities and understandings of school discipline'. *Research Papers in Education* 15 (1), 49–67.

Osler, A. and Starkey, H. (2010) *Teachers and Human Rights Education.* Stoke-on-Trent: Trentham Books.

Pantaleo, S. (2008) *Exploring Student Response to Contemporary Picturebooks.* Toronto: University of Toronto Press.

Pantaleo, S. and Sipe, L.R. (2008) 'Introduction: Postmodernism and picturebooks'. In *Postmodern Picturebooks: Play, parody and self-referentiality.* New York and London: Routledge.

Parsons, L.T. (2004) 'Ella evolving: Cinderella stories and the construction of gender-appropriate behaviour'. *Children's Literature in Education* 35 (2), 135–54.

Paynter, K.C. (2011) 'Gender stereotypes and representation of female characters in children's picture books'. Unpublished thesis, Liberty University.

Picower, B. (2012) 'Using their words: Six elements of social justice curriculum design for the elementary classroom'. *International Journal of Multicultural Education* 14 (1).

Purcell-Gates, V. (1988) 'Lexical and syntactic knowledge of written narrative held by well-read-to kindergartners and second graders'. *Research in the Teaching of English*, 22 (2), 128–60.

Reynolds, K. (2007) *Radical Children's Literature: Future visions and aesthetic transformations in juvenile fiction.* New York: Palgrave Macmillan.

Rochman, H. (1993) *Against Borders: Promoting books for a multicultural world.* Chicago: American Library Association.

Salisbury, M. and Styles, M. (2012) *Children's Picturebooks: The art of visual storytelling.* London: Laurence King.

Serafini, F. (2005) 'Voices in the park, voices in the classroom: Readers responding to postmodern picture books'. *Literacy Research and Instruction* 44 (3), 47–64.

— (2009) 'Understanding visual images in picturebooks'. In Evans, J. (ed.) *Talking beyond the Page: Reading and responding to picturebooks*. London and New York: Routledge.

— (2012) 'Interpreting visual images and design elements of contemporary picturebooks'. *Connecticut Reading Association Journal* 1 (1), 3–8.

Shome, R. (1999) 'Whiteness and the politics of London'. In Nakayama, T.K. and Martin, J.N. (eds) *Whiteness: The communication of social identity*. Thousand Oaks, CA: SAGE.

Short, K.G. (2009) 'Critically reading the word and the world: Building intercultural understanding through literature'. *Bookbird: A Journal of International Children's Literature* 47 (2), 1–10.

— (2011) 'Children taking action within global inquiries'. *Dragon Lode* 29 (2), 50–9.

Shulevitz, U. (1985) *Writing with Pictures: How to write and illustrate children's books*. New York: Watson-Guptill.

Sims, R. (1982) *Shadow and Substance: Afro-American experience in contemporary children's fiction*. Urbana, IL: National Council of Teachers of English.

Sipe, L.R. (1998) 'How picture books work: A semiotically framed theory of text-picture relationships'. *Children's Literature in Education* 29 (2), 97–108.

— (2002) 'Talking back and taking over: Young children's expressive engagement during storybook read-alouds'. *Reading Teacher* 55 (5), 476.

Sipe, L.R. and McGuire, C. (2009) 'Picturebook endpapers: Resources for literary and aesthetic interpretation'. In Evans, J. (ed.) *Talking beyond the Page: Reading and responding to picturebooks*. London and New York: Routledge.

Sipe, L.R. and Pantaleo, S.J. (2008) *Postmodern Picturebooks: Play, parody, and self-referentiality*. London: Routledge.

Smidt, S. (2012) *Reading the World: What young children learn from literature*. Stoke-on-Trent: Trentham Books.

Smolen, L.A. and Oswald, R.A. (2011) *Multicultural Literature and Response: Affirming diverse voices*. Santa Barbara, CA: Libraries Unlimited.

South African Government News Agency (2009) 'Madiba receives children's version of his book'. Online. www.sanews.gov.za/south-africa/madiba-receives-children's-version-his-book (Accessed 10 November 2013).

Spearman, M. and Eckhoff, A. (2012) 'Teaching young learners about sustainability'. *Childhood Education* 88 (6), 354–59.

Supple, C. (2007) *From Prejudice to Genocide: Learning about the Holocaust*. Stoke-on-Trent: Trentham Books.

Taylor, N., Nathan, S. and Coll, R.K. (2003) 'Education for sustainability in regional New South Wales, Australia: An exploratory study of some teachers' perceptions'. *International Research in Geographical and Environmental Education* 12 (4), 291–311.

Temple, C., Martinez, M., Yokota, J., Naylor, A., Freeman, E. and Naylor, E. (2010) *Children's Books in Children's Hands: An introduction to their literature*. 4th edn. New York: Pearson.

Tiffany, G. (2008) 'Lessons from detached youth work: Democratic education'. *Nuffield Review of 14–19 Education and Training, England and Wales.* Issues paper no 11. Online. www.nuffieldfoundation.org/sites/default/files/files/11%20 Lessons%20from%20Detached%20Youth%20Work%20Democratic%20 Education2.pdf (Accessed 7 May 2013).

Uitermark, J., Rossi, U. and van Houlton, H. (2005) 'Reinventing multiculturalism: Urban citizenship and the negotiation of ethnic diversity in Amsterdam'. *International Journal of Urban and Regional Research* 29, 1–39.

UN (1948) *The Universal Declaration of Human Rights.* Online. www.un.org/en/ documents/udhr/ (Accessed 20 June 2013).

— (1966) *International Covenant on Economic, Social and Cultural Rights.* Online. www.ohchr.org/EN/ProfessionalInterest/Pages/CESCR.aspx (Accessed 24 June 2013).

— (1998) *Kyoto Protocol to the United Nations Framework Convention on Climate Change.* Online. http://unfccc.int/resource/docs/convkp/kpeng.pdf (Accessed 20 June 2013).

UN Economic and Social Council (1951) *Convention Relating to the Status of Refugees.* Online. www.unhcr.org/pages/49da0e466.html (Accessed 9 May 2013).

UNESCO (2002) *Education for Sustainability – from Rio to Johannesburg: Lessons learnt from a decade of commitment.* Online. http://unesdoc.unesco.org/ images/0012/001271/127100e.pdf (Accessed 12 June 2012).

UNHCR (UN Refugee Agency) (2013) 'Website'. Online. www.unhcr.org.uk/ (Accessed 9 May 2013).

United States Holocaust Memorial Museum (2013) 'Website'. www.ushmm.org/ (Accessed 5 June 2013).

Vasquez, V.M. (2004) *Negotiating Critical Literacies with Young Children.* Mahwah, NJ: Lawrence Erlbaum.

Vasta, E. (2007) *Accommodating Diversity: Why current critiques of multiculturalism miss the point.* Working paper no 7–53. Online. www.compas. ox.ac.uk/fileadmin/files/Publications/working_papers/WP_2007/WP0753%20 Vasta.pdf (Accessed 6 March 2013).

Villegas, A.M. and Lucas, T. (2002) *Educating Culturally Responsive Teachers: A coherent approach.* New York: SUNY.

Wolfenbarger, C.D. and Sipe, L.R. (2007) 'A unique visual and literary art form: Recent research on picturebooks'. *Language Arts* 84 (3), 273.

Wolk, S. (2003) 'Teaching for critical literacy in social studies'. *The Social Studies* 94 (3), 101–6.

Yenika-Agbaw, V.S. (2008) *Representing Africa in Children's Literature: Old and new ways of seeing.* New York and London: Routledge.

Zeitler Hannibal, M.A., Vasiliev, R. and Lin, Q. (2002) 'Teaching young children basic concepts of geography: A literature-based approach'. *Early Childhood Education Journal* 30 (2), 81–6.

Building a curriculum based on respect, understanding and action

In this appendix, I present a list of picturebooks suitable for building a curriculum framework based on respect, understanding and action, and I indicate the approximate age targeted. The first consideration when choosing picturebooks is the learning needs and abilities of the children in the class. Picturebooks such as *One World* (Foreman, 2011) or *All the World* (Scanlon, 2009), which I have included in the 4–7 age category, can be successfully used as a stimulus for all age groups. Others, such as *One* (Otoshi, 2008), are accessible at different conceptual levels and therefore ages. The publication of the edition cited is given with the title of the book but this may not be the original date.

Some of these books can be used interchangeably between the categories of respect, understanding and action. The three concepts can be explored in detail through a layered analysis of one picturebook, such as *Gervelie's Journey: A refugee diary* (Robinson, 2009). Many development education themes – such as justice, fairness and equality – can be explored through these picturebooks. I have included additional categories, such as education, books, gender, versions of Cinderella and fairy tales.

Books to promote respect – for 4–7-year-olds

Atinuke and Tobia, L. (2012) *Anna Hibiscus' Song*. Walker.

— (2013) *Splash Anna Hibiscus*. Walker.

Base, G. (2001) *The Water Hole*. Viking.

Bash, B. (2002) *Tree of Life: The world of the African baobab*. Sierra Club.

Bergen, L. and Snyder, B. (2009) *Don't Throw That Away: A lift-the-flap book about recycling and reusing*. Little Green.

Browne, E. (2011) *Handa's Surprise*. Candlewick.

— (2011) *Handa's Hen*. Candlewick.

Chamberlin, M. and Chamberlin, R. (2005) *Mama Panya's Pancakes: A village tale from Kenya*. Barefoot.

Cunnane, K. and Juan, A. (2006) *For You Are a Kenyan Child*. Atheneum.

Daly, N. (2001) *What's Cooking, Jamela?* Farrar, Straus and Giroux.

— (2001) *Not so Fast, Songololo*. Frances Lincoln.

— (2004) *Where's Jamela?* Frances Lincoln.

— (2004) *Jamela's Dress*. Farrar, Straus and Giroux.

— (2006) *Happy Birthday Jamela!* Frances Lincoln.

— (2009) *A Song for Jamela*. Frances Lincoln.

— (2012) *The Herd Boy*. Frances Lincoln.

Diakité, P. and Diakité, B.W. (2006) *I Lost my Tooth in Africa*. Scholastic.

Foreman, M. (2011) *One World*. Andersen.

Fox, M. and Oxenbury, H. (2008) *Ten Little Fingers and Ten Little Toes*. Walker.

Fox, M. and Staub, L. (2001) *Whoever You Are*. Voyager.

Gliori, D. (2009) *The Trouble with Dragons*. Walker.

Green, J. and Gordon, M. (2005) *Why Should I Recycle?* Barron.

Heiman, S. and Avila, A. (2003) *Kenya ABCs: A book about the people and places of Kenya*. Picture Window.

Hoffman, M. (2007) *An Angel Just Like Me*. Frances Lincoln.

— (2007) *Grace and Family*. Frances Lincoln.

— (2007) *Amazing Grace*. Frances Lincoln.

Hoffman, M. and Van Wright, C. (2008) *Princess Grace*. Frances Lincoln.

— (2011) *Grace at Christmas*. Frances Lincoln.

Isadora, R. (2012) *There Was a Tree*. Nancy Paulsen.

Isadora, R. and Andersen, H.C. (2009) *The Ugly Duckling*. G.P. Putnam's Sons.

Jackson, J., Miller, S. and Diaz, D. (2009) *Let There Be Peace on Earth: And let it begin with me*. Tricycle.

Joosse, B.M. (2005) *Papa Do You Love Me?* Scholastic.

Kranz, L. (2006) *Only One You*. Rising Moon.

McQuinn, A. and Beardshaw, R. (2011) *Lulu Loves the Library*. Alanna.

— (2011) *Lulu Loves Stories*. Alanna.

— (2013) *Lulu Reads to Zeki*. Alanna.

Miller, D.S. and Schuett, S. (2003) *Are Trees Alive?* Walker.

Mitchell, S. and Andersen, H.C. (2007) *The Ugly Duckling*. Candlewick.

Moss, M. and Kennaway, A. (2000) *This is the Tree: A story of the baobab*. Frances Lincoln.

Muldrow, D. and Staake, B. (2010) *We Planted a Tree*. Random House.

Nayar, N. and Roy, P. (2009) *What Shall I Make?* Frances Lincoln.

Newell DePalma, M. (2005) *A Grand Old Tree*. Arthur A. Levine.

Onyefulu, I. (2004) *Welcome Dede: An African naming ceremony*. Frances Lincoln.

Pinkney, J. (2000) *Aesop's Fables*. Chronicle.

— (2002) *Noah's Ark*. Chronicle.

Pinkney, J., Aesop, Bessey, W. and Syarto, S. (2009) *The Lion and the Mouse*. Little, Brown.

Pinkney, J. and Andersen, H.C. (1999) *The Little Match Girl*. Phyllis Fogelman.

— (1999) *The Ugly Duckling*. Morrow Junior.

Roberts, L.H. and Readman, J. (2007) *George Saves the World by Lunchtime*. Transworld.

Roca, N. and Curto, R.M. (2007) *The Three R's: Reuse, reduce, recycle*. Barron.

Sammis, F. and Reeves, J. (1999) *Colours of Kenya*. Carolrhoda.

Scanlon, E.G. and Frazee, M. (2009) *All the World.* Beach Lane.

Tarpley, N. and Lewis, E.B. (2001) *I Love my Hair!* Little, Brown.

Wiley, T. (2009) *Big Earth, Little Me.* Paw Prints.

Wilkins, V.A. and Hunt, P. (2008) *Dave and the Tooth Fairy.* Transworld.

Williams, K.L. and Stock, C. (1991) *Galimoto.* HarperCollins.

Books to promote respect – for 7–10-year-olds

Aardema, V. (1999) *Bringing the Rain to Kapiti Plain.* Turtleback.

Abdullah, R.J.A., DiPucchio, K.S. and Tusa, T. (2010) *The Sandwich Swap.* Hyperion.

Argueta, J., Garay, L. and Amado, E. (2007) *Alfredito Flies Home.* Groundwood.

Barasch, L. (2009) *First Come the Zebra.* Lee & Low.

Brown, P. (2009) *The Curious Garden.* Little, Brown.

Bunting, E. and Soentpiet, C.K. (2001) *Jin Woo.* Clarion.

Choi, Y. (2001) *The Name Jar.* Knopf.

Conway, D. and Daly, J. (2011) *Lila and the Secret of Rain.* Frances Lincoln.

Curtiss, A.B. and Golino, M. (2003) *The Little Chapel that Stood.* Old Castle.

Deitz Shea, P. and Riggio, A. (1995) *The Whispering Cloth: A refugee's story.* Boyds Mills.

Dooley, N. and Thornton, P.J. (2005) *Everybody Brings Noodles.* Lerner.

— (2011) *Everybody Bakes Bread.* Lerner.

Garland, S. and Kiuchi, T. (1997) *The Lotus Seed.* Harcourt.

Gelman, R.G. and Choi, Y. (2000) *Rice Is Life.* Henry Holt.

Gerstein, M. (2003) *The Man who Walked Between the Towers.* Roaring Brook.

Gilmore, D.K.L. and Valiant, K. (2009) *Cora Cooks Pancit.* Shen's.

Handy, F., Carpenter, C. and Steele-Card, A. (2010) *Sandy's Incredible Shrinking Footprint.* Second Story.

Herzog, B. and Ayriss, L.H. (2009) *S is for Save the Planet: A how-to-be green alphabet.* Sleeping Bear.

Johnston, T. and Mazellan, R. (2008) *The Harmonica.* Charlesbridge Publishing.

Kimmelman, L. and Terry, W. (2011) *The Three Bully Goats.* Albert Whitman.

Krishnaswami, U. and Akib, J. (2006) *Bringing Asha Home.* Lee & Low.

Krishnaswami, U. and Sitaraman, S. (2003) *Chachaji's Cup.* Children's Book Press.

Kroll, V.L. and Carpenter, N. (2009) *Masai and I.* Baker and Taylor.

Kroll, V.L. and Cooper, F. (1998) *Faraway Drums.* Little, Brown.

Lord, M. and Hoshino, F. (2006) *Little Sap and Monsieur Rodin.* Lee & Low.

Lovell, P., Catrow, D., Island, D.C., Sprance, E. and Welsh, D. (2001) *Stand Tall, Molly Lou Melon.* G.P. Putnam's Sons.

Ludwig, T. and Gustavson, A. (2005) *Just Kidding.* Tricycle.

Ludwig, T. and Marble, A. (2003) *My Secret Bully.* River Wood.

Mollel, T.M. (1999) *My Rows and Piles of Coins.* Clarion.

Otoshi, K. (2008) *One.* Ko Kids.

O'Neill, A., Huliska-Beith, L., Abbott, G., Smith, C. and Labriola, A. (2008) *The Worst Best Friend.* Scholastic.

O'Neill, A., Huliska-Beith, L., Island, D.C. and Welsh, D. (2002) *The Recess Queen.* Scholastic.

Pedersen, J. (2005) *Pino and the Signora's Pasta.* Candlewick.

Recorvits, H. and Swiatkowska, G. (2003) *My Name is Yoon.* Frances Foster.

Reid, B. (2011) *Picture a Tree.* Scholastic.

Reynolds, J. (2011) *Only the Mountains Do Not Move: A Maasai story of culture and conservation.* Lee & Low.

Robbins, J. and Phelan, M. (2009) *Two of a Kind.* Atheneum.

Sheth, K. (2007) *My Dadima Wears a Sari.* Peachtree.

Thomas, J.C. (2008) *The Blacker the Berry.* Amistad.

Tutu, D. and Ford, A.G. (2013) *Desmond and the Very Mean Word.* Walker Books Ltd.

Walters, E. and Campbell, E. (2012) *The Matatu.* Orca.

Ward, H. (2001) *The Tin Forest.* Templar.

Wiles, D. and Lagarrigue, J. (2005) *Freedom Summer.* Demco Media.

Yang, B. (2004) *Hannah Is My Name.* Candlewick.

Young, E. (2006) *My Mei Mei.* Philomel.

Books to promote respect – for 9–13-year-olds

Baker, J. (1998) *Where the Forest Meets the Sea.* Greenwillow.

— (2002) *Window.* Greenwillow.

— (2007) *Belonging: Big book.* Walker.

Cha, D., Cha, C.T. and Cha, N.T. (2009) *Dia's Story Cloth: The Hmong people's journey of freedom.* Denver Museum of Natural History.

Danticat, E. (2010) *Eight Days: A story of Haiti.* Orchard.

Forler, N. (2009) *Bird Child.* Tundra.

Grimes, N. (2009) *Barack Obama: Son of promise, child of hope.* Simon & Schuster.

Kalman, M. (2002) *Fireboat: The heroic adventures of the John J. Harvey.* G.P. Putnam's Sons.

Light, J. and Evans, L. (2011) *The Flower.* Child's Play International.

McBrier, P. and Lohstoeter, L. (2001) *Beatrice's Goat.* Atheneum.

Meeks, A.R. (2010) *Enora and the Black Crane.* Magabala.

Michelson, R. (2008) *As Good as Anybody: Martin Luther King Jr. and Abraham Joshua Heschel's amazing march toward freedom.* Knopf.

Mortenson, G. and Roth, S.L. (2009) *Listen to the Wind: The story of Dr. Greg and three cups of tea.* Dial.

Obama, B. and Long, L. (2010) *Of Thee I Sing: A letter to my daughters.* RHCP Digital.

Stamaty, M.A. (2004) *Alia's Mission: Saving the books of Iraq.* Knopf.

Ward, H. and Craste, M. (2008) *Varmints.* Koala.

Winter, J. (2004) *September Roses.* Farrar, Straus and Giroux.

Books to foster understanding – for 4–7-year-olds

Clark, K.H. and Barton, P. (2010) *Sweet Moon Baby: An adoption tale.* Random House.

Damon, E. (2004) *What Is Peace?* Tango.

DiOrio, R. (2009) *What Does it Mean to Be Global?* Pickle.

— (2010) *What Does it Mean to Be Green?* Pickle.

— (2010) *What Does it Mean to Be Present?* Pickle.

James, S. (2008) *The Wild Woods*. Candlewick.

Jeffers, O. (2006) *Lost and Found*. HarperCollins.

Katz, K. (2001) *Over the Moon: An adoption tale*. Square Fish.

— (2006) *Can you Say Peace?* Henry Holt.

Larson, K., Nethery, M. and Cassels, J. (2008) *Two Bobbies: A true story of Hurricane Katrina, friendship, and survival*. Walker.

Miller, D. (2005) *Refugees*. Lothian.

Parr, T. (2005) *The Peace Book*. Little, Brown.

Stuve-Bodeen, S. and Hale, C. (2009) *Elizabeti's Doll*. Lee and Low.

Uhlberg, M. and Bootman, C. (2011) *A Storm Called Katrina*. Peachtree.

Williams, S. and Moriuchi, M. (2005) *Talk Peace*. Hodder.

Winter, J. (2006) *Mama: a true story in which a baby hippo loses his mama during a tsunami, but finds a new home, and a new mama*. Houghton Mifflin Harcourt.

Books to foster understanding – for 7–10-year-olds

Abebe, E. (2011) *Grandma's Humongous Suitcase: A tale of Ethiopian history and culture in a child voice*. Author House.

Alalou, E., Alalou, A. and Essakalli, J.K. (2008) *The Butter Man*. Charlesbridge.

Allen, D. and Nelson, K. (2003) *Dancing in the Wings*. Puffin.

Amnesty International (2008) *We Are all Born Free: The Universal Declaration of Human Rights in Pictures*. Frances Lincoln.

Baker, J. (2002) *Window*. Greenwillow.

Bunting, E. and Sylvada, P. (2005) *Gleam and Glow*. Houghton Mifflin Harcourt.

Castle, C., Burningham, J. and UNICEF (2001) *For Every Child: The UN Convention on the Rights of the Child in words and pictures*. Phyllis Fogelman.

Deacon, A. (2004) *Beegu*. Red Fox.

Durant, A. and Riddell, C. (2004) *Angus Rides the Goods Train*. Corgi.

English, K. and Weiner, J. (2009) *Nadia's Hands*. Boyds Mills.

Evans, S.W. (2011) *Underground: Finding the light to freedom*. Roaring Brook.

Fine, E.H., Josephson, J.P. and Sosa, H. (2007) *Armando and the Blue Tarp School*. Lee & Low.

Fleischman, P. and Ibatoulline, B. (2013) *The Matchbox Diary*. Candlewick Press.

Garay, L. (1997) *The Long Road*. Tundra.

Graber, J. and Mack, S. (2009) *Muktar and the Camels*. Henry Holt.

Grifalconi, A. (2009) *The Village that Vanished*. Ragged Bears.

Hathorn, L. and Stanley, E. (2002) *The Wishing Cupboard*. Lothian.

Hegamin, T.C. and Cabrera, C.A. (2009) *Most Loved in All the World*. Houghton Mifflin Harcourt.

Hoffman, M. (2002) *The Colour of Home*. Frances Lincoln.

Hopkinson, D. and Ransome, J.E. (1993) *Sweet Clara and the Freedom Quilt*. Knopf.

— (2005) *Under the Quilt of Night*. Simon & Schuster.

Kajikawa, K. and Young, E. (2009) *Tsunami!* Philomel.

Khan, R. and Christie, G. (2003) *Ruler of the Courtyard*. Viking.

Khan, R. and Kyong, Y. (2005) *Silly Chicken*. Viking.

Kyuchukov, C.S. and Eitzen, A. (2004) *My Name Was Hussein*. Boyds Mills.

Knight, M.B., Melnicove, M. and O'Brien, A.S. (2002) *Africa Is not a Country*. Lerner.

Kooser, T. and Root, B. (2010) *Bag in the Wind*. Candlewick.

Laiz, J. and Cafiero, T. (2006) *Elephants of the Tsunami*. EarthBound.

Malaspina, A. and Bootman, C. (2009) *Finding Lincoln*. Albert Whitman.

McKee, D. (2005) *The Conquerors*. Random House.

McKissack, P. and Cabrera, C.A. (2008) *Stitchin' and Pullin': A Gee's Bend quilt*. Random House.

Melrose, A. and Knight, K. (2010) *Kyoto: A big story about a boy and a little bear, and a little story about global warming*. BPR.

Nelson, V.M. and Bootman, C. (2003) *Almost to Freedom*. Carolrhoda.

Nye, N.S. and Carpenter, N. (1994) *Sitti's Secrets*. Paw Prints.

O'Brien, O. and Finn-Kelcey, N. (2009) *Perry the Playful Polar Bear*. BPR.

— (2010) *Perry the Polar Bear Goes Green: A story about global warming*. BPR.

Oelschlager, V. and Blanc, M. (2012) *I Came from the Water: One Haitian boy's incredible tale of survival*. Vanita.

Okimoto, J.D. and Trammell, J. (2007) *Winston of Churchill: One bear's battle against global warming*. Scholastic.

Pettitt, L., Darrow, S. and Gilchrist, J.S. (2010) *Yafi's Family: An Ethiopian boy's journey of love, loss, and adoption*. Amharic.

Polacco, P. (2003) *Mr Lincoln's Way*. Scholastic.

— (2009) *The Butterfly*. Penguin.

Radunsky, V. (2004) *What Does Peace Feel Like?* Simon & Schuster.

Rappaport, D., Collier, B. and Duncan, M.C. (2007) *Martin's Big Words: The life of Dr. Martin Luther King, Jr.* Weston Woods.

Park, F., Park, G. and Jenkins, D.R. (2010) *My Freedom Trip*. Boyds Mill.

Ramsey, C.A., Strauss, G. and Cooper, F. (2010) *Ruth and the Green Book*. Ebsco.

Rumford, J. (2008) *Silent Music: A story of Baghdad*. Roaring Brook.

Schroeder, A. and Pinkney, J. (2008) *Minty: A story of young Harriet Tubman*. Paw Prints.

Serres, A., Fronty, A. and Mixter, H. (2012) *I Have the Right to Be a Child*. Groundwood.

Shange, N. and Kadir, N. (2009) *Coretta Scott*. Katherine Tegen.

Shulevitz, U. (2008) *How I Learned Geography*. Farrar, Straus and Giroux.

Slade, S. and Bootman, C. (2010) *Climbing Lincoln's Steps: The African American journey*. Albert Whitman.

Tallec, O. (2012) *Waterloo and Trafalgar*. Enchanted Lion.

Vaugelade, A. (2007) *The War*. Lerner.

Visser, R. (2006) *Story of a Storm: A book about Hurricane Katrina*. Quail Ridge.

Watson, J.J. (2010) *Hope for Haiti*. Penguin.

Watson, R. and Strickland, S. (2010) *A Place where Hurricanes Happen.* Random House.

Whelan, G. and Benny, M. (2009) *The Listeners.* Sleeping Bear.

Woodson, J. and Ransome, J. (2013) *This Is the Rope: A story from the Great Migration.* Penguin Group (USA)

Woodruff, E. and Doolin, M. (1999) *The Memory Coat.* Scholastic.

Books to foster understanding – for 9–13-year-olds

Bogacki, T. (2009) *The Champion of Children: The story of Janusz Korczak.* Farrar, Straus and Giroux.

Branley, F.M. and Lloyd, M. (2005) *Earthquakes.* HarperCollins.

Bunting, E. (2006) *One Green Apple.* Houghton Mifflin Harcourt.

Burg, A.E. and Iskowitz, J. (2006) *Rebekkah's Journey: A World War II refugee story.* Sleeping Bear.

Cavouras, C. (2007) *Rainbow Bird.* Wakefield.

Cali, D. and Bloch, S. (2009) *The Enemy: A book about peace.* Random House.

Cunxin, L. and Spudvilas, A. (2008) *Dancing to Freedom: The true story of Mao's last dancer.* Walker.

Deedy, C.A. and Sorensen, H. (2002) *The Yellow Star: The legend of King Christian X of Denmark.* Cat's Whiskers.

Do, A. (2011) *The Little Refugee.* Allen & Unwin.

Douglis, C. and Kennaway, A. (2004) *Tessa and the Fishy Mystery.* United Nations Environment Programme.

— (2005) *Theo and the Giant Plastic Ball.* United Nations Environment Programme.

— (2005) *Tina and the Green City.* United Nations Environment Programme.

— (2006) *Tore and the Town on Thin Ice.* United Nations Environment Programme.

— (2006) *Trishna and the Dream of Water.* United Nations Environment Programme.

Elvgren, J.R. and Tadgell, N. (2006) *Josias, Hold the Book.* Boyds Mills.

Gabiann, M. and Grantford, J. (2008) *A True Person.* New Frontier.

Gallaz, C. and Innocenti, R. (2011) *Rose Blanche.* Creative Company.

Garland, S. (2012) *Azzi in Between.* Frances Lincoln.

Grady, C. and Wood, M. (2011) *I Lay my Stitches Down: Poems of American slavery.* William B. Eerdmans.

Greder, A. (2007) *The Island.* Allen & Unwin.

Gregorowski, C., Daly, N. and Tutu, D. (2008) *Fly, Eagle, Fly!: An African tale.* Aladdin.

Grossnickle Hines, A. (2011) *Peaceful Pieces: Poems and quilts about peace.* Henry Holt.

Heffernan, J. and McLean, A. (2001) *My Dog.* Scholastic.

Hesse, K. (2008) *The Cats in Krasinski Square.* Frances Lincoln.

Hoestlandt, J. (2000) *Star of Fear, Star of Hope.* Walker.

Javaherbin, M. and Ford, A.G. (2010) *Goal!* Candlewick.

Khan, R. and Himler, R. (2004) *The Roses in my Carpets.* Fitzhenry and Whiteside.

King, M.L. and Nelson, K. (2012) *I Have a Dream*. Random House Children's Books.

Landowne, Y. (2005) *Selavi, That Is Life: A Haitian story of hope*. Cinco Puntos.

— (2010) *Mali under the Night Sky: A Lao story of home*. Cinco Puntos.

Lauture, D. and Ruffins, R. (2000) *Running the Road to ABC*. Aladdin.

Lehman-Wilzig, T. and Orback, C. (2003) *Keeping the Promise: A Torah's journey*. Kar-Ben.

Levine, E. and Nelson, K. (2007) *Henry's Freedom Box*. Scholastic.

Lipp, F. (2009) *Running Shoes*. Zero to Ten.

Lipp, F. and Himler, R. (2001) *The Caged Birds of Phnom Penh*. Holiday House.

Littlesugar, A. and Low, W. (2006) *Willy and Max: A Holocaust story*. Philomel.

Lord, M. and Arihara, S. (2008) *A Song for Cambodia*. Lee & Low.

Lofthouse, L. and Ingpen, R. (2007) *Ziba Came on a Boat*. Penguin.

Marsden, J. and Ottley, M. (2008) *Home and Away*. Hachette.

Mbuthia, W. and Karanja, G.G. (2002) *My Sister's Wedding: A story of Kenya*. Soundprints.

McCann, M.R., Marshall, A.E. and Tryszynska-Frederick, L. (2003) *Luba: The angel of Bergen-Belsen*. Tricycle.

Mobin-Uddin, A. and Kiwak, B. (2005) *My Name Is Bilal*. Boyds Mills.

Mochizuki, K. and Lee, D. (1997) *Passage to Freedom: The Sugihara story*. Lee & Low.

Morley, B. (2009) *The Silence Seeker*. Transworld.

O'Brien, A.S. (2012) *A Path of Stars*. Charlesbridge.

Park, F., Park, G. and Jenkins, D.R. (2010) *My Freedom Trip: A child's escape from North Korea*. Boyds Mills Press.

Peet, M., Graham, E. and Wijngaard, J. (2010) *Cloud Tea Monkeys*. W.F. Howes.

Rappaport, D. and James, C. (2005) *The School Is not White: A true story of the Civil Rights Movement*. Jump at the Sun/Hyperion.

Raven, M.T. and Lewis, E.B. (2007) *Circle Unbroken*. Square Fish.

Robinson, A., Young, A. and Allan, J. (2009) *Gervelie's Journey: A refugee diary*. Frances Lincoln.

— (2009) *Hamzat's Journey: A refugee diary*. Frances Lincoln.

— (2009) *Mohammed's Journey: A refugee diary*. Frances Lincoln.

— (2010) *Meltem's Journey: A refugee diary*. Frances Lincoln.

Ruelle, K.G. and DeSaix, D.D. (2009) *The Grand Mosque of Paris: A story of how Muslims rescued Jews during the Holocaust*. Holiday House.

Say, A. (2008) *Grandfather's Journey*. Houghton Mifflin Harcourt.

Schur, M.R. and Pinkney, J.B. (1996) *When I Left my Village*. Dial.

Senker, C. (2007) *Why are People Refugees?* Hodder.

Seuss, Dr. (1984) *The Butter Battle Book*. San Val.

— (2009) *The Lorax*. HarperCollins.

Simon, S. (2006) *Earthquakes*. Perfection.

Smith, D.J. and Armstrong, S. (2011) *If the World Were a Village*. Allen & Unwin.

— (2011) *This Child, Every Child: A book about the world's children*. Kids Can.

Smith, I. and Nhem, S. (2010) *Half Spoon of Rice: A survival story of the Cambodian genocide*. East West Discovery.

Spielman, G. and Archambault, M. (2007) *Janusz Korczak's Children*. Kar-Ben.

Tan, S. (2000) *The Lost Thing*. Lothian.

— (2007) *The Arrival*. Arthur A. Levine.

— (2010) *The Red Tree*. Hachette.

Tan, S. and Marsden, J. (2010) *The Rabbits*. Hachette.

Vaugelade, A. (2007) *The War*. Lerner.

Whelan, G. and Milelli, P. (2009) *Waiting for the Owl's Call*. Sleeping Bear.

Williams, K.L. and Stone, W. (2011) *Beatrice's Dream: A story of Kibera slum*. Frances Lincoln.

Williams, M. and Christie, R.G. (2005) *Brothers in Hope: The story of the lost boys of Sudan*. Lee & Low.

Wiviott, M. and Bisaillon, J. (2010) *Benno and the Night of Broken Glass*. Kar-Ben.

Woodson, J. and Lewis, B. (2001) *The Other Side*. G.P. Putnam's Sons.

Yolen, J. and Shannon, D. (1996) *Encounter*. Voyager.

Books that consider action – for 4–7-year-olds

Boelts, M. (2009) *Those Shoes*. Candlewick.

Child, L. and Hurst, B. (2009) *We Are Extremely Very Good Recyclers*. Dial.

— (2010) *Lola: I really, really need actual ice skates*. Dial.

Cronin, D. (2006) *Duck for President*. Abdo.

Cronin, D., Lewin, B., Travis, R., Huff, S. and Reynolds, R. (2000) *Click, Clack, Moo: Cows that type*. Simon & Schuster.

DiPucchio, K.S. and Pham, L.U. (2008) *Grace for President*. Hyperion.

Jeffers, O. (2009) *The Great Paper Caper*. Philomel.

Paratore, C. (2008) *26 Big Things Small Hands Do*. Free Spirit.

Pingry, P.A. and Walker, S. (2007) *The Story of Rosa Parks*. Candy Cane.

Proimos, J. (2009) *Paulie Pastrami Achieves World Peace*. Little, Brown.

Reynolds, P.H. (2005) *The Dot*. Candlewick.

Waddell, M., Oxenbury, H. and Enfield, H. (2006) *Farmer Duck*. Mantra Lingua.

Walsh, M. (2008) *10 Things I Can Do to Help My World*. Candlewick.

Books that consider action – for 7–10-year-olds

Alexander, J., Shore, D.Z. and Ransome, J. (2009) *This Is the Dream*. HarperCollins.

Aston, D.H. and Roth, S.L. (2011) *Dream Something Big*. Penguin.

Bouler, O. (2011) *Olivia's Birds: Saving the Gulf*. Sterling.

DiSalvo-Ryan, D.A. (2000) *Grandpa's Corner Store*. HarperCollins.

— (2001) *A Castle on Viola Street*. HarperCollins.

Drummond, A. and Borden, L.W. (2005) *The Journey that Saved Curious George: The true wartime escape of Margret and H.A. Rey*. Houghton Mifflin Harcourt.

Evans, S. (2012) *We March*. Roaring Brook.

Farris, C.K. (2008) *March On: The day my brother Martin changed the world*. Scholastic.

Farris, C.K. and Soentpiet, C.K. (2003) *My Brother Martin: A sister remembers growing up with the Rev. Dr. Martin Luther King*. Simon & Schuster.

Foreman, M. (2007) *Mia's Story: A sketchbook of hopes and dreams*. Walker.

Giovanni, N. and Collier, B. (2005) *Rosa*. Henry Holt.

Hess, I., Carpenter, S. and Network, F.T.R. (2010) *Think Fair Trade First*. Global Gifts.

Johnson, A. and Velasquez, E. (2008) *A Sweet Smell of Roses*. Perfection.

King, M.L. and King, C.S. (2008) *The Words of Martin Luther King, Jr.* William Morrow.

Kittinger, J.S. and Walker, S. (2010) *Rosa's Bus*. Boyds Mills.

Manning, M. (2011) *Planet Patrol: A book about global warming*. Hodder.

Moore, J.R. and Wummer, A. (2001) *The Story of Martin Luther King, Jr.* Candy Cane.

Muth, J.J. (2003) *Stone Soup*. Scholastic.

Nelson, K. (2013) *Nelson Mandela*. HarperCollins.

Rappaport, D. and Nelson, K. (2008) *Abe's Honest Words: The life of Abraham Lincoln*. Hyperion.

Reynolds, A. and Cooper, F. (2010) *Back of the Bus*. Philomel.

Rockliff, M. and Low, W. (2012) *Me and Momma and Big John*. Candlewick.

Roth, S.L. and Trombore, C. (2011) *The Mangrove Tree: Planting trees to feed families*. Lee & Low.

Schrock, J.W. and Darragh, A. (2008) *Give a Goat*. Tilbury House.

Siddals, M.M.K. and Wolff, A. (2010) *Compost Stew: An A-to-Z recipe for the earth*. Ten Speed.

Sisulu, E.B. and Wilson, S. (2009) *The Day Gogo Went to Vote*. Little, Brown.

Smothers, E.F. and Holyfield, J. (2003) *The Hard-Times Jar*. Farrar, Straus and Giroux.

Stuve-Bodeen, S. and Boyd, A. (2003) *Babu's Song*. Lee & Low.

van Wyk, C., Bouma, P. and Mandela, N. (2009) *Nelson Mandela: Long Walk to Freedom*. Roaring Brook.

Warren, S.E. and Casilla, R. (2012) *Dolores Huerta: A hero to migrant workers*. Amazon.

Williams, K.L. and Saport, L. (2011) *Circles of Hope*. William B. Eerdmans Publishing Co.

Wilson, L. and Cornelison, S. (2010) *Sofia's Dream*. Little Pickle.

Young Shelton, P. and Colon, R. (2009) *Child of the Civil Rights Movement*. Random House.

Books that consider action – for 9–13-year-olds

Cole, H. (2012) *Unspoken: A story from the Underground Railroad*. Scholastic.

Corcoran, J. and Jepson, J.B. (2012) *Dare to Dream: Change the world*. Kane Miller.

Cullerton Johnson, J. (2010) *Seeds of Change: Planting a path to peace*. Lee & Low.

Deedy, C.A. (2009) *14 Cows for America*. Peachtree.

Deitz, Shea, P. and Morin, L. (2006) *The Carpet Boy's Gift*. Tilbury.

Farris, C.K. (2008) *March On: The day my brother Martin changed the world*. Scholastic.

Fitzpatrick, M.L. and Deer, G.W. (2001) *The Long March: The Choctaw's gift to Irish Famine Relief*. Random House.

Kamkwamba, W. and Mealer, B. (2012) *The Boy who Harnessed the Wind*. Dial.

McGinty, A.B. and Gonzalez, T. (2013) *Gandhi: A march to the sea*. Two Lions.

McGrath, B.B. (2006) *The Storm: Students of Biloxi, Mississippi, remember Hurricane Katrina*. Charlesbridge.

Milway, K.S. (2008) *One Hen: How one small loan made a big difference*. Kids Can.

Milway, K.S. and Daigneault, S. (2010) *The Good Garden: How one family went from hunger to having enough*. Kids Can.

Napoli, D.J. (2010) *Mama Miti: Wangari Maathai and the trees of Kenya*. Simon & Schuster/Paula Wiseman.

Nivola, C.A. (2008) *Planting the Trees of Kenya: The story of Wangari Maathai*. Farrar, Straus and Giroux.

Nolen, J. and Nelson, K. (2003) *Big Jabe*. HarperCollins.

Oelschlager, V., Blackwood, K. and Blanc, M. (2010) *Bonyo Bonyo: The true story of a brave boy from Kenya*. Vanita.

Pinkney, A. and Pinkney, B. (2010) *Sit-In: How four friends stood up by sitting down*. Little, Brown.

Ringgold, F. (2003) *If a Bus Could Talk: The story of Rosa Parks*. Paw Prints.

Rumford, J. (2010) *Rain School*. Houghton Mifflin Harcourt.

Shange, N. and Brown, R. (2009) *We Troubled the Waters*. HarperCollins.

Shange, N. and Nelson, K. (2004) *Ellington Was Not a Street*. Simon & Schuster.

Shoveller, H. (2006) *Ryan and Jimmy: And the well in Africa that brought them together*. Kids Can.

Watkins, A.F. and Velasquez, E. (2010) *My Uncle Martin's Big Heart*. Harry N. Abrams.

— (2011) *My Uncle Martin's Words for America: Martin Luther King Jr.'s niece tells how he made a difference*. Harry N. Abrams.

Weatherford, C.B. and Lagarrigue, J. (2007) *Freedom on the Menu: The Greensboro sit-ins*. Paw Prints.

Weatherford, C.B. and Nelson, K. (2006) *Moses: When Harriet Tubman led her people to freedom*. Hyperion.

Williams, K.L., Mohammed, K. and Chayka, D. (2007) *Four Feet, Two Sandals*. William B. Eerdmans.

Williams, K.L., Mohammed, K. and Stock, C. (2009) *My Name Is Sangoel*. William B. Eerdmans.

Winter, J. (2008) *Wangari's Trees of Peace: A true story from Africa*. Houghton Mifflin Harcourt.

Zalben, J.B. (2006) *Paths to Peace: People who changed the world*. Recording for the Blind & Dyslexic.

Books about perspective

Browne, A. (2008) *Voices in the Park*. Dorling Kindersley.

— (2010) *Me and You*. Farrar, Straus and Giroux.

Macaulay, D. (1990) *Black and White*. Houghton Mifflin Harcourt.

Muth, J.J. (2002) *The Three Questions*. Scholastic.

— (2005) *Zen Shorts*. Scholastic.

— (2008) *Zen Ties*. Scholastic.

— (2010) *Zen Ghosts*. Scholastic.

Scieszka, J. and Johnson, S. (2009) *The Frog Prince Continued*. Puffin.

Scieszka, J. and Smith, L. (2007) *The Stinky Cheese Man and Other Fairly Stupid Tales*. Penguin.

— (2009) *The True Story of the Three Little Pigs*. Paw Prints.

Singer, M. and Massee, J.E. (2010) *Mirror Mirror: A book of reversible verse*. Dutton.

Smith, L. (2010) *It's a Book*. Roaring Brook.

Wiesner, D. (2001) *The Three Pigs*. Clarion.

Woodson, J. and Lewis, B. (2001) *The Other Side*. G.P. Putnam's Sons.

Books about the right to education

Amnesty International (2008) *We Are all Born Free: The Universal Declaration of Human Rights in pictures*. Frances Lincoln.

Castle, C., Burningham, J. and UNICEF (2001) *For Every Child: The UN Convention on the Rights of the Child in words and pictures*. P. Fogelman.

Cline-Ransome, L. and Ransome, J.E. (2013) *Light in the Darkness: A story about how slaves learned in secret*. Hyperion.

Cunxin, L. and Spudvilas, A. (2008) *Dancing to Freedom: The true story of Mao's last dancer*. Walker.

Fine, E.H., Josephson, J.P. and Sosa, H. (2007) *Armando and the Blue Tarp School*. Lee & Low.

Hughes, S. (2011) *Off to Class: Incredible and unusual schools around the world*. Turtleback.

Park, F., Park, G. and Zhang, C.Z. (2008) *The Royal Bee*. Paw Prints.

Rappaport, D. and James, C. (2005) *The School Is Not White: A true story of the Civil Rights Movement*. Jump at the Sun/Hyperion.

Ruurs, M. (2009) *My School in the Rain Forest: How children attend school around the world*. Boyds Mills.

Smith, P. and Shalev, Z. (2007) *A School Like Mine: A unique celebration of schools around the world*. Dorling Kindersley.

Williams, M. and Christie, R.G. (2005) *Brothers in Hope: The story of the lost boys of Sudan*. Lee & Low.

Winter, J. (2009) *Nasreen's Secret School: A true story from Afghanistan*. Simon & Schuster.

Books about libraries and books

Brown, M. and Parra, J. (2011) *Waiting for the Biblioburro*. Random House.

Elvgren, J.R. and Tadgell, N. (2006) *Josias, Hold the Book*. Boyds Mills.

Roth, S.L. and Abouraya, K.L. (2012) *Hands Around the Library: Protecting Egypt's treasured books*. Dial.

Ruurs, M. (2005) *My Librarian Is a Camel: How books are brought to children around the world*. Boyds Mills.

Stamaty, M.A. (2004) *Alia's Mission: Saving the books of Iraq*. Knopf.

Winter, J. (2005) *The Librarian of Basra: A true story from Iraq*. Harcourt.

— (2011) *Biblioburro: A true story from Colombia*. Beach Lane.

Fairy tales and fractured fairy tales

Ada, A.F. (2007) *Extra Extra: Fairy tale news from hidden forest*. Atheneum.

Ada, A.F. and Tryon, L. (2005) *Yours Truly, Goldilocks*. Aladdin.

— (2009) *With Love, Little Red Hen*. Paw Prints.

Ahlberg, A. and Ahlberg, J. (2006) *The Jolly Postman*. Little, Brown.

Ahlberg, A. and Ingman, B. (2011) *Previously*. Candlewick.

Allen, D. and Nelson, K. (2009) *Brothers of the Knight*. Paw Prints.

Alley, Z. and Alley, R.W. (2008) *There's a Wolf at the Door*. Roaring Brook.

Andersen, H.C., Lewis, N. and Birmingham, C. (2011) *The Little Mermaid*. Walker.

Aston, D.H. and Murphy, K. (2003) *Loony Little*. Candlewick.

Auch, M.J. and Auch, H. (2002) *The Princess and the Pizza*. Scholastic.

— (2006) *Chickerella*. Holiday House.

Baker, L. (2009) *Snow White and the Seven Dwarfs: A read-aloud storybook*. Random House.

Bateman, T. and Cravath, L.W. (2002) *The Princesses Have a Ball*. Albert Whitman.

Briggs, R. (2008) *Jim and the Beanstalk*. Paw Prints.

Child, L. (2013) *Beware of the Storybook Wolves*. Hodder & Stoughton.

Child, L. and Borland, P. (2006) *The Princess and the Pea*. Hyperion.

Cole, B. (2009) *Princess Smartypants*. Puffin.

— (2009) *Prince Cinders*. Penguin.

Disney, W. (2005) *Walt Disney's Cinderella*. Disney.

Elya, S.M. and McDonald, M. (2005) *Fairy Trails*. Bloomsbury.

Emberley, M. (1990) *Ruby*. Little, Brown.

Ernst, L.C. (2005) *Little Red Riding Hood: A newfangled prairie tale*. Aladdin.

— (2006) *The Gingerbread Girl*. Scholastic.

— (2009) *Goldilocks Returns*. Paw Prints.

Fearnley, J. (2004) *Mr Wolf and the Three Bears*. Egmont.

Fierstein, H. and Cole, H. (2005) *The Sissy Duckling*. Simon & Schuster.

Fleming, C. and Lambert, S.A. (2004) *Gator Gumbo: A spicy-hot tale*. Farrar, Straus and Giroux.

French, F. (2009) *Snow White in New York*. Marco.

Geist, K. and Gorton, J. (2007) *The Three Little Fish and the Big Bad Shark*. Cartwheel/Scholastic.

Gibb, S. (2011) *Rapunzel*. Albert Whitman.

Goode, D. (2000) *Cinderella: The dog and her little glass*. Blue Sky.

Grey, M. (2011) *The very Smart Pea and the Princess-to-be*. Random House.

Hale, B. and Fine, H. (2008) *Snoring Beauty*. Houghton Mifflin Harcourt.

Hartman, B. and Raglin, T. (2009) *The Wolf Who Cried Boy*. Scholastic.

Hassett, A. and Hassett, J. (2006) *The Three Silly Girls Grubb*. Houghton Mifflin Harcourt.

Hawkins, C. (2005) *Fairy Tale News*. Walker.

Hoberman, M.A. and Emberley, M. (2012) *You Read to Me, I'll Read to You: (3) very short fairy tales to read together*. Little, Brown.

Kellogg, S. (2009) *The Pied Piper's Magic*. Dial.

Kloske, G. and Blitt, B. (2005) *Once Upon a Time, the End (Asleep in 60 Seconds)*. Atheneum.

Lasky, K. and Manders, J. (2004) *Humphrey, Albert, and the Flying Machine*. Harcourt.

Lorenz, A. and Schleh, J. (2002) *Jack and the Beanstalk: How a small fellow solved a big problem*. Harry N. Abrams.

Martin, J.M.C. (2004) *12 Fabulously Funny Folktale Plays*. Scholastic.

Meddaugh, S. (2002) *Cinderella's Rat Pa*. Houghton Mifflin Harcourt.

Morgan, M. (2008) *Dragon Pizzeria*. Random House.

Osborne, M.P. and Potter, G. (2005) *Kate and the Beanstalk*. Aladdin.

Osborne, W., Osborne, M.P. and Potter, G. (2005) *Sleeping Bobby*. Atheneum.

Palatini, M. and Moser, B. (2005) *The Three Silly Billies*. Simon & Schuster.

Pichon, L. (2010) *The Three Horrid Little Pigs*. Tiger Tales.

Pinkney, J. and Andersen, H.C. (1999) *The Ugly Duckling*. Morrow.

Rubin, V. and Montijo, R. (2007) *The Three Swingin' Pigs*. Henry Holt.

Scieszka, J. and Johnson, S. (2009) *The Frog Prince Continued*. Puffin.

Scieszka, J. and Smith, L. (2007) *The Stinky Cheese Man and Other Fairly Stupid Tales*. Penguin.

— (2009) *The True Story of The Three Little Pigs*. Paw Prints.

Shulman, L. and Litzinger, R. (2007) *The Matzo Ball Boy*. Puffin.

Stanley, D. (2002) *Rumpelstiltskin's Daughter*. HarperCollins.

— (2004) *The Giant and the Beanstalk*. HarperCollins.

— (2007) *Goldie and the Three Bears*. HarperCollins.

Sturges, P. and Walrod, A. (2002) *The Little Red Hen Makes a Pizza*. Puffin.

Sweet, M. (2008) *Carmine: A little more red*. Houghton Mifflin Harcourt.

Trivizas, E. and Oxenbury, H. (2009) *The Three Little Wolves and the Big Bad Pig*. Paw Prints.

Umansky, K. and Fisher, C. (2004) *A Chair for Baby Bear*. Barron.

Whipple, L. and Beingessner, L. (2002) *If the Shoe Fits: Voices from Cinderella*. Margaret K. McElderry.

Wiesner, D. (2001) *The Three Pigs*. Clarion.

Wilcox, L. and Monks, L. (2005) *Falling for Rapunzel*. Puffin.

— (2011) *Waking Beauty*. Puffin.

Willard, N., Dyer, J. and Perrault, C. (2004) *Cinderella's Dress*. Blue Sky.

Willems, M. (2012) *Goldilocks and the Three Dinosaurs*. HarperCollins. .

Yolen, J. and Dyer, J. (1987) *The Three Bears Rhyme Book*. Harcourt Brace Jovanovich.

Yolen, J. and Stanley, D. (2009) *Sleeping Ugly*. Paw Prints.

Youngquist, C.V. and Sorra, K. (2002) *The Three Billygoats Gruff and Mean Calypso Joe*. Simon & Schuster.

Versions of the Cinderella story

Buehner, C. and Buehner, M. (2009) *Fanny's Dream*. Paw Prints.

Climo, S. and Heller, R. (1992) *The Egyptian Cinderella*. Harper Collins.

— (2009) *The Korean Cinderella*. Paw Prints.

Climo, S. and Krupinski, L. (2000) *The Irish Cinderlad*. Harper Collins.

Coburn, J.R. and Flotte, E. (1998) *Angkat: The Cambodian Cinderella*. Shen's Books.

Coburn, J.R., Lee, T.C. and O'Brien, A.S. (1996) *Jouanah: A Hmong Cinderella*. Shen's.

Coburn, J.R. and McLennan, C. (2000) *Domítila: A Cinderella tale from the Mexican tradition*. Shen's.

Daly, J. (2005) *Fair, Brown and Trembling: An Irish Cinderella story*. Farrar, Straus and Giroux.

De La Paz, M.J. and Tang, Y.S. (2001) *Abadeha: The Philippine Cinderella*. Shen's.

DePaola, T. (2004) *Adelita: A Mexican Cinderella story*. Puffin.

— (2009) *Adelita: A Mexican Cinderella story*. Paw Prints.

Dwyer, M. (2004) *The Salmon Princess: An Alaska Cinderella story*. Sasquatch.

Fleischman, P. and Paschkis, J. (2007) *Glass Slipper, Gold Sandal: A worldwide Cinderella*. Henry Holt.

Gilani, F. and Adams, S. (2011) *Cinderella: An Islamic tale*. Consortium.

Hickox, R. and Hillenbrand, W. (1999) *The Golden Sandal: A Middle Eastern Cinderella story*. Holiday House.

Jaffe, N. and August, L. (1998) *The Way Meat Loves Salt: A Cinderella tale from the Jewish tradition*. Henry Holt.

Ketteman, H. and Warhola, J. (1997) *Bubba the Cowboy Prince: A fractured Texas tale*. Scholastic.

Louie, A.L. and Young, E. (1996) *Yeh-Shen: A Cinderella story from China*. Puffin.

Manna, A.L., Mitakidou, A.L.M.S., Mitakidou, C. and Potter, G. (2011) *The Orphan: A Cinderella story from Greece*. Random House.

Martin, R. and Shannon, D. (1998) *The Rough Face Girl*. Puffin.

Mehta, L., Brucker, M.B. and Tang, Y. (2002) *Anklet for a Princess: A Cinderella tale from India*. Shen's.

Minters, F. and Karas, G.B. (1997) *Cinder-Elly*. Puffin.

Monnar, A., Franklin, L. and Michaud, N. (2008) *Adelaida: A Cuban Cinderella*. Readers Are Leaders.

Onyefulu, O. and Safarewicz, E. (1995) *Chinye*. Frances Lincoln.

Perrault, C. and Crane, W. (2011) *Cendrillon ou la petite pantoufle de verre*. Planet.

Perrault, C. and Crane, W. (2011) *Cinderella, Or the Little Glass Slipper (Illustrated by Walter Crane)*. Planet.

Perrault, C. and Innocenti, R. (2001) *Cinderella*. Creative Company.

Pollock, P. and Young, E. (1996) *The Turkey Girl: A Zuni Cinderella story*. Little, Brown.

Quoc, M. and Long, M. (2007) *Tam and Cam: The ancient Vietnamese Cinderella story*. East West Discovery.

Schroeder, A., Sneed, B. and Perrault, C. (2009) *Smoky Mountain Rose: An Appalachian Cinderella*. Paw Prints.

Sierra, J. and Ruffins, R. (2000) *The Gift of the Crocodile: A Cinderella story*. Simon & Schuster.

Silverman, E. and Gaber, S. (2008) *Raisel's Riddle*. Paw Prints.

Souci, D.S. (2010) *Sootface: An Ojibwa Cinderella story*. Perfection.

Souci, R.D.S. and Pinkney, B. (2002) *Cendrillon: A Caribbean Cinderella*. Aladdin.

Steptoe, J. (2001) *Mufaro's Beautiful Daughters: An African tale*. Houghton Mifflin Harcourt.

Books that highlight gender issues

Boelts, M. and Jones, N.Z. (2009) *Those Shoes*. Candlewick.

Bradley, K.B. and Alley, R.W. (2006) *Ballerino Nate*. Dial.

Browne, A. (1986) *Piggybook*. Knopf.

Child, L. and Hurst, B. (2010) *I Really, Really Need Actual Ice Skates*. Dial.

Chin-Lee, C., Halsey, M. and Addy, S. (2008) *Amelia to Zora: 26 women who changed the world*. Charlesbridge.

Codell, E.R. and Plecas, J. (2011) *The Basket Ball*. Harry N. Abrams.

Funke, C. and Meyer, K. (2008) *A Princess, a Pirate, and one Wild Brother*. Scholastic.

Geeslin, C. and Juan, A. (2011) *Elena's Serenade*. Atheneum.

Gravett, E. (2011) *The Odd Egg*. Pan Macmillan.

Heap, S. and Sharratt, N. (2007) *Red Rockets and Rainbow Jelly*. Puffin.

Hilton, P. and Hill, J. (2011) *The Boy with Pink Hair*. Celebra.

Kemp, A. and Ogilvie, S. (2010) *Dogs Don't Do Ballet*. Simon & Schuster.

Kessler, C. and Jenkins, L. (2006) *The Best Beekeeper of Lalibela: A tale from Africa*. Holiday House.

Kilodavis, C. and DeSimone, S. (2011) *My Princess Boy*. Aladdin.

Meyer, K. (2004) *The Princess Knight*. Scholastic.

Munsch, R.N. and Martchenko, M. (2009) *The Paper Bag Princess*. Annick.

Ray, R. and Ewert, M. (2008) *10,000 Dresses*. Seven Stories.

Smothers, E.F. and Holyfield, J. (2003) *The Hard Times Jar*. Farrar, Straus and Giroux.

Stuve-Bodeen, S. and Bodeen, S.A. (2008) *Babu's Song*. Lee & Low.

Resources for selecting suitable picturebooks

Every year new picturebooks are published. This resource section is designed to help school librarians, teachers and student teachers access recently published high-quality picturebooks. Many resources available to teachers include websites, YouTube clips, blogs and book awards for children's literature. This section lists a selection of such resources to keep readers up to date.

Journals

Bookbird: A Journal of International Children's Literature	www.ibby.org
Booklist	www.ala.org/booklist/
Book Links	www.booklistonline.com/booklinks
Bulletin of the Center for Children's Books	http://bccb.lis.illinois.edu/
Children's Literature Association Quarterly	http://muse.jhu.edu/journals/chq/
Children's Literature in Education	http://link.springer.com/journal/10583
Horn Book Magazine	www.hbook.com/
International Research in Children's Literature	www.euppublishing.com/journal/ircl
The Lion and the Unicorn	http://muse.jhu.edu/journals/uni/
Signal	www.claas-kazzer.de/signal/about.html
School Library Journal	www.slj.com/

In addition, *The English Journal*, *Journal of Adolescent & Adult Literacy*, *Journal of Children's Literature* and the *School Library Journal* also feature picturebooks.

Websites

Most authors and illustrators have their own websites.

Love Reading for Kids	www.lovereading4kids.co.uk/genre/pw/Book-Awards.html
Children's Books Ireland	www.childrensbooksireland.ie/about-cbi/
The Children's Book Review	www.thechildrensbookreview.com/
Picturing Books	http://picturingbooks.com/
Children's Books	http://childrensbooks.about.com/
The Guardian	www.theguardian.com/books/picture-books
About.Com Children's Books	http://childrensbooks.about.com/od/picturebooks/Picture_Books.htm
PaperTigers	www.papertigers.org/home.html
Children's Laureate	www.childrenslaureate.org.uk/
Saffron Tree	www.saffrontree.org/

Blogs

Picture book den	http://picturebookden.blogspot.ie/
Picture book party	www.picturebookparty.co.uk/
Passionate about picturebooks by Sandie Mourão	http://picturebooksinelt.blogspot.ie/
The official blog of the Society of Children's Book Writers and Illustrators	http://scbwi.blogspot.ie/
Through the Looking Glass: Children's Book Reviews	http://lookingglassreview.blogspot.ie/
Teach with picture books	http://teachwithpicturebooks.blogspot.ie/

Book awards
The Coretta Scott King Awards
Established to commemorate the life and works of Dr Martin Luther King Jr and to honour Mrs Coretta Scott King for her courage and determination to continue the work for peace and world brotherhood, this award is given to an African American author and an African American illustrator for an outstanding, inspirational and educational book.
www.ala.org/emiert/cskbookawards

Notable Books for a Global Society Award
The NBGS list was established in 1995 to help students, teachers and families identify books that promote appreciation for the world's diverse cultures and ethnic and racial groups. The NBGS Committee undertook to identify 25 books each year that promote understanding across lines of culture, race, sexual orientation, values and ethnicity.
http://clrsig.org/nbgs.php

The Pura Belpré Award
Established in 1996, the Pura Belpré Award is presented annually to a Latino/Latina writer and illustrator whose work best portrays, affirms and celebrates the Latino cultural experience in an outstanding work of literature for children and youth. The award is named after Pura Belpré, the first Latina librarian at the New York Public Library.
www.ala.org/alsc/awardsgrants/bookmedia/belpremedal

Children's Africana Book Awards
These awards are designed to encourage the publication of accurate, balanced children's materials on Africa, to recognize literary excellence and to acknowledge the research achievements of outstanding authors and illustrators.
www.africaaccessreview.org/aar/awards

The Ezra Jack Keats New Writer and New Illustrator Awards for Children's Books
Known collectively as the Ezra Jack Keats Book Award, the New Writer Award was established in 1985 and the New Illustrator Award in 2001 to recognize and encourage authors and illustrators starting out in the field of children's books.
www.ezra-jack-keats.org/

The Charlotte Zolotow Award

This American literary award, presented annually for outstanding writing in a picturebook published in the United States, was established in 1998 by the Cooperative Children's Book Center (CCBC) at the University of Wisconsin–Madison.
http://ccbc.education.wisc.edu/books/zolotow.asp

The Caldecott Medal

The Caldecott Medal, named in honour of nineteenth-century English illustrator Randolph Caldecott, is for outstanding illustration in a picturebook. It is awarded annually by the Association for Library Service to Children.
www.ala.org/alsc/awardsgrants/bookmedia/caldecottmedal/caldecottmedal

The Children's Book of the Year Awards

The Children's Book Council of Australia celebrates and supports Australian authors and illustrators of books for children and young adults, primarily though the Children's Book of the Year Awards.
http://cbca.org.au/awards.htm

Children's Books Ireland (CBI)

The CBI Book of the Year Awards (formerly the Bisto Awards) are the leading annual children's book awards in Ireland, now in their third decade.
www.childrensbooksireland.ie/the-cbi-awards/

Amelia Bloomer Project

The Amelia Bloomer Project is an annual book list published by the Feminist Task Force of the American Library Association's Social Responsibilities Round Table since 2002.
http://ameliabloomer.wordpress.com/2013/01/28/the-2013-amelia-bloomer-project/

The Kate Greenaway Medal

Established in 1955, for distinguished illustration in a book for children, the medal is awarded annually for an outstandingly well-illustrated book.
www.carnegiegreenaway.org.uk/greenaway

The Jane Addams Children's Book Awards

Presented annually since 1953 by the Women's International League for Peace and Freedom (WILPF) and the Jane Addams Peace Association, the awards, which include a picturebook category, recognize books that promote the cause of peace, social justice, world community and the equality of the sexes.
www.janeaddamspeace.org/_books/

Green Earth Book Awards

The Green Earth Book Award is an environmental stewardship book award for children and young adult books. Over 80 books have been honoured since 2005.

www.natgen.org/green-earth-book-awards/

Hans Christian Andersen Award

Every other year, iBbY (International Board on Books for Young People) presents the Hans Christian Andersen Awards to a living author and illustrator whose complete works have made a lasting contribution to children's literature.

www.ibby.org

The Golden Kite Awards

Presented by the SCBWI (Society of Children's Book Writers and Illustrators), the Golden Kite Awards recognize excellence in children's literatures in four categories: Fiction, Non-fiction, Picturebook text and Picturebook illustration.

www.scbwi.org/awards/golden-kite-award/

Index